Organize your email so that it works for you!

Protect yourself from nasty spam, viruses, and worms!

D1304801

DEgunKing

your EMAIL, SPAM, and VIRUSES

Jeff Duntemann

 PARAGLYPH PRESS

President
Keith Weiskamp

Editor-at-Large
Jeff Duntemann

Vice President, Sales, Marketing, and Distribution
Steve Sayre

Vice President, International Sales and Marketing
Cynthia Caldwell

Production Manager
Kim Eoff

Cover Designers
Kris Sotelo and Jesse Dunn

Degunking Email, Spam, and Viruses ™

Limits of Liability and Disclaimer of Warranty

The author and publisher of this book have used their best efforts in preparing the book and the programs contained in it. These efforts include the development, research, and testing of the theories and programs to determine their effectiveness. The author and publisher make no warranty of any kind, expressed or implied, with regard to these programs or the documentation contained in this book.

The author and publisher shall not be liable in the event of incidental or consequential damages in connection with, or arising out of, the furnishing, performance, or use of the programs, associated instructions, and/or claims of productivity gains.

Trademarks

Trademarked names appear throughout this book. Rather than list the names and entities that own the trademarks or insert a trademark symbol with each mention of the trademarked name, the publisher states that it is using the names for editorial purposes only and to the benefit of the trademark owner, with no intention of infringing upon that trademark.

Paraglyph Press, Inc.
4015 N. 78th Street, #115
Scottsdale, Arizona 85251
Phone: 602-749-8787
www.paraglyphpress.com

Paraglyph Press ISBN: 1-932111-93-X

Printed in the United States of America
10 9 8 7 6 5 4 3 2 1

⚡ **PARAGLYPH**
P R E S S

The Paraglyph Mission

This book you've purchased is a collaborative creation involving the work of many hands, from authors to editors to designers and to technical reviewers. At Paraglyph Press, we like to think that everything we create, develop, and publish is the result of one form creating another. And as this cycle continues on, we believe that your suggestions, ideas, feedback, and comments on how you've used our books is an important part of the process for us and our authors.

We've created Paraglyph Press with the sole mission of producing and publishing books that make a difference. The last thing we all need is yet another tech book on the same tired, old topic. So we ask our authors and all of the many creative hands who touch our publications to do a little extra, dig a little deeper, think a little harder, and create a better book. The founders of Paraglyph are dedicated to finding the best authors, developing the best books, and helping you find the solutions you need.

As you use this book, please take a moment to drop us a line at **feedback@paraglyphpress.com** and let us know how we are doing—and how we can keep producing and publishing the kinds of books that you can't live without.

Sincerely,

Keith Weiskamp & Jeff Duntemann
Paraglyph Press Founders
4015 N. 78th Street, #115
Scottsdale, Arizona 85251
email: **feedback@paraglyphpress.com**
Web: **www.paraglyphpress.com**

To the Eternal Memory of

Louis J. Pryes 1916-1990

Black sheep uncle and Yankee tinkerer

Who believed in me when nobody else did.

❧

About the Author

Jeff Duntemann is an author, editor, lecturer, and industry analyst specializing in networking and computer security/performance topics. In his thirty years in the technology industry he has been a programmer and systems analyst for Xerox Corporation, a technical journal editor for Ziff-Davis Publications, Editor-in-Chief of *Turbo Technix*, *PC Techniques* and *Visual Developer Magazine*, and Editorial Director for Coriolis Group Books. He has at least a dozen books under his belt, the most recent including *Jeff Duntemann's Wi-Fi Guide* and *Degunking Windows* (with Joli Ballew.) See Jeff's Web site at www.duntemann.com. He lives with his wife Carol in Colorado Springs, Colorado.

Acknowledgments

Once again, my most amazing co-workers get a tip of the hat for making this thing happen: Keith Weiskamp, Cynthia Caldwell, Steve Sayre, and Kim Eoff, with Ben Sawyer always in there somewhere with sage advice.

Thanks are also due to Trevor Wise and Ben Oram, who both sent me Gmail invites, and to David Beers, for technical advice and welcome friendship throughout the process.

As always, inexpressible gratitude goes to my spouse Carol, who made room in her life for the project, gave me time to create, and urged me through the walls as I hit them.

Contents at a Glance

Contents

Chapter 3
Using the Right Email Client 35

Chapter 4
Developing Good Email Habits 49

Chapter 5
Read and Degunk Your Email from Anywhere 67

Chapter 6
Cleaning and Organizing Your Mailbase 89

Chapter 7
Avoid Becoming a Spam Magnet! 109

Chapter 8
Understand the Spam Filtering Conundrum 125

Chapter 15
Degunk Nigerian Rhapsodies, Hoaxes, and Other Smelly Phish...................................... 285

Chapter 16
Degunking After a Malware Attack 301

Index 323

Introduction

Email and Viruses: Who's to Be the Master?

Email: Pure magic! Just click that button and stuff comes in. *Well, yeah: And apples fall out of trees. What's your point?* The point is this: Email is one of those things that's so fundamental—and yet so simple—that most of us don't think about it very much at all. We install it and we use it without question, and without thinking much about it, most of us eventually remold our work and even our personal lives around its quirks and its rhythms and its dangers. Viruses ride in on its attachments. Worms exploit obscure flaws in our email client software and in the Web browsers used to render messages on our screens. It's all a package, inextricably linked and thoroughly stuck to the mouse-clicking fingers of the Heavily Networked Generation.

Email is now the inescapable morning ritual for hundreds of millions of globally aware human beings. Coffee used to be the centerpiece at the launching of a new day. Now your coffee just sits on its AOL Free 10,000 Hours! Signup CD while you stare at the screen and mutter. Another visit from the Bagle or Netsky viruses. Another pitch (or 15 or 20) to enlarge body parts that half of us don't even have. Another obscure stock is up 700 percent, as it has been every day this month—yeah, right. Another notification that a new Internet worm is on the prowl, targeting (of course!) Internet Explorer. Nuke nuke, file file, mutter mutter—and eventually the coffee is stone cold and another hour of your life has vanished into history.

Why do we do it? Well, it's the way we touch *the Internet!* In most people's eyes, email and the Web are like the laws of physics, a mysterious presence that's just out there, demanding to be saluted, heard, and obeyed. The real question, if we dare to ask it, is one we inherited from Humpty Dumpty: *Who's to be the master?* You or email? You or the spam and the scams and the worms and the spyware and the clutter and digital noise that I call *gunk* with a completely straight face?

Take Back Your Inbox!

In the context of this book, "gunk" means any and all unwanted items that come in to your PC by way of the Internet. This includes old email messages that you've long since forgotten, new messages that you didn't really want to receive, spam, scams, viruses, worms, outrageous offers, spyware that reports all your browsing habits back to its shadowy HQ, home page hijackers, Trojan horse back-door systems, spam relays, and anything else that slows down your PC, violates your privacy, and breaks your concentration while you're trying to get your work done.

It's gunk because it's sticky—hard to get rid of—and it slows down the wheels of your mind as you constantly have to dodge it and duck it and work around it. It's down there in the cracks of your workday, soaking up your energy and attention. Like dust on the knickknacks and grease on the wall behind the wok, it builds up over time until it dominates everything you do…unless you take the lead, first to clean it up and then to prevent it from accumulating in the future.

When you first began using your current email setup, it probably wasn't all cluttered up with thousands of messages dropped randomly in several badly chosen folders. But now it seems that handling your email is getting more complicated by the day. Over time, the needs of home, office, and family have led to multiple email accounts, each of which generates its own fountain of complexity. Spam is probably overwhelming your inbox. Shadowy network "black hats" are clawing at the door to get in. Virus threats are a constant concern. Your wireless connection is a big source of worry. One of your kids has just downloaded an amazing game that came in with a virus that's wreaking havoc on all your computers. You don't know the difference between a virus, a worm, spyware, a Trojan horse, a phish, and a mad cow.

I wrote this book to help you take back your inbox and your PC by ridding them of the Internet-related gunk that they've accumulated over time, whether from poor housekeeping on your part or by your doing the "wrong things" on an increasingly hazardous Internet. With a little psychology, a little technology, and a dash of disciplined effort, you can keep the email chaos, spam, viruses, worms, phishers, and various other troublemakers off of your PC and out of your life. Just read through this book, chapter by chapter, follow the steps provided, and you'll be amazed at how much simpler your networked life will become—and how much better your PC will run!

How This Book Is Organized

I've divided this book into four parts, reflecting the four general issues involved in coping with email, spam, viruses, and spyware.

I. Creating a Gunk-Free Email Strategy

Before you can do anything to rescue your day from email gunk, you have to rethink the way you work with email. You will need to create a set of strategies that fit who you are, what you do, and how you work with computers. This includes what email client you use, what email addresses you obtain, and what tools you use to keep the spam at bay. That's what this first part of the book covers, and once you've laid down this foundation, all the rest can happen with a lot less trouble and effort.

II. Degunking Your Email

If you've been using email for more than a few months, the gunk is there and I'll bet you know it. In Part II, I'll explain how you can develop the discipline of both cleaning it out and keeping it from collecting in the future. Some of this involves effective use of technology, but the greater part is just the same personal discipline you call upon to schedule regular dental cleaning appointments. Sure, it's not fun…but if you spend a little time now, you can forestall a *huge* amount of pain down the road.

III. Degunking Spam

Spam is the Great Curse of the email world, and alas, it will get a lot worse before it gets any better. Part III gives you your choice of ways to fight it. How you deal with spam depends on who you are, what you do with your PC, and how much spam you get, and what sort of spam it is. Prevention is much easier than cure, and again, personal discipline plays a big part. Sure, you're curious…but just *opening* that spam is an invitation to huge problems. Understand how spam works, and you'll make fewer mistakes that put you in spammer crosshairs.

IV. Degunking Viruses, Worms, and Spyware

Some viruses still propagate as they did in the old days: by attaching themselves to existing, respectable computer programs. Today, most viruses travel more or less by themselves, and they travel by email. Work smart when you use email (and put some fairly simple virus precautions in place) and you won't get bit.

The most fearsome invaders of your PC, however, aren't really viruses at all but related code-creatures called *worms,* which don't need an invitation to wreak havoc on your computer. They just walk in, sit down, and take over your PC unless you erect certain barriers between you and the greater networked world. (And don't think you're safe if you use a dialup connection!) Here, technology probably has the edge over personal discipline, but in Part IV, I'll show you how to establish and maintain your defenses so that bad guys will have to work so hard to break in that they'll just leave you alone and go down the street.

How to Use This Book

In this world of the Incredible Shrinking Attention Span, a lot of people tend to hunt through a computer book for just the right solution to the problem that's plaguing them *right now.* Keep in mind that putting out fires as they happen is much less effective over the long run than cleaning out the deadwood before the fires start. The whole degunking concept is really a 12-step program, and for best results, you should start at the beginning and work your way through the whole process. It's not only a matter of fixing things on your PC. As I'll say again and again in this book, it's about fixing your own work strategies so that clutter and hazards don't pile up and eventually get the better of you. These strategies interlock in a lot of nonobvious ways, and if you skip some of the earlier ones, the later ones won't work as well, and might not work at all.

A Note on Operating Systems

Given its roots in ARPANet, email has always been a global, operating-system-independent activity. It's really about information moving between networks according to well-defined protocols. As you might expect, how you approach email as a discipline depends less on what computer you're using than on the way you yourself organize complexity and budget your time between creative tasks and system maintenance. Like a lot of things that depend on the human element in computing, it's more psychology than technology.

Individual email clients are very much tied to individual operating systems, as are all of the viruses and worms that beset us. So even though a lot of the "big picture" issues and strategies in this book will apply to any email system running on any computer anywhere, eventually you have to find the right button and click it. Where I return to specific computer platforms, I'll be talking about Windows because of its near-monopoly on desktop computing around the world.

For many of the same reasons that market leaders attract most of the attention and most of the press, Windows tends to attract most of the gunk. As I'll explain later, virus writers concentrate on Windows not because Windows is necessarily more vulnerable than Linux or Mac, but because viruses need a "critical mass" of accessible computers in order to propagate. Viruses are machine specific, and if only 1 machine out of 20 is a Mac, a Mac virus may not find enough other Mac machines in its owner's address book to "break out" and become a serious problem.

Windows gets the majority of both gunk and glory, and thus Windows is a good part of what I'll be talking about here. (Paraglyph Press, of which I am a founder, has published *Degunking Your Mac* for Mac-specific issues, including a thorough discussion of email gunk.) Most of what I say here applies to all of the 32-bit Windows versions (Windows 95 through XP).

Finally, a word to my fellow geeks: I'm writing this book primarily for non-technical users of email and (especially) Windows. Please don't feel slighted if I don't spend chapters on manually editing the Windows Registry or monitoring malware with a packet sniffer. In conversations with my friends and clients, I found that the real need was a book for "ordinary people," rather than the technically adept. Look at it this way: The more I help them, the less they'll be calling you to help them when the spam, the scammers, and the viruses strike!

Why Is Your Computer Suffering from Email and Virus Gunk?

Degunking Checklist:

√ Make sure you understand the three basic processes involved in degunking: degunking your email, degunking spam, and degunking viruses.

√ Learn about the 10 key causes for email gunk and the 10 key causes for virus gunk.

√ Make sure you understand that the best email and virus degunking results can be obtained by performing cleanup tasks in a specific order.

√ Learn the degunking 12-step program and put it into practice.

I've been in the computer industry since 1976, and I've seen a lot of gunk. As those who have read my previous book *Degunking Windows* (with Joli Ballew) may know, we're not talking about dog hair on your mouse ball. (If only *all* computer gunk were as easy to beat as that!) What we're talking about is *digital* gunk: information that piles up needlessly or gets scrambled or scattered or lost. We're also talking about ugly stuff from outside: spam and *malware,* which is software that invades your PC, slowing it down or even damaging it. Viruses, Trojans horses, and worms, oh my! It gets scarier day by day.

If you've used your PC a lot, and for any significant amount of time, you're probably deluged with email and malware gunk. For years I used to wade through a mountain of spam every morning, and I'm still always on my guard for the latest killer virus with crosshairs set on my PC. As much of a tech freak as I am, there are still moments when I really yearn for the simple days when every email message I got was a real one and when I could use my PC without having to worry about worms lurking at my network connection or some shadowy guy in a black hat, working behind the scenes trying to steal my identity. Identity theft is at an all-time high. People around the world are losing millions of dollars every year to online scammers, and they are at risk to lose even more unless they learn how to protect themselves.

Fortunately, with a little bit of knowledge and a little time and effort, you can take charge of your PC and reduce the amount of email and malware gunk that comes in. In this chapter I'll explain why your PC has likely become a magnet for both email and malware gunk. In the second part of the chapter I'll introduce you to the strategy I've devised for degunking your PC. I'll present some of the important questions that you need to ask yourself to help you see how your computer is getting gunked up, and then I'll introduce you to the very important degunking 12-step program that this book is based on.

The most important thing to understand about the email and virus degunking process presented in this book is that you'll get the best results if you follow the process that I outline. If you have a little experience using your PC, you might be tempted to skip around in this book. Try to resist. Stick with the strategy that I'll be presenting. What I'll be showing you are techniques that I've been using myself for years and have successfully taught my co-workers and clients. It works. Really! Follow the degunking plan and you'll get the best possible results.

What the Experts Know

What I'm about to show you isn't as difficult and doesn't take as much time as you might think. Nor is it unrelentingly, eye-crossingly technical. Much of it consists of simple common sense and organizational skills that you could apply to organizing your closets or your desk as easily as to your files and software. By following these steps in order, you can keep your PC much safer and make your email much easier to manage.

Basic email housekeeping 101. Here I'll focus on how to get everything email related set up properly and how to rid yourself of all the email gunk you don't need. After you complete this first step you'll feel as good as you do when you clean out a really gunked-up garage or medicine cabinet. You'll learn how to set up a good email degunking strategy, how to choose the best email client to help you manage your email, how to put good email habits to work, and how to really clean and organize your mailbase. I'll even show you a set of special degunkng techniques and tips you can use to help you with your email while you are on the road.

Basic spam degunking and prevention. Once you've culled your mailbase and set up your system to manage your email more efficiently, it's time to roll out the heavy artillery and take aim at spam. You can think of this process as both "deep cleaning" and prevention. Here you'll learn how to apply techniques that really work to combat spam—and also what techniques work badly or have unacceptable side effects. I'll begin by explaining how spammers pull their scurvy tricks and how you can avoid being a magnet for spam. After that you'll learn how to decide which of several anti-spam technologies to use: content filtering, server-side filtering, challenge-response spam suppression, or Bayesian spam filtering.

Degunking malware: viruses, worms, adware, and spyware. The last stage of our deep cleaning process involves degunking the creatures that can really wreak havoc on your PC: viruses, Trojans horses, worms, adware, and spyware. The types of viruses that the black hats can dream up might seem endless, but there are smart degunking procedures you can put into place right away to protect yourself. I'll begin the discussion of this part of the degunking process by explaining the different categories of viruses so that you can better understand what you're up against, and then I'll show you the best ways to chose and set up a successful virus protection system. You'll also learn how to degunk some of the more troublesome gunk, including phish, adware, and spyware. A lot of it is psychology more than technology: Like it or not, the global network has changed the way we use our PCs, and we have to be careful in ways we didn't have to even five or six years ago. I'll help you protect yourself against online scams and identity theft, which has become a *huge* problem, especially for nontechnical Internet users. Finally, I'll explain how to set up your own personal firewall to block those nasty network worms right at the gate.

Understanding How You Got So Gunked Up

If you've been using your PC for a while (and "awhile" may be only a single year—or as little as eight or nine months!), you've probably noticed that it doesn't run as fast as it did when you took it out of the box that glorious first day home from Best Buy. Yes, entropy applies to Windows, just as surely as it applies to chemistry and physics. Those mundane everyday activities of checking email, uploading and downloading files, and installing programs have gunked up your PC and made it run slower. There's nothing "evil" about those activities or the software that you use to perform them—but hard drives get fragmented and Registries get clogged nonetheless. (You *did* read my last book, *Degunking Windows,* didn't you?)

Defragging your hard drive and cleaning up your Registry is a good start, but it's *only* a start. The blizzard of email and spam that you receive can make it almost impossible for you to find important messages and attachment files. If you're like most people who have used email a lot for a period of years, you probably have a mailbase that already contains thousands of messages that you've sent and received and don't quite know what to do with or how to manage. (The scariest thing I ever saw in computing was a co-worker's email inbox with *12,000* messages in it! Boo!)

You might eventually get to the point where your PC gets so horribly gunked up with spam, viruses, spyware, and abandoned files that you might think "it's worn out" or otherwise beyond hope, making you suspect that you need a new PC. And if you're really unlucky, you could have a bad system crash or malware attack that could wipe out your mailbase entirely—and unless it was backed up, you'll lose your only copy of all those important messages that you've been saving for future reference.

Fortunately, you can reverse "Windows entropy" and greatly improve the performance of your PC by following a set of proven techniques to get all that gunk out. But before you roll up your sleeves to begin degunking, it's important to understand how your PC got gunked up to begin with. Let's look at the causes of gunk for email (including spam) and at the causes of virus gunk, which includes malware.

The 10 Key Causes of Email Gunk

Our strategy for cleaning out and then preventing email and spam gunk must take into consideration the 10 key causes of email gunk on your PC:

1. Email piles up in your inbox and you don't act on it.
2. Sent messages pile up in your Sent Items folder and you don't routinely delete them.
3. Email attachments pile up in your Attach folder and you don't archive or delete them.
4. You read your email too frequently during the day, breaking your concentration and interrupting your "real" work.
5. Your folder hierarchy isn't effective and it makes it easy to forget where messages are stored.
6. You use your primary email address on e-commerce sites and Usenet newsgroups, where spambots are known to roam.
7. You don't have an effective spam filtering technology in place.
8. Your email client doesn't block spam beacons in its preview pane.
9. You've attempted to opt out of spammer mailings using their links or opt-out email addresses.
10. A virus or worm has stolen your address book or planted a spam proxy on your PC.

These 10 causes account for virtually all of the gunk that you've accumulated through the use of email. The last one is a slightly odd one, but no less important for that: It's a direct cause of email gunk on *other people's* PCs—and other people who disregard Item #10 are causing email gunk on *your* PC. So by addressing #10, you'll be helping everybody else out, and by doing so helping yourself too. *Spam and malware are everybody's problem.*

All of these gunk-generating problems are easily addressed with a little discipline and a little helper technology, none of which is expensive and the best of which, remarkably enough, is completely free. I'm going to go down the list in this book and address them all, and in every case present you with a step-by-step strategy for cleaning it out and putting it right. When you're done, you'll be processing your email more quickly and more efficiently—and your PC will run faster too.

Spam

Spam hardly needs any introduction—it's the bane of anyone with an email account. These unsolicited commercial email ads are like weeds in our gardens. The more we try to get rid of them, the faster they come back. Eventually, they overwhelm us one way or the other. We end up with mailbases teeming with irrelevant files, making them slow to sort, search, and compress. Spam messages average 10 to 20 times larger than "real" email messages, so having scads of them in your email client wastes a significant amount of your hard drive space. Many people I've helped with spam have more megabytes of disk tied up in spam than in their legitimate messages!

If you've fought the spam wars in vain for any period of time, you may have convinced yourself that it's pointless and that there is nothing you can do about it. But as you'll learn in this book, there are strategies you can put to work right away to greatly reduce your exposure to spam. Many users I talk to simply throw in the towel on spam, and some spend up to an hour every day sorting through their email and deleting spam messages and the attachments that ride in with them. If you take a more proactive approach by using more than one email address, using good trainable spam filters, and avoiding activities that attract spam in the first place, you can save a *lot* of time, energy, and torn hair.

The 10 Key Causes of Virus Gunk

Unfortunately, keeping your email under control is only half of the battle. Spam-planted spyware, email-borne viruses and worm-planted "back doors" all slow your PC down and clutter up the Windows Registry—and those are only the nondestructive effects. Some of this malware will delete or corrupt files, mess with your system settings, and in extreme cases, render your PC unbootable.

Malware attacks are not due to bad luck, some shadowy conspiracy, or evil spirits. It's just technology, and truth be told, a good deal of it is caused by bad habits and carelessness on your part. Here are the 10 key causes of virus gunk:

1. Not having an antivirus utility installed on your PC.

2. Not keeping your antivirus utility update subscription current and in force.

3. Opening email attachments without scanning them for malware first.

4. Double-clicking on files in Windows Explorer "just to see what they are," especially if you've allowed Windows to hide file extensions.

5. Installing and running software downloaded from newsgroups or peer-to-peer networks without letting it "cool off" for a week (to allow your antivirus software to""catch up") and then scanning it for malware.

6. Booting from an infected diskette or (much more rarely) an infected CD or Zip disk.

7. Keeping macros enabled in Microsoft Office applications.

8. Keeping "install on demand" enabled in your Web browser, particularly Internet Explorer.

9. Letting other people use your PC indiscriminately and without supervision, especially if you allow them to log in as administrator.

10. Frequenting porn, warez, and cracks sites on the Web while logged in as administrator.

The Spyware and Adware Bogeyman

Spyware and *adware* are products that are "free," at the cost of forcing you to watch banner ads or pop-ups while they're running. Adware simply shows you the ads. Spyware, however, reports information on your Web surfing habits back to its creators' HQ, and may set you up for targeted email marketing (spam attack!). Spyware has become more aggressive in recent years, and some spyware technologies don't show up in your installed programs directory but rather run in the background (as Windows services) 24/7, eating processor power and memory *even when the "free" application isn't running.* This makes them hard to find, hard to uninstall, and, worst of all, hard to clean up after.

In fairness, most spyware is relatively innocuous—it won't raid your hard drive or report the balance of your bank account to black hat types in the Ukraine. However, spyware and adware will consume processor cycles and available memory and slow down your machine—especially if more than one of them is installed. They can also conflict with the operation of other software.

They are gunk in the purest sense of the word, and you are best to be rid of them.

Identity Theft

Perhaps the newest threat to come in on the Internet's magic carpet is *phishing,* which is an online masquerade that persuades you to enter your credit card or ATM card numbers into a phony Web site that looks like your familiar Citibank online banking site—but is actually a server somewhere in the Third World, run by shadowy black hats. It's an interesting question that you should ask yourself: How do you know that the Web site you think you're on is really the Web site you want? Even technical people can be fooled. Don't be one of them. I can explain how not to be phished, and will.

The Strategy Behind Degunking

Perhaps the most difficult part of getting your PC gunk-free involves dedicating the time to do it. There's definitely a "degunk me now, or degunk me later" psychology about it: If you keep to the strategy and do a little bit every day, it'll never get so bad as to require a week of your time to climb out of the morass. The strategy I'll present in this book is what it is for a reason, and if you follow it, you'll end up spending the least amount of time for the greatest benefit.

As we work through all the different degunking techniques presented in this book, I'll arrange the necessary tasks in the order that will likely get you the best results in the shortest amount of time. My approach will be to show you not only how to fix things, but how things really work so that you can take charge and think things through on your own. I'll also show you how to get yourself on a maintenance program so that your computer runs well on an ongoing basis. If you're new to the world of email, spam, and viruses, don't worry. Degunking is much easier than assembling a gas grill in the backyard or doing your taxes on the "short form."

The basic strategy behind degunking your email and viruses is based on how your PC operates in the first place:

√ How different email clients store emails and attachments

√ How email programs set up filters to block unwanted spam messages

√ How keyword filtering operates with different email clients

√ How spammers use different tricks to get past spam filters and into your personal mailbox

√ How black hats create and distribute malware on the Internet

√ How more recent black hat techniques such as phishing can put you at risk for identity theft

√ How tools such as backup programs and firewalls can help you protect yourself and minimize damage in the event of a malware attack

As you'll learn in this book, the more you understand about the basics of how email, spam, and malware operates, the better you'll get at degunking and saving yourself time and headaches. Of course, you don't need to be an expert on email and viruses to make your PC run better and protect yourself. A little bit of common sense and the ability to learn from the experience of experts goes a long, long way.

Important Questions to Ask Yourself

As you use your computer on a regular basis, you need to ask yourself some of the following questions:

√ Does it seem that I'm having more difficulty sending and receiving email than I once did?

√ Am I spending too much time trying to locate copies of messages that I have sent or received?

√ When was the last time that I went through my email and deleted the messages I no longer need?

√ Am I getting so much spam that I don't even have enough time to read or manage my legitimate email?

√ Am I losing legitimate messages that are being sent to me because they're getting mistakenly snagged by a spam filter?

√ When was the last time I set up a virus protection program or did a scan of my hard drive to see if it was free of viruses or other malware?

√ Do I have a firewall in place to keep network worms from gunking up my PC?

Let's continue by putting together a degunking strategy that first explores how email and viruses operate. Once you're familiar with how email and viruses work, you'll be able to see how my 12-step degunking program (see the end of this chapter) will help improve your life.

Email Management 101

Your email system (whether you realize it or not) eats up a lot of space on your hard drive. Different email programs (more properly called email *clients*) store messages in a relatively similar fashion, in a species of database. (I'll be using the term *mailbase* in this book for your email database.) Unfortunately, each email client stores its message data using a different database technology, so it's not a situation where one size (or technique) fits all. The good news is that no matter what email client you use, you can apply some sound degunking techniques to manage your email better, reduce the amount of spam you receive, and better organize the email you receive and send out.

The email clients I'll focus on in this book include Outlook, Outlook Express, Eudora, Poco Mail, and Mozilla Thunderbird.

Fortunately, the degunking process is pretty much the same, no matter what email client you use:

1. Process messages as they come in.

2. Create a comprehensible folder hierarchy for storing "keeper" messages, and sort your inbox into that folder hierarchy.

3. Move messages that must be held temporarily for later action into a folder created for that purpose—and check it periodically to delete abandoned mail.

4. Delete or deep-archive messages in your Sent Items folder once they get to be 60 or 90 days old.

5. Scan your attachments folder for attachment files that can be deleted or archived, making sure your virus protection is in place. (Viruses *love* to hide in attachments!)

6. Check your Drafts folder to make sure abandoned drafts aren't piling up.

7. Make sure you don't have multiple (and forgotten) copies of your mailbase lying around the odd corners of your hard drive.

Combating Spam with Filtering Techniques

Keeping spam from overwhelming your inbox is a matter of choosing a spam filtering technology, putting it in place, and maintaining it. There is no such thing as "set it and forget it" spam filtering. Every technology that works well (and has no undesirable side effects) requires a little bit of tweaking over time. The trick is to use a filtering technology that matches your own email situation and the severity of your spam burden. Content filtering works well for people who receive a little or a moderate amount of spam from a few different spammers; Bayesian (trainable) filters work much better for people who get mountains of spam from every scumbag in the observable universe.

Prevention is, of course, vital in the spam wars, and you need to be vigilant in certain ways:

√ Choose email addresses that are not vulnerable to dictionary attacks.

√ Use a "disposable" email address to deal with all but the most trusted e-commerce sites.

√ Never respond *in any way* to a spam message. Neither buy goods nor take surveys sent by spammers. (The surveys are only used to verify your email address!)

√ Never attempt to unsubscribe from spammer mailing lists.

√ Don't post your email address (or allow other people to post it) on the Web or in Usenet newsgroups.

1. Disable image downloading in the preview pane of your email client to avoid spam beacons—and if image downloading can't be disabled, get a better email client!

Setting Up a Virus Protection System

Spotting viruses as they attempt to enter your PC is the core mission of a virus protection system. Modern virus protection is part caution and part antivirus technology. The technology is something you buy and install, and make sure to keep updated. A *signature file* contains characteristic data patterns by which a particular virus may be recognized. Most modern antivirus utilities can be configured to automatically download updated virus signature files on a weekly or even a daily basis. Without those ongoing updates, newly released viruses will *not* be spotted and they *will* infect your PC!

Needless to say, keep your updates subscription current. After all, $20 to $40 a year is a small price to pay, weighed against the havoc that a bad virus can wreak on your PC.

Newer antivirus utilities try to do a great deal and make heavy demands on your PC. If you have an older PC, it becomes important to shop for an antivirus utility that "goes easy" on the computer and won't bog down a three- or four-year-old system.

A good deal of your antivirus strategy are common-sense points of caution:

√ Don't open email attachments without scanning them for viruses, even if they come from someone well known to you.

√ Don't install software without scanning it for viruses.

√ Keep downloaded software from untrusted sources for a week before scanning it, to allow updated virus signatures to reach your antivirus utility. A brand-new virus could reach your PC and infect it before the antivirus companies have a chance to isolate and distribute signatures. (New viruses are often first released on newsgroups and peer-to-peer networks.)

√ Disable "install on demand" in your Web browser.

√ If you must surf to dicey sites (think porn, warez, cracks), create a limited-privileges user under Windows, and log in as that user before setting out on the Web. A limited privileges account will limit the damage that malware can do to your PC.

Preventing the Installation of Spyware and Adware

There are two kinds of "free": Really and truly free and ad-supported. Ad-supported software may not cost money out of pocket, but it will install some kind of rotating pop-up or banner ad system that continuously circulates ads in front of your eyes while you use the software. Worse than adware is spyware, which actually sends data back to some unknown location, pinpointing your Web surfing destinations. Such ad systems may not be directly destructive, but get several of them operating at once and they will slow your PC to a crawl. They are also difficult to remove and may conflict with other software.

Preventing the installation of spyware and adware is relatively simple:

1. Disable install on demand in your Web browser. Some nasty spyware will install itself as soon as you surf to its Web site if install on demand is enabled.

2. Carefully research any free product you may be considering on the Web to see if others have found it to contain adware or spyware.

3. Resist installing free goodies like smiley collections or toolbars. Some of the worst spyware hides behind these relatively worthless items.

4. Choose open-source free software when such software is available to do the job you need done. Open-source software *never* contains adware or spyware.

5. Don't be cheap. Avoiding the aggravation and distraction that adware and spyware will cost you is worth far more than the $30 or $40 you might have to spend on an adware-free version of some software package.

6. Scan your PC periodically with an anti-adware utility like Ad-Aware or Spybot Search & Destroy to spot and remove any suspicious items that may have gotten past you.

Protecting Yourself from Identity Theft

Over the past year, countless people have received emails demanding that they "verify their account" by clicking a URL in an email message that appears to come from a bank or auction site. Clicking the URL takes them to an authentic-looking Web form, complete with familiar Web design, graphics, and logos. It looks like a bank, and it's asking for bank information like account numbers, ATM passwords, credit card numbers, and PINs.

All phony, all stolen. Anyone can download the elements of a Web site and repost them with subtle changes that direct the output of Web forms to a server anywhere in the world. If you click the URL in this "phishing" message, you'll run the risk of entering financial information that identity thieves will use to pick your bones clean.

Avoiding these identity theft attacks is easy:

1. Never, but *never* click to a bank, PayPal, or auction site from a URL sent to you via email. Legitimate financial sites will never ask you to "verify an account" in an email.

2. When you go to a finance- or auction-related Web site, *type the Web address into the URL bar.* (It doesn't take that long to type "www.ebay.com," anyway.)

3. Don't even click a saved bookmark! Black hats have written malware that creates phony bookmarks (pointing to banks or auction sites) that say Citibank but take you to their outlaw servers.

Setting Up a Firewall to Protect Against Internet Worms

Perhaps the very worst species of malware are worms, which are related to viruses but much more subtle. A worm doesn't always need you to open an attachment to make it run. (Some worms do ride in on email attachments, but in those cases we call them "blended threat" malware because they act like both worms and viruses at the same time. Ugly!) Worms take advantage of "security holes" in common software to simply jump from one PC to another over the Internet. You don't have to make some kind of mistake to let them in. Unless you put a firewall in place, they will enter your PC, infect it, and leap to other unprotected PCs around the world.

A firewall is a piece of software that blocks certain kinds of traffic into (or out of) your PC, using its network connection. If you connect to the Internet without a firewall, even through a slow dialup connection, it's only a matter of time before a worm scans your network port and makes its jump into your PC.

Worm protection can be summarized this way:

1. Install a firewall of some kind before you ever connect to the Internet for the first time.

2. If you have a broadband connection, buy a router (wired or wireless) with a Network Address Translation (NAT) firewall inside.

3. For any type of Internet connection (broadband or dialup), install a software firewall like ZoneAlarm Pro. Do this even if you install a router. Software firewalls can also stop worms and viruses from propagating *out* of your PC if they somehow get established.

4. If you can avoid it, don't use Microsoft Outlook or Internet Explorer. These products are the first choice of black hats looking for network security holes to exploit in their worms and viruses. Other products also have security holes—but other products don't have 95 percent of the market!

Oh, and Don't Forget Your Backups!

Needless to say, all defenses have cracks, and all defenders—even deep geeks—occasionally slip up. I've gotten stung by viruses under odd circumstances. It happens, and the more you work on your PC, the more likely it is that you'll take a hit. The hurricanes that pounded Florida in the summer of 2004 remind us that the world is a messy place. There are fires, floods, and earthquakes, not to mention petty thieves with a crowbar and a drug habit to support. Lots of things can render your PC useless—or missing.

These threats from both the Internet and the physical world make it absolutely crucial to back up your mailbase and other critical information on a regular basis and in a systematic way. There are many excellent backup utilities on the market, but even manually backing up to CD-R or DVD-R is better than leaving your irreplaceable data exposed and vulnerable.

Here's a backup strategy that makes sense:

1. Because making removable media (CD-R, DVD-R, Zip, etc.) involves some manual labor, create a backups folder on a drive unit *other* than your main drive unit (C:) and use this as a destination for your daily backups. If you have two physical drives in your PC, put the backup folder on a physical drive separate from C:.

2. Every few days, or at the very least weekly, copy your data to a removable medium of some kind.

3. Keep a four-copy "rolling backup" in a safe place at home, ideally in a different room from the PC.

4. Once a month, take the oldest copy from your rolling backup and put it in your safe deposit box. If you have data that doesn't change much over time (mp3s, digital photos, etc.), keep a copy in your safe deposit box as well.

5. Keep a six-month rolling backup in your safe deposit box, and destroy the oldest copy each time you place a new copy in the box.

The Email and Malware 12-Step Degunking Program

Here is the basic 12-step degunking process that you'll follow in this book:

1. Create an email strategy that fits who you are and what you do with email (Chapter 2).

2. Select an email client that complements the way that you work (Chapter 3).

3. Develop a good set of email habits that help you get and stay organized, reduce clutter, and protect you against spam and malware as much as possible (Chapter 4).

4. Choose a system for managing your email while you're on the road, and make sure the system doesn't allow you to "fork your mailbase" (Chapter 5).

5. Clean and organize your mailbase on a regular basis so that email gunk doesn't accumulate (Chapter 6).

6. Set up a basic keyword filtering system to reduce the amount of spam getting to your inbox (Chapters 7 and 8).

7. If your spam volume makes keyword filtering bothersome or ineffective, install a more powerful Bayesian spam filtering system like the free utility POPFile. Also learn to avoid spam control methods that don't work (Chapters 9 and 10).

8. Choose, install, and maintain a virus protection system. Keep that update subscription current (Chapters 11 and 12).

9. Prevent the installation of adware and spyware, and scan regularly for spyware elements that get past you (Chapter 13).

10. Set up a software firewall. If you have a broadband Internet connection, also install a router that includes a Network Address Translation (NAT) firewall. The two are not the same, but together they provide almost complete protection against worms (Chapter 14).

11. Protect yourself against identity theft. Never click URLs in email to navigate to a financial or auction site (Chapter 15).

12. Back up your mailbase (and all your data) on a regular basis according to a system that you define for yourself and hold to. Also make sure you know what to do if you suffer a really bad malware attack (Chapter 16).

Gunk Be Gone

The most difficult part about degunking your email and malware involves dedicating a little time to the doing. But once you start degunking, you'll be amazed at how much time and aggravation you can save. The best part about the process is that all of the tasks that I'll be showing you how to do are not difficult at all. I'll also be explaining all of the important background issues as we go along. If you follow the degunking process in the way that I've described in this chapter, you'll not only protect your computer (and yourself), you'll also make your PC run so much better.

Creating Your Email Degunking Strategy

Degunking Checklist:

√ Determine your email profile and learn which of four categories of email users you belong to.

√ Determine how many email addresses you are likely to need, and why.

√ Learn where email addresses come from so that you can get the best possible addresses.

√ Obtain the email addresses you need.

√ Develop a backup strategy to get onto the Internet.

√ Learn how to register your own Internet domain to get maximum control.

√ Learn how to obtain and use disposable email addresses to provide you with more security.

Why are you up to your eyebrows in email? Simple: *You don't have a degunking plan.* Email is a little like your front lawn. Unless you mow it, weed it, and trim the edges on a regular basis, it will become a meadow. And maybe a meadow is what you want—but it's important to remember the difference between a lawn and a meadow: A lawn grows *your* way. A meadow grows its own way. And if it gets deep and dense enough, it can hide all sorts of interesting things, including things you need to find (like the lawn clippers) and things you'd just as soon *not* find (moles, snakes, and thistles).

Without a strategy for managing your email lawn, it will become an email meadow and you'll be knee-deep in interesting things, some of which can draw blood. This first section of the book is about mowing your email meadow so that it becomes a lawn again, and keeping it mowed over the long haul. Doing this requires time and discipline, but mostly it requires a strategy. That strategy depends on who you are, how you make your living, and how much you depend on digital communication. All these things add up to your *email profile,* and once you know your email profile, you can get a better handle on ways to keep your email from growing wild.

What's Your Email Profile?

Everyone has different needs and organizes their lives in different ways, but I'm struck more by the similarities among my many friends and contacts than by their differences. In terms of the ways that they've integrated email into their lives, the people I know fall into four broad categories: Public Professional, Private Professional, Student-Enthusiast, and Casual Communicator. Let's run down the list, and as I do, ask yourself where you might fit in. This is an important early step to help you get on the fast track to degunking success.

The Public Professional

Here, think doctors, lawyers, salespeople, journalists, tech support people, and independent consultants of many kinds. Public Professionals use email not only daily but almost constantly, and email is a crucial element in getting their work done. More than that, Public Professionals are visible to the outside world and must be easily reachable by total strangers. Like all professionals, the Public Professional has both a public and a private life, and keeping those two lives separate is usually desirable, although not always easily achieved. These two lives have two separate and only modestly overlapping universes of contacts, often maintained by two separate computer tools.

The Private Professional

The Private Professional is very much like the Public Professional, but with an important difference: no public visibility. Good examples include department managers, government office workers, and front-line staff in private companies who do not deal with the general public. A Private Professional uses email regularly during the day to get a job done and may communicate with family and friends. A Private Professional does not usually have a personal Web page. Although Private Professionals understand computers well and use them effectively, they are not typically geeks and don't compute for the sheer fun (or compulsion) of it.

The Student-Enthusiast

The Student-Enthusiast is usually young and has had a computer since childhood. The Student-Enthusiast uses digital communication daily, sometimes constantly, and considers it a given and not something exotic. They are often gadget freaks and may have both a PDA and a high-end pocket phone. More than someone in any of the other categories, the Student-Enthusiast regularly uses multiple communications modes (phone, IM, email) and is fluent with all of them. These days, tech savvy is less a geek specialty and more equally present among young men and women.

The Casual Communicator

Casual Communicators are people who do not often use a computer at work. They may be retired, work out in the field in the skilled trades, or work in one of the service industries that does not involve office computing. Their computers are at home, and they uses them to keep in touch with family and friends, or to look things up on the Web. They value their privacy and prefer not to be contacted by people they don't know, and they have a circle of contacts that may consist of no more than 10 or 20 people total. Casual Communicators are not enthusiasts and use their computers only when they feel they need them.

Pick Your Profile

Now, where do you fit in? I'll be citing these four categories frequently during the rest of this book, so you'll need to be honest, look in the mirror, and decide which category is most nearly yours. Few people will fit in any single category precisely, but the categories are really there to be used as starting points. Once you decide which category comes closest to the way you work and use digital communication, dealing with the unique circumstances of your individual situation becomes a *whole* lot easier. Once you decide which category you fit into, you can tailor the settings on your computer to minimize the type of gunk that you are most likely to accumulate. For example, if you are a Student-Enthusiast, you likely don't need to get email from companies that are trying to sell you professional-level products or services. Or if you are a Public Professional, you need to be careful that your spam-fighting machinery does not make you difficult to contact by the general public.

The Three Kinds of Email Addresses

At the core of your email degunking strategy lie your email addresses. (Yes, plural!) Your email address may seem a simple and singular thing, but for a lot of people, their first mistake is assuming that only one email address is necessary. You should probably have two, and may need more than two. (I have *seven*— but then again, I'm both a Public Professional and a world-class geek.) Having multiple email addresses may seem like much more fussy work, but in truth, reading multiple email accounts is no more difficult than reading one. As you'll see in the next chapter, all common email clients can read mail from several email addresses, and whatever additional effort is involved is all done up front and only needs to be done once. The biggest hazard of having multiple email addresses is, in fact, forgetting that you have them, as I'll explain later on.

There are three general categories of email addresses:

√   Your primary email address or addresses
√   Your backup email address
√   Disposable email addresses

Let's take a closer look at these categories and why they're necessary.

Using Your Primary Email Address(es)

Your primary email address is the one you use most of the time, on a daily basis. It's the one you give to your friends and business associates. If you have a business card, it's the address on your business card. It's the primary way that you want the world to be able to reach you.

It's possible (and often necessary) to have more than one primary email address. Here's one place where your email profile makes a big difference. Many Public Professionals try very hard to keep their public and personal lives separate, and one way to do this is to maintain a separate primary email address for each. You give the world your public address, and you give your family and close friends your private address—and guard that address as best you can. (The big challenge will be persuading your inner circle not to spread it around.)

Even if you're a Private Professional, having two primary email addresses is a good idea. These days, almost anyone who works in an office is given an email address for work use. Time was when most companies didn't care if you took your work email address home with you and used it from your home PC to message friends and family members. These days, company email policies have been tightened greatly, and your email traffic may in fact be monitored. This has been done for various reasons, all of them related to both network security (think viruses!) and a desire to keep employees from spending company time chatting with non-company people about non-company matters. You may actually be forbidden to use your company email for after-work sorts of things, especially things like online shopping.

If your workplace does not impose restrictions like that, a single primary address may suffice for Private Professionals. (Keep in mind that company policies can change overnight, especially if some serious technology crisis involving email occurs.) Student-Enthusiasts often get by with one primary address, especially if they have a university broadband account at school. Where Student-Enthusiasts have more than one primary address, it's usually to separately cover time spent at school and time spent at home, where a university email account may not be accessible.

If you're a Casual Communicator and do not use email as part of your day job, a single primary email address is usually all that you need.

Using Your Backup Email Address

Your backup email address is just that: a second email account, obtained from a separate email hosting company. The key attribute of a backup email address is that it be *completely independent of your primary email address.* In case the mail servers at the company that hosts your primary email address are down for some reason, you can use your backup email address to communicate until such time as your primary address comes back online.

Any time you sign up for a broadband Internet account, you will receive an email address as part of the deal. I always recommend to friends and clients that this email address *not* be used as a primary email address, but rather as your backup email address. I say this for two important reasons:

√   In most cases, an email address associated with a broadband Internet connection can only be read from where your broadband connection is. Go out on the road and the account is likely to be inaccessible, or perhaps only accessible through a very lame Web-based screen.

√   It's often difficult, and sometimes impossible, to change the email address that comes with a broadband connection. If the spammers find it, you may not be able to shut it down and request a new (and different) address from your broadband provider.

Like a spare tire, a backup email address should be treated as such and used only in an emergency. Even using it to communicate with your friends is a bad idea, for this reason: If your backup email address ends up in too many people's address books, you raise the likelihood that an address-book virus will harvest your address from someone else's machine. You could find your backup account pounded by virus attacks, or added to a shadowy spammer address database.

TIP: A dialup Internet account can provide a good backup email address. Because it's a dialup, and slow, you won't be tempted to use it very much.

Using Disposable Email Addresses

Disposable email addresses are just that: disposable. You choose them and use them and turn them off at any point and never miss them. Needless to say, you don't use them to communicate with friends, family, or business associates.

Disposable addresses are often obtained from free Web mail sites. They exist to be used for online commerce and other circumstances where you don't trust someone not to misuse the address. If anyone *does* misuse a disposable address, you simply cancel the address and obtain a new one.

Online firms now offer special email addresses that "time out" and go away after a period of time or a given number of uses. I'll describe these and how they're used in more detail later in this chapter.

Understand Where Email Addresses Come From

For a long time, you got your email address from the same entity that gave you access to the Internet, and that was the only email address you had. For some folks, this meant accessing the Net at work, with a company email address. For others, this meant an account with an Internet service provider (ISP) and an address from that provider.

Today, the picture is much more complex. You can get email accounts in a number of different ways, from several different types of organizations. Let's run down the list quickly, so you know what's available.

ISP Internet Accounts

Anytime you establish an account with an Internet service provider (ISP), you will receive an email address. This is true whether the account is for cable, DSL, or dialup service. For the majority of Internet users, this is the only email address they have.

If you're a Casual Communicator, that may be OK. The big disadvantage to most ISP email addresses is that they can only be read via an email client like Outlook Express from home, where your Internet connection is. If you go traveling and want to check your email, you can't connect with the email client program you're accustomed to using. Some ISPs provide a Web-based mail client feature so that you can check your mail while connecting from a hotel or coffee shop somewhere on the road, but that's not universal. Worse, many Web mail accounts have restrictions on sending or receiving attachments. Most road warrior types make heavy use of such attachments, and not being able to send and receive binary documents is a serious problem.

ISP email accounts make good backup accounts, but I don't recommend them as your primary email account, especially if your email needs place you in the Public Professional, Private Professional, or Student-Enthusiast category.

Your Employer's Email System

For a long time, people who had "work" email addresses were the envy of the neighborhood. Not only did such Internet access (including email) cost them nothing, but companies often had T1 access, which was expensive but very fast. (These days, many broadband systems are very nearly as fast as T1 lines.)

When the Internet was young, innocent, and relatively undisturbed by constant virus, worm, and black hat attacks, having email at work was a grand thing. Unfortunately, many companies have put restrictions in place governing the use of company email servers, and a few even have keyword monitoring systems that examine incoming and outgoing messages for certain "interesting" terms (*eBay, porn, Amazon,* and so on) and archive them to disk. Some company email systems forbid sending and receiving attachments. Viruses ride in on attachments, and company secrets (think documents and spreadsheets) ride out on them. Companies rightfully want to limit the amount of personal email stored on company servers and, more to the point, are leery of the time that staffers spend monitoring online auctions and sending email to family and friends.

It's just not much fun on the company server anymore. If you're a Private Professional and have no particular desire to use email for personal matters, you might get by simply having a company email address. But unless it's *you* who owns the company, you're unlikely to be able to use company email without the sense that somebody's looking over your shoulder.

Web Hosting Service Email Accounts

The high road for email service is to register and own your own Internet domain, so that your email address is in the form **me@my-very-own-domain.com**. This costs a little money and takes a little work, but if you're in the Public Professional category, you probably need the benefits it provides. A little later in this chapter, I'll explain how registering and owning a domain works and what it usually costs.

The key is this: When you establish a Web hosting account with most Web hosting firms, you also get a slice of an email server and some email addresses as part of the deal. How many email addresses you get depends on the nature of the plan, but even the cheap, $4.99/month bargain Web hosting plans that I see everywhere come with 5 email addresses. The more expensive plans can give you 20 or even 30 addresses, which should be enough for anybody. So for $5 a month, you can have a modest Web page and five email addresses, which should be enough for almost anyone, even those in the Public Professional category.

TIP: Note that Web hosting plans do not include Internet access. You need to have some way of getting onto the Internet as well. This is what you pay your broadband or dialup ISP for.

GunkBuster's Notebook: Finding a Low-Cost Web Hosting Service

Very recently, I have begun seeing Web hosting firms offering email-only hosting plans that do *not* include Web space. These can be quite inexpensive. GoDaddy.com, based in Scottsdale, Arizona, is a leader here and will give you a spam-filtered email account with a single address for $9.95 per year—basically $0.83 cents per month. A plan with five addresses is $19.95 per year. This is ideal for Private Professionals who do not need or want a Web page but would like to have multiple email addresses. Web hosting firms are legion, and one of the best ways to find one is to ask your tech-savvy friends which ones they use. Nothing works as well as word of mouth, especially if your friends have been with a hosting service for a year or more.

Free Web Mail Accounts

Web mail is just that: email that you can only read by logging in to a page on the Web. Sometimes when you get a conventional POP (Post Office Protocol) email account from an ISP, you will also receive a Web mail login. What I'm talking about here are Web-based services that offer email independent of any ISP and often without POP access. In a lot of these services, the only way you can read or send messages is through a form on a Web page operated by the service. (Some also offer POP access.) To use a Web mail account, of course, you first need access to the Internet through a conventional ISP.

GunkBuster's Notebook: Tips on Selecting a Web Mail Service

The majority of Web mail services these days do not charge at all for an email address on the service. How can they do this? Easy: Ads. You'll be presented with ads anytime you're logged in to the Web mail site, and some Web mail services will append ads to the bottom of every message that you send. I find this irritating, but most people don't even notice the ads after a few days, and ad-based Web mail now is a well-established institution in the Internet world.

Yahoo! Mail is probably the best known Web mail service, but I don't recommend it based on some experiences I have had, involving the release of my email addresses to spammers. Before you choose a service, shop around, ask your friends what they use, and use Google to see if people have had complaints about a particular Web mail provider.

Before you choose a Web mail provider, check its feature list and terms of service for the following:

√ How many messages can be stored on the Web mail server? Most Web mail services won't quote you a number of messages (since messages are of different sizes) but of storage capacity in megabytes. If you have a sense for how large your typical messages are, you can do the math and work it out. The good news is that disk storage is getting cheaper and competition is forcing hosting services to provide more storage for mail—sometimes as much as a gigabyte of storage, which is a *lot* of messages!

√ Does it support sending or receiving binary attachments? If so, how many megabytes (MB) of storage are available to store mail and attachments? Are there size limits on any single attachment? Many mail hosting services limit the size of attachments to one or two megabytes. The amount of storage quoted for an account is typically shared by mail and attachments, and this amount is getting bigger all the time. (See the previous point.)

√ Will the account be deleted if you don't use it for a period of time? If so, how long is that period of time?

√ Does the service provide access from a POP mail client (like Outlook Express) in addition to the Web form?

√ Is there server-side spam filtering? This is not necessarily a good thing! Read Chapter 10 to get a balanced perspective on this issue. The kind of filtering done at the server is critical. Some filters are overly aggressive and will lose real mail for you. If server-side filtering is available, can it be turned off?

√ Is there a Web-based address book for your contacts? If you use Web mail as your primary email, this will be important. If Web mail becomes your backup email strategy and your address book is on your PC, you won't need this. For privacy and availability reasons, I think it's better to keep your address book locally, on your PC.

√ Does the service provide several domains that you can choose from when you select your email address? Some domains "make a statement" reflecting hobbies or philosophical leanings, while others may simply be easier to remember. If you have a choice, choose one that's easy to spell!

√ Is there online help for the service? Without some sort of help system, you'll be figuring things out by trial and error, and errors can sometimes lose you mail you'd prefer to keep.

Some Web mail services provide additional features like message encryption and the ability to import messages and contacts from your PC-based mail clients and address books. Shop carefully. If you can stomach the ads, and if storing your messages and contacts on somebody else's server somewhere else in the world doesn't bother you, Web mail can work really well. Web mail accounts make excellent disposable email addresses because the accounts cost nothing to create and can be deleted without losing anything.

Freenets and Community Networks

In that strange, little-known period between 1989, when the Internet was first opened to the public, and 1994, when *the Web* became mostly synonymous with *the Internet,* email ruled the Net and there were wonderful dialup text-only Internet accounts called *freenets.* These were genuinely free access points to the Net, run by volunteers and nonprofit 501(c)(3) community organizations. Although freenets could access text-only Web pages after the Web was created in 1993, text-only Web pages are currently about as popular as fat-free potato chips. Over the years, freenets slipped more and more into obscurity—which is actually where many of them prefer to be. If you can find a freenet, a text-only email account makes a dandy, zero-cost backup account. All you need is a dialup modem and the patience to configure it correctly. Be aware that you probably won't be able to send or accept binary attachments. In the freenet world, text-only really means text *only.*

The best list of freenets and community networks that I've seen can be found here:

www.lights.com/freenet/

AzTeC is still around, but freenets are pretty sparse. Consider it pure serendipity if you have one within dialup range, and don't be afraid to use it!

Back Up Your Internet Access

Most of us take our Internet access for granted, assuming it will always be there—and we get very grumpy when it inevitably goes down for a few hours…or days. Having a backup route for getting onto the Net is a good idea, because if you can't get on the Net, all the email addresses in the world won't help you a bit.

Most people who have Internet access at work use their work access if their home access goes down. In years past this was a no-brainer, but many companies are increasingly twitchy about staff using the company network for personal things. Check first, and if you can find backup access elsewhere, grab it.

For many years I've used a separate dialup account with a national dialup provider as my backup Internet access. This works well, and I've also depended on the account for Net access when I travel. If you travel a lot, a dialup account is almost essential. More and more hotels are installing built-in broadband (be it wired or wireless), but it will be some years, if ever, before such systems are universal. AOL, whatever its flaws, is very good this way. I've used AT&T dialup since 2000 and have no complaints.

Wi-Fi hotspots make for excellent backup Internet access, if there's one convenient to you. Most public hotspots are fee based, but more and more are "going free" as customer bait. The leader here is Panera Bread, a national bread/soup/coffee shop that has rolled out free hotspots in hundreds of locations nationwide. Another is Shlotzky's Deli. Check around. I've seen free hotspots everywhere from Best Buy to Dairy Queen.

TIP: *Many folks hit upon the idea of simply connecting to the Net through a neighbor's broadband connection using their unprotected wireless network. About 60 percent of wireless network owners do not turn on encryption, and therefore anyone with a laptop and a wireless client can just hook in, surf the Web, or download mail. Resist the temptation. First of all, this is illegal—and besides, if your broadband connection is down, chances are your neighbors' will be down as well.*

GunkBuster's Notebook: Beware of "Free" Internet Service Providers

People who go searching for freenets sometimes scratch their heads when I tell them that freenets are scarce and getting scarcer. They point to several Web-based lists of "free ISPs," and these seem to be present in nearly every large and middling American city. So what's going on?

The problem is that there are two kinds of "free": There is really and truly free, like the nonprofit, community-based freenets, and then the commercial ISPs offering accounts for "free, as long as you let us do certain things." These "certain things" generally involve advertising of some sort and may subject you to pop-up ads, "commercials" that interrupt your online work, or in some cases install the sorts of spyware and adware that I warn against in Chapter 13. (Be careful not to confuse free Internet access with free Web mail! Web mail accounts are often ad supported, but the ads are all Web based and do not install anything on your PC.)

So how do you tell? Some of the lists are reasonably honest; see **www.all-free-isp.com** for starters. Many of the so-called "free" ISPs offer free accounts with intrusive banner ads and draconian restrictions on how many hours per month you can connect and how you can use the account. (Most, for example, will not work with POP mail clients like Outlook Express and Mozilla Thunderbird.) Many charge hugely for technical support. As incredible as it may seem, these companies hook a lot of customers

with free accounts that are so irritating that they upgrade to a paid account. More than a few will install advertising systems that "phone home" with your browsing destinations and statistics.

My take on free ISPs is this: Unless you stumble across a genuine, community-based freenet, free ISPs are not worth what they cost you: attention, irritation, spyware, adware.

Register Your Own Internet Domain

For relatively little money, you can register and own an Internet domain. Way back in 1997 I registered **duntemann.com** as my own domain, and I have been using it ever since, for both my primary email address and for my personal Web site. I pay about $20 per year to keep the domain registration in force. The price sometimes depends on which top-level domain (TLD) you want. A TLD is the part of a domain name "after the dot." The common ones include **.com**, **.net**, **.org**, and **.biz**, but there are many, many more. Some are country-specific, and some (like **.gov** and **.edu**) require you to be in a certain sort of organization and require that you prove it.

For a long time, the only way to register a domain was through Network Solutions and its corporate predecessors, and while that was the case, prices were quite high. In the last few years, domain registration has been opened up to competition and prices have fallen tremendously. If you shop, you can find domain registration that is quite cheap. One of the country's largest domain registrars, Go Daddy (**www.godaddy.com**) charges as little as $5 per year to register certain of the "off-brand" TLDs like **.us**. Most of the time you'll pay between $9 and $20 per year. If you pay for several years at once, the per-year cost usually goes down.

The easiest way to register a domain is to work through an Internet hosting service. The well-known ones that I recommend include Interland, Go Daddy, and SectorLink. There are, however, literally thousands more to choose from. Most hosting services offer domain registration through a Web form. Figure 2.1 shows Go Daddy's registration page.

To register a domain, you must first determine if it's available; let's just say that elvis.com and money.com (and almost any other ordinary word in the dictionary) were snapped up years ago. Whatever service you're working through to register a domain will have a search screen. Type in the domain and cross your fingers.

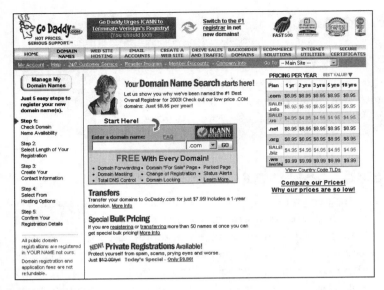

Figure 2.1

Domain Registration at GoDaddy.com.

If the domain is available, you can continue through the registration process, which typically requires entry of a credit card number and your billing information. If the precise domain you typed is not available, some systems will search for the same name under other TLDs like **.org**, **.net.**, **.biz**, and so on. If the **.com** form of your desired domain isn't available, the **.org** or **.us** form may be.

GunkBuster's Notebook: Choosing a Domain to Register

Finding a domain to register for your personal use or for business use is as much art as it is science. Since the Internet has become so commercialized over the past five years, it has become much more difficult to find a domain that hasn't been already taken. Here are some tips I can give you to help you save time and resources in choosing a domain:

√ Dictionary words are gone. Really—even obscure dictionary words. I tried to register **contrapositive.com** years ago and it was already gone. Sometimes you can find a dictionary word under a second- or third-shelf TLD like **.info**, but your best bet is to be creative and assemble something from several words instead.

√ Steer clear of domains that contain trademarks, especially big-company trademarks, even if the domain itself is

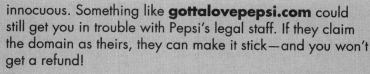

innocuous. Something like **gottalovepepsi.com** could still get you in trouble with Pepsi's legal staff. If they claim the domain as theirs, they can make it stick—and you won't get a refund!

√ The jury is out on whether hyphens are a good or a bad thing. Is it easier for people to remember st-fidgets-old-catholic-church or stfidgetsoldcastholicchurch? Nobody knows—but for sure, if you use hyphens between words, use hyphens between *all* words.

Remember this wisdom: *People will try typing a domain name only twice before giving up.* Help them get it right the first time!

Obtain and Use "Evaporating" Email Addresses

A disposable email address can be any email address that you wouldn't mind losing in a minute. You use disposable addresses when dealing with businesses online, when posting to Usenet newsgroups, and when communicating with people or organizations that you can't trust not to misuse your address. Many people use addresses from free Web mail accounts for this purpose, and they work well. However, very recently online services have appeared that specialize in disposable email addresses of a particular sort: addresses that are used only once (say, to make a purchase on the Web from a site known to be untrustworthy) and allow communication from the Web site for a period of time and then "evaporate" and go away.

There are some minor differences among these "evaporating email address" services, but they all work pretty much the same way:

1. You establish an account with a disposable email service. They are generally not free, but they don't cost very much—usually something like $10 per year. (At least one service I've tried—**spamgourmet.com**—is free.)

2. You give your primary email address to the service.

3. Whenever you need to communicate with an untrustworthy entity, the service generates an evaporating address for you, sometimes by having you install a browser button in your Web browser. When you click the browser button, a dialog pops up that creates and configures an evaporating address. The address can be configured so that it will "last" for a set period of time or else evaporate after a certain number of messages are sent to it.

4.   You give the evaporating address to a person, Web site, or other entity that you don't trust. When this entity sends a message to the disposable address, the address service forwards the entity's message to your primary email address. You get the message at your usual address, but the untrusted entity never gets your "real" email address.

5.   Typically, when you buy something from a Web site, you engage in a *short* (two or three message) conversation with that Web site. After all the shipping confirmations and so on have been sent, you don't need to keep receiving email from the Web site. If the Web site begins sending you spam, you may only get a message or two before the evaporating address evaporates. Your primary email address is never revealed—and remains clean of spam.

I've tried this, and while it works as advertised, it seems like a lot of bother to me, especially when free Web mail accounts are so easy to get and delete. So are evaporating email addresses for you? Here are some points to consider:

√   If you only buy online from the largest and most reputable e-commerce vendors—Amazon, Barnes & Noble, Half.com, and so on—you don't need to use an evaporating address. I've found that the largest vendors don't sell your address to spammers and will respect requests not to send you their own promotional mail. Use a single Web mail address for these "trustworthy" e-commerce sites. If you start getting spam, kill it and get another. I've had my current "trusted" e-commerce address for almost two years and it gets no spam.

√   If you post a lot on Usenet newsgroups, an evaporating address can be quite useful because spambots crawl newsgroups constantly, trolling for email addresses in the headers of postings. Newsgroups are a problem, spam-wise, and I'll have more to say about them in the spam section of this book.

√   If you're a real Web freak and are constantly registering for forums and newsletters and buying odd things from odd sites, evaporating addresses are just the ticket because this surfing style will generate *huge* amounts of spam for you.

√   If you own your own Internet domain and have a large number of uncommitted email addresses as part of your hosting account, you can create and destroy your own disposable email addresses any time you want. This is what I do, and I recommend it for Public Professionals who have their own domains.

In the meantime, here are three characteristic services for evaporating email addresses. I've tried them all and they work well:

Emailias	**www.emailias.com**	$20/year	Feature rich, may be overkill
SpamEx	**www.spamex.com**	$10/year	Easy and inexpensive
SpamGourmet	**www.spamgourmet.com**	Free	Good but takes some study

Summing Up

The first part of your new gunk-free email strategy is obtaining the right sort of email addresses—and enough of them to do what you need to do. Table 2.1 summarizes my recommendations in this area.

The general principles are these:

√ Don't use your ISP email address as your primary address unless you use email very little, don't travel, and don't buy things through e-commerce sites.

√ Don't use your work address for anything but company communications if you can avoid it. In any event, be aware of company policies pertaining to the use of company email and don't cross them!

√ Registering your own Internet domain gives you maximum control, and (usually) all the email addresses you'll ever need. If you're not intimidated by the technology and don't mind the modest extra expense, it's a great way to go.

√ Always use disposable or evaporating email addresses for e-commerce,, newsgroups, and online newsletters. Most spam comes from these sources.

Table 2.1   Email Address Recommendations.

User Type	Primary Address(es)	Backup Address	Disposable Addresses
Public Professional	Register a domain; define one address for public use, another for private use	ISP address, or email-only account with a *different* Web host	Define as needed under own domain
Private Professional	Email-only account with a Web host	ISP address, or employer email if policies permit	Free Web mail or evaporating address service
Student-Enthusiast	Register a domain; define addresses as needed	School email, ISP address, or employer email if policies permit	Define as needed under own domain or use evaporating address service
Casual Communicator	Free Web mail	ISP address	Free Web mail

Using the Right Email Client

Degunking Checklist:

√ Learn what a good email client is.

√ Pick an email client that matches your needs.

√ Find out what software monoculture is and why the overwhelming popularity of some email clients is a serious problem.

√ Determine whether a POP or IMAP account is better for you.

√ Find out how to travel with your entire mailbase intact, wherever you go.

√ Compare email choices and options.

Decades ago, when I was taking square dance lessons, the dance caller would cajole us into asking the girls to dance by hollering in a faux-western drawl, "Pick one, they's all good!" And while it's true that they were all suitable square dance partners, some of the girls were more graceful than others and some were lots prettier, and the, let's say, essential chemistry between some of the girls and some of the boys (including this one) was just not there.

That's roughly how I feel about email client programs: You have to pick one to play the email game, and any of them will do the basic job. Each of them has points of special brilliance, and each of them has flaws. Which one you choose depends completely on how and how much you intend to use email and on other factors that I can only describe as personal chemistry.

If you're already using an email client that you've learned and are comfortable with, and if you've been using it now for some time, moving to another is probably more bother than it's worth.

That said, this chapter will be of greatest interest if either one of the following applies:

√   You don't already use email and need to pick a client program.

√   You hate the program you're using and have to switch.

The types—and amount—of email gunk that you receive depends very heavily on the email client that you use. This is not simply a matter of spam, either. Some email clients have "security holes" that make them hazardous to use if you don't take certain precautions, and there's no gunk like malware gunk!

On the other hand, if you like what you've got, it's OK to skim to the end of the chapter—but it might be smart to read along instead and see what you might be missing!

What Makes a Good Email Client?

I've been an Internet email user since early 1994, and before that made heavy use of CompuServe, MCI Mail, and (earlier still) ARPANet, back while I worked at Xerox. I've used more email clients than I can count, and certainly I've used all the major ones, some of them for years running. Out of this experience, I've isolated 15 characteristics that any good email client should exhibit. Let's talk a little bit about each.

Easy to Learn and Use

Some software is just more difficult to learn and use than other software. Some part of the issue is good design, but a lot of it is just straightforwardness and familiarity in menu structures, window layouts, and so on. Like it or not, the "Outlook-style" user interface (UI) for email clients is now a strong standard, and any client that doesn't look like Outlook in terms of how the menus are set up and where the major panes appear will be harder to learn. This is not always stubbornness or a "not-invented-here" mind-set on the part of client vendors. Eudora has been around since 1991, long before Outlook, and its tabbed UI operates differently from everything else out there. If you've ever used something that looks like the Outlooks, you'll have to un-learn a lot before you can become truly comfortable with Eudora.

Pegasus Mail is an extremely powerful and feature-rich program, but it has a deserved reputation for being difficult to learn. Part of this is due to errors in the online help (which refers to the "New" button when it really means the "Add" button) and part to unnecessary complexity, errors that beep without any explanation of what is wrong, and so on. It has what I call the "Unix disease," which is a general disregard for ease of use and an assumption that all users are equally willing to toil endlessly with a program until they figure it out.

On the flip side, newer email clients like The Bat, Poco Mail, and Mozilla Thunderbird all have the general look and feel of Outlook and Outlook Express and are a great deal easier to learn, especially if you have one of the Outlooks at work and learned how to use email on it.

Multiple Mail Accounts

As I explained in Chapter 1, one email address is not enough. Working effectively requires at least two and probably several. A good email client must be able to send and receive mail from multiple email accounts with minimal difficulty and hoop-jumping. The good news is that virtually all modern email clients can.

Hierarchical Folders or Mailboxes

As I'll explain a little later in this book, nothing helps conquer email gunk like a good hierarchical folder system. This means allowing you to create folders within folders, with a vertical folder management pane that can expand or collapse folder subtrees as needed.

As with support for multiple accounts, hierarchical folder management is now almost universal in email clients. But be sure to read the fine print before committing to an off-brand client.

Binary Attachments

Email has evolved from a simple text messaging system to a general system for moving data around. Some of that data is binary in nature—not text—like images, spreadsheets, database files, programs, and so on. Almost all clients now give you the option of sending and receive such binary data as a sort of "ride along" attached to the message. There are hazards in receiving attachments that I'll cover in the last section of this book, but they don't outweigh the usefulness of binary attachments. These days, you simply have to have that ability.

HTML and Plain-Text Mail

All the major email clients allow you to choose between HTML and plain-text mail. It's increasingly important for a simple reason: Virtually all spam uses HTML encoding. Some people have become so desperate to keep ahead of spam that they trash all messages encoded using HTML. Never use HTML-formatted email unless you absolutely must. On more and more people's email systems, it's a quick trip to the trash bin.

Protection Against "Spam Beacon" Image Downloads

This is all about the "preview pane" and the window that displays the actual message when opened. A good client must allow you to disable image downloads in the preview pane and message display window. HTML-formatted messages often bring down images from a remote server, and these images can be encoded to your specific email address. If you bring down the image, the spammer knows that the message was opened and therefore that your email address is "live." You need to avoid that at all costs. Email clients that use Microsoft Internet Explorer as the preview pane or message viewer (like both Outlooks) have this problem. (The latest Outlook has a partial solution.) Clients with their own message viewers usually do not. Pegasus Mail, The Bat, Poco Mail, and Mozilla Thunderbird are very good in this respect. Eudora gives you the option of using either IE or its own message viewer.

Protection Against Scripts in HTML Messages

Messages formatted as HTML may contain *malware,* which refers to programs that run and do things that aren't in your interest. This may include changing your Web browser home page, launching windows hawking pornography, installing spyware, and worse. Much malware takes the form of scripts embedded in the HTML code. If your preview pane or message viewer is an HTML viewer that runs scripts, malware may be given control of your PC, to do their gunk-y and often damaging thing. (I'll have a lot more to say about this in the last section of this book.) If your email client uses Internet Explorer as its preview pane and message viewer, you have to manually configure IE to ignore scripts. Better, in my view, is to use an email client with a separate HTML viewer that either does not understand scripts or that defaults to ignoring them. There is almost no reason to allow scripts to run in email messages, and these days only spammers and system hijackers use them. The Outlooks are bad in this regard, especially Express. Pegasus Mail, The Bat, Poco Mail, Mozilla Thunderbird, and Eudora are generally safe if you keep the defaults set by the installer.

Imports Mail from Many Email Clients

These days, most people already have a *mailbase*; that is, a number of email messages that they have received in the past and wish to retain. When you change email clients, it's extremely important to be able to transfer your mailbase to the new client. The easiest way to do this is to use an import feature built into the new client. Most email clients will import messages from the industry leaders: Outlook, Outlook Express, and Eudora. It's far less common to import from clients with less market share. If you're looking to change email clients, read the fine print to see if the new client can import from the old client or if the old client can export a mailbase to a format that the new client can import. See the next point.

Exports Mail to Standard Formats

Exporting messages and mailboxes is an important feature, especially if you're forward-looking enough to think you may need to jump to another email client in the future. Many email clients can export messages and address books to common formats, like the RFC822 mailbox format. If you can export your mailbase and address book to a common format, a new email client is more likely to be able to import the data. Outlook, Outlook Express, and Eudora do not export data very well. The Bat probably does a better job with imports and exports than any other major client, with Poco Mail a close second.

Uses the Windows Address Book

Address books are a problem. Although virtually all email clients include a built-in address book feature, many people already have contact information stored in the Windows Address Book (WAB). Unfortunately, no major non-Microsoft email client makes direct use of the WAB. There's at least a partial reason for this: The WAB uses an interface called Messaging Application Programming Interface (MAPI), which has some extremely serious security holes. Unfortunately, Outlook and Outlook Express make direct use of the WAB, but no others do. For other email clients, you have to import it. Eudora and The Bat import contact information from the WAB, and Poco Mail offers a free utility that will do the job outside of Poco Mail itself. For import-challenged mail clients, you can use a third-party package like Fookes Software's Mailbag Assistant.

User-Defined Message Filters

Whether you use it to knock out spam or to sort incoming messages into folders automatically, filtering is an inescapable part of your gunk-fighting arsenal. Any good client must have some sort of filtering system that allows users to define their own filters. All the major email clients allow you to do filtering, though some (Outlook and Pegasus particularly) are better at it than others.

Easy Backup of Your Mailbase

Most email clients do not store your entire mailbase in one single, easy-to-back-up file. Each mail folder may be stored in a separate file, and there may be additional files for indexes. Furthermore, email attachments may be stored in a separate folder. Backing up all the various fragments of your mailbase must be done carefully, and the best email clients have a built-in backup feature so that your mailbase may be copied to a separate location on your hard drive or network with a single command. Poco Mail and The Bat are the best in this regard. For most other mail clients, you will have to locate and back up your mailbase manually. I'll explain more about this in later chapters.

Support for POP and IMAP Mailboxes

The vast majority of email servers use Post Office Protocol (POP) mailboxes, but there is another very useful email protocol named Internet Message Access Protocol (IMAP). IMAP keeps messages in mail folders maintained on a central server. Periodically, the user "synchronizes" folders on a local PC with their corresponding folders on the IMAP server. This makes it very easy to read your mail from multiple locations (like work and home). IMAP is usually not available with typical ISP mail accounts. It's most often used in company mail servers, so if your email access comes from your employer, you're more likely to have access to IMAP. The real problem with IMAP is that it's a *much* more complex protocol than POP, and some email clients implement it better than others. The best IMAP email client that I know of is Mozilla Thunderbird, followed by Outlook Express (which I don't recommend) and Poco Mail.

Cheap or Free

The technology behind email clients is not rocket science, and they should not cost more than $50. Outlook is expensive because it generally comes with Microsoft Office. It also contains a lot of other non-email features, like the appointment calendar, which you may not need. If cost is an issue, both Pegasus Mail and Mozilla Thunderbird are free, and Thunderbird, at least, is very easy to set up and use.

Not Too Popular

Huh? This last point is extremely important from a gunk perspective, and it's peculiar enough to warrant some extended discussion in a section of its own. There are non-obvious dangers when "everyone" uses the same email client—or any networking software, like Web browsers. Let's talk about that in more detail.

The Problem of Software Monoculture

If you're not already using Microsoft Outlook or Outlook Express, I recommend not choosing them or switching to them. This has nothing to do with whether I like Microsoft or not. It doesn't even have to do with whether the Outlooks are quality software. (They are!) Both programs have their quirks (which I'll explain later), but their real problem is much simpler, if more controversial: *They are too popular.* The technical term for this problem is *software monoculture.* Quite simply, when a single product or family of software gains an overwhelming proportion of market share, bad things happen more easily. This is true of most software categories, including operating systems, but it is particularly true of software like email clients that handle communication among different computers.

The best way to demonstrate the dangers of software monoculture involves viruses and worms. (I'll explain viruses and worms in much more detail later in this book.) Nearly all viruses and worms exploit security flaws in particular programs. A worm might be a specialist in, for example, Internet Explorer. That worm won't affect Netscape or Opera. Worms and viruses are all specialists and need the vulnerable program for which they were written to be running before they can take over and propagate themselves. Once an email virus is running on a PC, it emails itself to other PCs by locating and using the email addresses stored in the PC's address book.

So follow me carefully here: If 60 percent of all the users listed in someone's address book are running Outlook Express, a virus is very likely to take hold on at least one or two of those users' PCs. (All the other users of Outlook Express in the address book are smart and have a virus scanner, or at least don't open attachments.)

On the other hand, if only 10 percent of the users listed in someone's address book are running Eudora, a virus is unlikely to encounter a user without virus protection. Unless the virus can mail itself to a system that both has the vulnerable software and lacks virus protection, *it cannot propagate.*

Virus writers know this. They've done the math and they understand that writing an email virus that exploits a weakness on an email client with only 6 percent market share is a waste of time. That virus will never find a critical mass of unprotected machines, so it's basically dead on arrival.

What this means is pretty simple: You're safer using Internet software with relatively little market share. On the flip side, you're in more danger using software that "owns the market" because such software is constantly in the crosshairs of virus and worm authors. Given Microsoft's overwhelming domination of the Windows software market, this generally cooks down to not using Microsoft's Outlook email clients or its Internet Explorer Web browser.

Again, this has little or nothing to do with technical quality. Microsoft's software is no worse than that of other companies in that regard and is probably better, for no other reason than all the negative attention they get when security breaches come to light. Security vulnerabilities are regularly reported in other software. On May 7, 2004, a major buffer-overflow vulnerability was confirmed to exist in the Eudora email client versions 5 and later. If exploited, the vulnerability could allow an intruder to completely take over the underlying copy of Windows. Although Eudora is fairly popular, it's not nearly as popular as Outlook or Outlook Express. Finding a Eudora user at random out on the Internet is a lot tougher than finding an Outlook Express user, so even though the vulnerabilities may exist in Eudora and other minority-player email clients, few of the black hats will bother looking for copies of Eudora when there are so many, many more copies of Outlook Express to attack!

So understand me when I offer the following advice, because it has nothing to do with Microsoft itself but everything to do with the percentages of Microsoft's market share: Using Outlook, Outlook Express, and Internet Explorer carries risks that using other software does not. Although I cover the Outlooks in this book, I don't think using them is an especially good idea. I'll explain in much more detail why not in the spam and malware chapters later in this book.

POP or IMAP?

Virtually all email accounts that you get from an ISP will be Post Office Protocol (POP) accounts. POP is a simple and ancient protocol that is very well understood and has long since shaken out. In a POP account, all your email messages are downloaded from the POP server and live on your hard drive. Taken as a group, these messages constitute your *mailbase*.

One problem with using POP-based email turns up when you have to process email from multiple locations: work, home, or on the road. Your mailbase exists in a single place, and if you download messages to multiple PCs (say, your home PC, your work PC, and your laptop), there is no easy way to make sure that all messages downloaded to all PCs are eventually gathered into your mailbase. If email is important to your work or hobbies and you retain messages for future reference, it's a bad idea to allow messages to be scattered among several different PCs.

Internet Message Access Protocol (IMAP) fixes this problem. If you have an IMAP-based email account, all your messages are stored on a central IMAP server. You can create folders on the server just as you can create folders in an email client. The view of your mailbase that you see on your email client mirrors the structure of your mailbase as it exists on the central server. If you buy a new laptop for work on the road, you connect to your IMAP server with the new laptop and your email client will download an image of your mailbase from the IMAP server to your laptop. Changes made to any image of your centrally stored mailbase will be synchronized to the central copy, so no matter where you go, you can download a completely current image of your mailbase, typically with one click in your email client.

Typically.

The problem with IMAP is that it's quite complex, and also relatively new and still in flux around the edges. There have been attempts in the best email clients to fully implement IMAP and keep up with its changes, but some do a better job than others, and in a few (like Calypso), it's barely implemented at all.

I used IMAP for almost a year under Outlook 2000, and it left a bad taste in my mouth. Synchronizing my central mailbase (which has always been very large) with my several copies of Outlook was a *very* slow process. Strange things would happen, and sometimes folders on the server would become corrupt. From what I hear, such things still happen and are very hard to troubleshoot.

Still, if you do a lot of traveling and need to manage email from multiple locations (like work, home, satellite offices, and on the road), IMAP has a lot going for it. Over time, the major email clients are getting better at handling it. Ironically, one of the very best IMAP email clients is the free, open-source Mozilla Thunderbird. If you decide to use IMAP, nothing comes even close in terms of reliability and speed. (On the Mac, Microsoft's new Entourage client is also excellent for IMAP.)

Because IMAP accounts require a lot of storage on the server side, few ISPs provide it, and where they do, you may be faced with extra charges and strict limits on the size of your mailbase. (All the more reason to keep the gunk level down!) Most of the time, when you have an IMAP account, it will be through your employer. This won't help you with your personal email, which I do recommend keeping separate from your work email. (This may be a condition of employment, as well. Be careful!)

My recommendations: If you are a Public Professional and have access to an IMAP email server, use it, making sure that your email clients fully support the IMAP standard. Other categories of email users should probably stick with POP, especially those folks who are nontechnical. IMAP has a lot more features and options than POP, and sorting them out so as to use them most effectively takes a lot of study and practice. Using IMAP badly can be a good way to accumulate email gunk. (Even something as simple as deleting a message is, well, "nuanced.") If you decide to use IMAP, *take the time to learn it thoroughly!*

My Recommendations

There are a lot of different choices to be made in the email world, and it can get bewildering at times. To wrap up this chapter, I'd like to provide some insights to help you get your head around the choices you need to make. I recognize that some of these choices may have been made for you already, especially if your sole access to email is through your employer. But keep in mind that employment situations can change abruptly, and it never hurts to know a little more about technology than you need to so whatever jumping you have to do isn't done blindly!

Figure 3.2 summarizes how the major Windows email clients stack up in terms of the 15 points I set forth at the beginning of this chapter. In the chart, filled circles are good and empty circles are bad. The more black a given client has in its column, the more that client adheres to my 15 characteristics of good email clients.

Protocols: POP vs. IMAP

√ If you are basically nontechnical, do not use IMAP. It is complex and subtle, and not all email clients implement it completely.

√ If your only email access is through your employer, IMAP may be a given. If it is, take advantage of any courses or seminars that teach you how to use it. The learning curve is much stiffer than for POP.

√ If you travel a lot or have PCs in multiple locations, IMAP may be worth using irrespective of its learning curve because it allows you to keep your mailbase on a central server and download it to any PC on which you happen to be working.

Protocols: Client Choices

√ Virtually all email clients implement POP completely and well. If you're using POP, the decision about which client to use will depend on other things. Keep reading.

√ If you're using IMAP through your employer, you may be given a client at the office and will not have a choice. If so, use the same email client at home. IMAP is hard enough to learn. Don't complicate your situation by trying to learn the way two different clients handle it.

√ If you're using IMAP and have a choice of clients, I *strongly* recommend Mozilla Thunderbird over all others. Furthermore, this recommendation takes priority over almost all other factors because a bad implementation of IMAP will do nothing but make you crazy and Thunderbird's is as good as any I've encountered.

Clients and Your Experience Level

√ If you are a nontechnical Casual Communicator (see Chapter 2), almost nothing beats Mozilla Thunderbird. It's free and extremely easy to figure out and use.

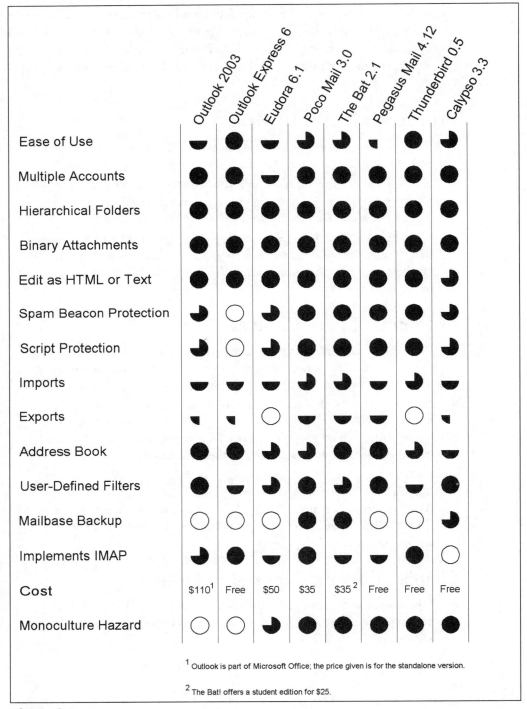

Figure 3.1
Email Clients Comparison Chart

√ If you are a Public Professional (see Chapter 2) and use email a great deal, the more powerful clients (Outlook, Poco Mail, The Bat, Pegasus) are a much better choice. Migrating your mailbase to a more powerful client is *much* more difficult than simply learning a more powerful client to begin with.

√ If you are a Casual Communicator or are generally nontechnical, do not use Outlook. The reasons center on ensuring that all necessary Microsoft security updates are always installed, not only those that exist but those that will doubtless be released in the future. Without those updates, your PC is at grave risk of being compromised by network intruders. Also, when using Outlook, it is *imperative* that you use a firewall like ZoneAlarm Pro. All this requires knowing more about firewalls and Windows updates than nontechnical people typically do.

Clients and the Nature of your Work

√ If you travel a great deal and process a lot of email on the road, choose a client that makes it easy to move your mailbase between your desktop PC and your laptop. IMAP is one way to do this, but if you can't use IMAP, Poco Mail and The Bat are probably your best choices. The Bat is the champ here because it's the only email client I've tested with a true two-way mailbase synchronization feature. (More on mailbase synchronization in Chapter 5.)

√ If you do a lot of research in public libraries or work in other places (like Internet cafés) where Internet-connected PCs are available for your use, you can use a specialty client like Poco Systems's EmailVoyager, which is a USB Flash drive preloaded with a self-contained version of Poco Mail. Your client and mailbase are thus stored together in something that fits in your pocket and will work in any USB-port-equipped Windows 2000 or XP computer. (If you already have a Flash drive, you can buy Poco Mail Portable Edition separately.) More on EmailVoyager and how it's used in Chapter 5.

The concept of using email from multiple locations is a complex one, and I've devoted the entirety of Chapter 5 to it.

Summing Up—Have Client. Will Email!

This chapter has mostly been for those who are actively looking for a new email client. If you already have an email client and you're comfortable with it, stick with it. No email client is immune to email gunk, and as I'll explain in later chapters, spam and malware are often handled most effectively outside your email client. In the next chapter, I'll get down to the key issue in preventing email gunk: good working habits and developing the discipline of dealing with the inevitable gunk before it piles up in unmanageable quantities.

Developing Good Email Habits

Degunking Checklist:

√ Process mail when it comes in. Don't let it pile up.

√ Cancel unnecessary email newsletters or listservs to reduce the amount of mail you get.

√ For each incoming message, ask yourself three questions: Keep? Hold? Or Pitch? Be decisive.

√ Create a separate folder for mail that can't be processed right now so that it won't "go below the fold."

√ Try to impose a 100-message limit on your inbox. A *single-screen* limit is ideal.

√ Configure your email client so that attachment files are deleted when the messages they came in on are deleted.

√ Don't read email too often — it slows down your other work.

√ Use an email notifier to prioritize your mail and reduce the number of times you read it.

√ Create an email backup strategy and stick with it.

T he secret behind quick housecleaning is really nothing more than living a reasonably tidy, organized life: Don't dump your dirty socks in the corner; don't let dirty dishes get so deep in the sink that you can't find the faucets. The less the mess piles up, the quicker you'll be able to go through and be done with the cleaning.

Keeping email gunk at bay is a similar challenge, and a lot of it is simply developing and maintaining good email habits. That's what this chapter is about: Getting a routine underway that keeps the mail moving smoothly, whether it's headed for your archival folders or on a quick path to the trash. Later on in this book I'll explain how to handle periodic cleaning of your mailbase. For the moment, let's talk about the simple everyday habits of processing mail as it comes in.

Sort Your Email: Keep, Hold, or Pitch?

The Prime Directive in the war against email gunk is so obvious that it may make you groan: *Process email when it comes in.* Too many people ignore messages in their inboxes until they get lost in a huge pile of email. In most cases, old messages are simply ignored until they're months old, at which time they're simply deleted, even if it would be smarter to answer them or file them for future reference.

You have to do the work. You do it now, or you do it (a lot more of it) later. Ducking the work merely allows "real" email to become gunk, and slogging through the gunk at a later date simply makes the inevitable that much more work. If you feel you're getting too much email, consider whether your email newsletters or listservs are necessary, or whether Cousin Suzie needs to be told to stop forwarding you those prayer chain letters. (If your inbox is choked with spam, there are other things you can do, and I'll explain them in detail later in this book.)

In general, any email message falls into one of three categories:

1. Mail with lasting value, which should be retained indefinitely (keep).
2. Mail that is associated with a current project or otherwise limited by a calendar date and needs to be held for a period of time and then archived or deleted (hold).
3. Mail that can be dealt with right now and then deleted immediately (pitch).

These three categories of mail require action that you could characterize as keep, hold, or pitch. Each time you look at a message entering your inbox, those three words should be kept in mind.

Beware the Fold!

Your overall goal is to keep the size of your inbox down. The reason is simple: If you can't see a message on your screen, you're much more likely to forget that it's there. Once a message scrolls off the top (or the bottom, on some clients) of the message header pane, we say it "goes below the fold," which is an old journalists' expression from the newspaper industry. The stuff that gets and keeps attention is the stuff you can see without having to unfold the paper—or scroll up the message header pane. Email inboxes get out of control when too many messages go "below the fold" and are forgotten. Useful stuff may be lurking in the shadows of your inbox, lost amidst the gunk that should have been deleted or filed in a folder the day it came in.

This is what "Keep, Hold, or Pitch" helps remind you to do. It doesn't have to be done in that order; in fact, I've found it effective to make three separate scans of my inbox each time I sit down to process email, and they're actually in the order *Pitch…Hold…Keep.* The reason for the order is this: You want to eliminate everything that doesn't have to be retained permanently *first,* so you're less tempted to keep unnecessary messages and grow your mailbase needlessly. Remember: *Unnecessary messages are gunk!*

Do it like this:

1. *Pitch:* First delete anything that can be deleted without further action. Don't worry too much that you might need it later in case something related comes in. This is what the Trash folder is for. (In some clients, this folder is called Deleted Items.) You can delete something by moving it to Trash, and it will stay there against the odd chance that you might need to retrieve it over the next couple of days. The key, of course, is not to empty Trash too often. Leave messages in Trash for at least four days and ideally a week. If you get a lot of spam, don't have your filters send it to Trash. Create a separate folder called Spam and make it your spam filter's target folder. Delete spam from the Spam folder once a day.

2. *Hold:* Move messages that you can't handle immediately to a separate folder. You may be waiting on someone else for status on their part of a project, or you may need to finish a spreadsheet or some analysis to provide a useful answer. "Hold" messages may have to hang fire for a few days, and if you get a lot of mail, some of them will definitely go below the fold in your inbox and might get lost. Here's how you handle them: Create a Pending Items folder and move anything that you can't process *right now* into it. (Be *very* sure that the item actually needs special attention and can't simply be read and deleted!) The single toughest discipline in handling email well is forcing yourself to go back to your Pending Items folder regularly to deal with what's there. My rule of thumb: Nothing should be left in Pending Items for

more than 30 days. If you can't handle it in that time, bounce it back to its sender with an apology or an explanation.

3. *Keep:* Once you've deleted what you don't need and moved anything that must wait to Pending Items, process what's left and either delete it or sort it to one of your folders for archived messages. This is the real work of email, and you'll spend most of your time on this step.

TIP: One reason that quantities of useful messages accumulate in your inbox is that you haven't created folders for them yet. These "orphan keepers" will pile up on you, sometimes without your noticing. Scan your inbox periodically and see if there are several messages on the same general topic. If they're really keepers, create a folder to store them in, or find an existing folder where they may fit. If they're not really keepers, well, you know what to do!

The 100-Message Rule

Most people who depend on email try to adhere to a 100-message rule for their inboxes. Keep an eye on the number of messages your inbox contains, and when it tops 100, budget some time *right now* to get it down to about 50—or fewer. When you have more than 100 messages in your inbox, chances are that the oldest are forgotten and just sit there gathering dust and making searches more difficult and time consuming.

If you're *really* disciplined, try to adhere to a *single-screen* rule. In other words, keep no more messages in your inbox than will display on a single screen. Especially if you're busy and transact a lot of communication over email, this will be extremely hard. Don't feel like a failure if you can't manage it. It's an ideal to strive for, not a requirement!

GunkBuster's Notebook: Don't Abandon Attachments!

Attachments are files that come in with an email message but are not themselves part of the message. Nearly all email clients can accept attachments with incoming mail, but attachments are a potent source of email gunk if you don't handle them properly. The #1 priority is to make sure your email client is set up so that when you delete an email message, *any attachments it came in with are deleted with it.* If you don't do this, abandoned attachment files (which are often quite large) will accumulate in your attachments folder until you may literally have hundreds of megabytes of them. (Do your friends send you images or MP3 music files? I rest my case!)

Every client handles this differently, *sigh*. Here are some pointers for those clients that give you some control over how attachments are deleted:

√ Poco Mail: Be sure the "Query to delete attachments when deleting messages" item is checked in the Reading Mail section in the Options window.

√ The Bat: Be sure the "Delete attached files when the message is deleted from the trash folder" item is checked in the Files & Directories section in the Account Properties window.

√ Eudora: Be sure that the "Delete attachments when emptying trash" item is checked, in the Attachments section in the Options window.

Note that in Outlook and Outlook Express, attachments are always deleted with messages they came in with. Delete the messages, and their attachments are always gone.

Cleaning out your attachments folder regularly is essential. I'll have more to say about that later in this book when we talk about cleaning up email gunk after the fact.

Prioritize Your Email with Email Notifiers

One thing I've told a lot of my friends and clients that has surprised them but then helped them a great deal is this: *You're reading email too often.* Most email clients have an option specifying how often the email client should go up to your server and fetch down mail. An amazing number of people set this option at 10 minutes, or even 5—meaning that they are actually checking their mail as often as 20 times an hour.

Some years back I remember hanging out in a corporate cube farm and hearing that cute little xylophone riff used by Eudora to announce incoming mail what seemed like every few *seconds*. Get enough people in the same room reading Eudora email out of synch every five minutes and you'll be hearing that riff in your sleep.

The problem is really one of distraction and splintered concentration. Every time the xylophone goes off, the human tendency is to drop what you're doing and pop up the client to see what came in. It takes a mighty will to ignore the siren song of an email announcement. Stopping to read email breaks your concentration on the task at hand, and the total time you spend on email (counting the time you spend bringing up the client, scanning the message list, taking several deep breaths, and pondering all the other matters that come to mind as you scan the displayed message headers) will be a *lot* more than if you read mail only a few times a day.

I strongly recommend reading email only three times a day at work, and maybe once or twice at home in the evening. Most people object that their work often depends on responding to certain emails very quickly. Waiting three or four hours to respond to messages from the boss or from important customers is a non-starter—and so the xylophone goes off every five minutes.

Notifiers: Your Silent Email Partner

There is a solution. The key here is "certain emails." Not all of them. Certainly not spam. What you need is a utility that will frequently and silently check the mail on your server and alert you when mail from certain people arrives or mail containing certain character strings in the header. You decide what indicates a critical message and the notifier will watch for them.

These utilities exist, and they're called *email notifiers.* They live in your PC's taskbar tray, silently checking the mail on your POP server every so often. You install one and tell it what messages to watch for. When a message comes in that triggers one of its filters, a talk-balloon pops up over the tray, telling you that a priority message has arrived. At that point, you can bring up your regular email client and bring down mail.

Of course, at that point your client brings down all the other mail that has been gathering on your server as well, but assuming that you don't consider too many different senders as "critical," you'll be breaking concentration a lot less to read email during the course of an ordinary day.

POPTray: Free and Easy

One of the best email notifiers I've tried is also the easiest to use—and they don't get any cheaper. POPTray does just about everything an email notifier should do, and it's completely free and open source. It supports POP, IMAP4, IMAP4 SSL, and Hotmail out of the box, and there is a plug-in interface allowing programmers to create support for other mail protocols. You can download it from the product home page: **www.poptray.org**.

Install POPTray

The POPTray installer is an executable file: Run it and the install wizard guides you through the process. There isn't much to the install—most of the configuration is done from the Options tab after the program is fully installed. The only trick to be aware of during installation is shown in Figure 4.1. By default, POPTray supports several (human) languages, but if your native language is English, you can save over a megabyte of disk space by not installing the others. Uncheck the Language Files option on the tab shown in Figure 4.1.

Once POPTray installation is complete, it will be minimized to the taskbar tray. You need to set a number of options before using it. Right-click the POPTray tray icon and select Options. First of all, decide how often you want POPTray to go up and check your email server. The Interval item is the top item on the Options screen. You can set it for any reasonable interval. I use one minute, which may seem excessive, but that ensures that I will hear about any critical email within a minute of its arrival while not being bothered by spam or low-priority mail.

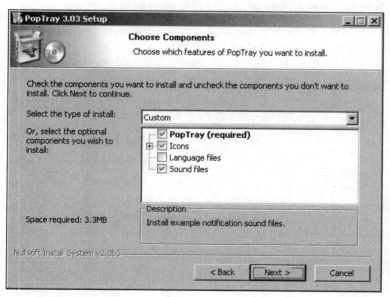

Figure 4.1

Deselecting Language Files during POPTray installation.

Perhaps the most important thing is to set up your email account or accounts. POPTray can handle several at once, but you have to enter login data for each one separately. To set up accounts, click the Accounts tab on the right margin. Click the Add Account icon at the top of the window to set up an email account. I show the Add Account window in Figure 4.2.

The "empty" account gets a default name of NoName. Enter a name for the account; this is not the account's email address! Enter the mail server name, login, and password, just as you did for the account when you set it up in your email client program. The default protocol is POP3. If you're using an IMAP4 or IMAP4 SSL account, you must download the plug-ins for those protocols separately and follow the included instructions for installing them. A plug-in for Hotmail is also available for download.

You can select a display color for the account. POPTray periodically displays the number of messages waiting as a colored number in the middle of its taskbar tray icon. If you only have one account the color doesn't matter. However, if you use POPTray to monitor several accounts, it's handy to have a distinct color for each so that you can tell at a glance if mail is piling up in a particular account.

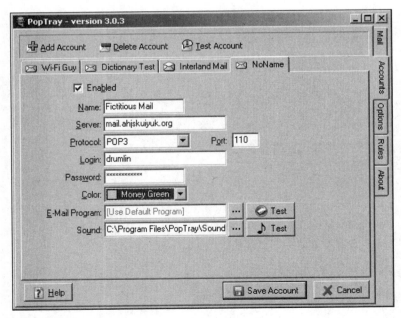

Figure 4.2
Setting up an email account in POPTray.

When setting up an account, you can specify a sound that POPTray will play whenever new mail is detected on the server. The default is no sound, and I think that's a good idea, especially if you're trying to avoid having your email be a distraction! Sound has its uses with POPTray, as I'll describe in the next section.

Once you have the account set up the way you like, click Save Account.

Create POPTray Rules for Critical Senders

POPTray really doesn't do anything especially useful until you define one or more rules for it to follow while checking mail on your servers. These rules can do many things, but they have two primary uses:

1. Alerting you to the arrival of critical messages
2. Detecting and deleting spam

I'll have more to say about POPTray's uses in fighting the spam wars later in this book. To create a rule, bring up the POPTray window and click the Rules tab in the right margin. Click Add Rule at the top. A new rule will be created, and you must fill out the new rule's various parameters. This window is shown in Figure 4.3.

Note that most of the rules shown in Figure 4.3 are actually my traps set for spammers and not rules defining critical senders. I'll speak more of POPTray spam traps later on in this book.

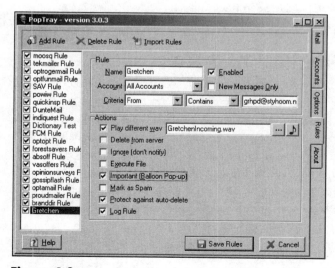

Figure 4.3

Creating a new rule in POPTray.

To create a rule defining a critical sender, follow these steps:

1. Give the rule a short descriptive name. In the example, it is Gretchen.

2. Specify which account is to be monitored by this rule. If you don't specify a single account, POPTray will apply the rule to all accounts.

3. The Criteria line is the key to the process. You have many options here, though most are useful only in rare circumstances. Most of the time you want to specify that the From field must contain a particular email address. So select From, which is the default.

4. Select Contains, which is the default.

5. Type the full email address that you wish to consider critical.

6. Under Actions, you tell POPTray what to do if all of the parameters in the Criteria line are found to be true for a message. Most of the time, you want to be notified. You have two different notification methods to choose from: A pop-up talk balloon and an audio announcement. Each has a separate check box. If you select them both, you will receive both a visual and audio notification.

7. If you check Play Different WAV, you can select a sound file in WAV format by clicking the browse (…) button. POPTray comes with several different canned messages, but, although they're in English, the woman speaking them has a strong European accent and some of them are a little hard to understand. If you have a microphone, I suggest recording your own announcements in your own voice, using your sound card. Your own voice saying "Mail from the Boss!" is hard to misunderstand!

8. When all the parameters have been filled out, click Save Rules at the bottom to save the new rule.

Let POPTray Prioritize Your Mail

When it's running, POPTray checks your mail server periodically according to the Interval parameter, and it will display the number of messages waiting on the server in a colored number at the center of its taskbar tray icon. When a critical message comes in for which you've defined a rule, a talk balloon will appear over the taskbar tray, as well as an audible alert if you've selected sound. At that point, you can double-click the POPTray taskbar tray icon to launch your default email client. (You don't have to bring up POPTray itself! To bring up POPTray, right-click the tray icon instead.) When you download your mail in your email client, your critical message will be there.

All the rest of your mail (and spam) will come down too, of course, and you might as well deal with it along with your critical messages. The point is to download mail only when it's important to download mail and not every 5 or 10 minutes throughout the day.

TIP: Try to avoid the error of defining too many senders as critical. If you have 50 rules declaring that almost every person from whom you ever get email is critical, POPTray will be interrupting you many times during the day and you might as well not bother installing it. The point is to prioritize your email. If more than five or six senders are considered critical, you may need to go back and do some serious thinking about priorities. Not everything (nor everybody) is priority #1!

Back Up Your Email

Unless you're a Casual Communicator and use email only for day-to-day contact with friends, you will build up a mailbase of messages worth keeping. Storing them securely means backing them up regularly, at least once a week or (if you're an email maniac) at the end of every day, when you back up all your other work as well.

Backing up your mailbase doesn't necessarily mean copying it out to some kind of removable media, at least not every time you perform a backup. Backing up your mailbase simply means copying it to some location in addition to where it "lives"; that is, where your email client stores it as messages come in.

Have an Email Backup Strategy

Establish a backup strategy for your mailbase and stick to it. Such a strategy depends on how valuable you consider the messages in your mailbase, how much email you get, and which email client you use. The key point is how often to back up your mailbase, and my recommendation is simple: At *minimum,* every time you get at least 25 new messages in your mailbase, do a backup. Note that these 25 new messages in the mailbase do *not* include spam or messages that you read and immediately pitch. I'm talking about 25 messages that need to be retained, either short term (in your Pending Items folder) or for good. If using email is crucial to your career and you consider the messages in your mailbase valuable, it's good to back up your mailbase every night—and keep a copy of your mailbase off-site, in a safe place.

At this point, let me recommend an email backup strategy for the four categories of email users.

Public Professional

Create a backup folder somewhere on your hard drive. If your hard drive is divided into multiple drive units (in other words, C:, D:, and E:), create the backup folder on a drive unit *other* than the primary folder where your mailbase is stored. For example, if your mail client maintains your mailbase on drive C:, create your backup folder on drive D: or E:. Better still: If you have a network, create the backup folder on another PC somewhere on your network. The idea is to have your backup in a place where a malfunction that destroys your primary mailbase folder is less likely to destroy your backup folder as well.

1. Back up your mailbase to the backup folder *every* night.

2. Every week, burn a copy of your mailbase to a CD, DVD, or other removable medium.

3. Keep a four-week "rolling backup" stack of these backup copies somewhere safe at home, ideally away from your PC so that if your PC is stolen, your backup copies are less likely to go with it.

4. Once a month, take the oldest of the four copies and place it in some off-site storage location. Your safe deposit box is the obvious place, but at the home of a trusted friend or family member is another option. I keep a six-month rolling backup in my safe deposit box and destroy the oldest copy from the safe deposit box each month as I add the newest.

Private Professional

Create a backup folder as described for Public Professionals (in the preceding section).

1. At least once a week, but preferably every night, back up your mailbase to the backup folder.

2. Once a month, burn your mailbase to CD or DVD. Keep this copy somewhere safe, preferably somewhere physically secure and away from your computer system, like in the basement or in a home safe. If you have a safe deposit box at a bank, it's a good idea place a copy in it periodically.

Student-Enthusiast

Your strategy should be the same as for the Private Professional. If you have multiple PCs on a network, it's always a good idea to create your backup folder on a PC elsewhere on your network so that if your main PC is destroyed by fire or power surge or is stolen, your backup is less likely to go with it.

I have heard of students in networked university housing "trading backups" with one another. This means that you back up your mailbase to a folder on a trusted friend's PC down the hall (not your roommate!) and your friend backs up their mailbase to a folder on your PC. If your operating system supports password-protecting individual folders, you can encrypt your backup mail folder on your friend's machine and vice versa. University security policies may make this impossible; certainly check and see.

Casual Communicator

Your mailbase is likely to be very modest in size and won't grow very quickly. At least once a month (and every week if you're ambitious), save your entire mailbase out to a CD-R. If your email client supports easy backup from its own menus, saving the mailbase to a different location on your hard drive is a good idea, and some clients (especially Poco Mail and The Bat) make it so easy that there's no reason not to do it weekly or nightly.

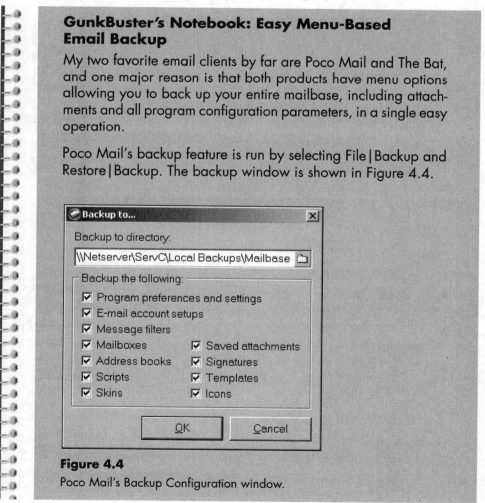

GunkBuster's Notebook: Easy Menu-Based Email Backup

My two favorite email clients by far are Poco Mail and The Bat, and one major reason is that both products have menu options allowing you to back up your entire mailbase, including attachments and all program configuration parameters, in a single easy operation.

Poco Mail's backup feature is run by selecting File | Backup and Restore | Backup. The backup window is shown in Figure 4.4.

Figure 4.4
Poco Mail's Backup Configuration window.

The default is to back up everything associated with your mailbase and email accounts, but you can selectively back up or not back up the separate mailbase and account elements if you choose. You can also navigate to different folders on your PC and even to shared hard drives on PCs elsewhere on your network.

The Bat's backup feature is more powerful but not quite as easy to use. You run the backup feature by selecting File | Backup. The window that appears is called the Maintenance Centre, and you must browse to a folder somewhere and type the name of the backup file, which ends in .tbk. (There is no default file name, unfortunately. You have to invent one and type it.) See Figure 4.5. The Bat allows you to password-protect the resulting backup archive if you choose.

Note that The Bat supports mailbase synchronization, which is related to but not the same as mailbase backup. I'll discuss mailbase synchronization in the next chapter.

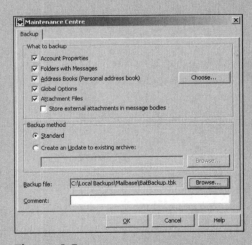

Figure 4.5
The Bat's Maintenance Centre window.

Find Your Mailbase

Some email clients make it extremely easy to back up your mailbase, especially Poco Mail and The Bat. Others have no menu-based backup feature at all, and a few (Outlook and Outlook Express, especially) go so far as to make it difficult to even *find* your mailbase on your hard drive.

But basically, if you can't find it, you can't back it up. In this section, I'll present some tips to help you locate where your email client keeps your mailbase. Keep in mind that it's possible to change the location of the mailbase with most email clients, and if you're "inheriting" a computer with an email client already installed on it, the mailbase location may not be the default location.

√ *Outlook:* The mailbase for "big" Outlook is stored in a file with a .pst extension. Do a search of your hard drives from Windows Explorer for *.pst. The default name for the file is outlook.pst, but advanced Outlook users can store their mailbases in a .pst file with a different name and path. However, the default path for the outlook.pst file is a good place to look first:

C:\Documents and Settings\<user name>\Local Settings\Application Data\Microsoft\Outlook

√ *Outlook Express:* The easy way to find it is to use Windows Explorer and search for inbox.dbx, which is the name of the Outlook Express inbox. Outlook Express mailbases are stored with each folder in a separate file, so the mailbase will be in several or many files. The default location is down a twisted path under **C:\Documents and Settings\Local settings\Identities**. An identity has an ID code that looks something like {6F9F294F-A7FC-49CC-8F6D-E6744ECD54FE}, and under that awful mess will be further subdirectories ending in one named Outlook Express. Outlook Express allows you to change the location of the mailbase by selecting Tools | Options and clicking on the Maintenance tab. Click the Store Folder button to enter a new path to your mailbase. I recommend changing to a mailbase path a little less complex than the default, especially if you do not define multiple identities.

√ *Eudora 6.1:* The easy way is to search for the file eudora.ini, which contains Eudora's preferences. The file will be in the same directory as Eudora's mailbase. The default mailbase path is this:

C:\Documents and Settings\<user name>\Application Data\Qualcomm\Eudora

√ *Poco Mail 3:* Search for the file in.idx, which is one part of Poco Mail's inbox. (Each mail folder is represented by two files, one with an .idx extension and the other with a .dat extension.) The default mailbase path is simple:

C:\Program Files\PocoMail3\Mail

√ *The Bat 2.1:* Search for the file thebat.abd. All files in the found directory, plus all subdirectories beneath it, are considered part of the mailbase. The default mailbase path resembles Eudora's:

C:\Documents and Settings\<user name>\Application Data\The Bat!

√ *Mozilla Thunderbird:* This is the default mailbase path:

C:\Documents and Settings\\<user name>\Application Data\Thunderbird\Profiles\default

Note that anything (files and folders both) at this path and below it should be considered part of the Thunderbird mailbase and saved out as part of your mailbase backup.

Backup Media

Once you know where your mailbase is, doing the actual backup is fairly easy. Using Windows Explorer, you can drag and drop the entire mailbase directory tree to another place on your hard drive, or to a place on another PC somewhere on your network. If your mailbase is small enough to drag and drop onto a single 1.44 MB diskette (remember those?), consider yourself lucky—but also consider this to be a temporary situation. The fact that mailbases *grow* was my primary motivation for writing this book, and a mailbase is unlikely to be diskette-small for long. Zip disks are common and reasonably inexpensive, and the 250 MB versions will hold almost any mailbase (including my own, which is almost 200 MB in size), but they are bulky and less reliable than I'd like them to be.

TIP: *Magnetic media (which includes diskettes, Zip disks, and Imation Superdisks) degrade over time, and my experience with Zip drives indicates that Zip media degrade fairly quickly. Don't expect a backup copy of your mailbase to last even three years on a Zip drive without a "refresh." For your long-haul backups, use CD-R or DVD-R media!*

It may not be quite as easy if you have a CD-R or DVD-R burner on your PC. Many of these are not (yet) configured to act as drag-and-drop media, indistinguishable from a diskette or Zip drive. Some can be configured for drag and drop: Easy CD Creator 5 has a "DirectCD" feature that allows you to format a CD-R so that you can drop files on it from Windows Explorer. Most of the older CD burners require that you run a special utility to write data to a CD-R.

GunkBuster's Notebook: When Drag and Drop Is a Drag

Be careful when you drag and drop directory trees from one place to another. If you drag a directory tree to another location on the same drive unit (in other words, from somewhere on C: to another place on C:), *the directory tree will be moved, not copied.* It will vanish from its original location and reappear at the location where you dropped it—and if the directory tree contains your mailbase, your email client will no longer be able to find it!

I always advise people to locate their backup copies of their mailbase (or anything else) on another drive unit entirely. If something wipes out your C: drive, it's better if your mailbase and its backup copy are not still both on C:. Still, if you must copy your mailbase from one location to another on the same drive unit, press the Ctrl key while you do the drag-and-drop operation. If Ctrl is depressed, the directory tree will be copied, not moved, and the original will remain in its accustomed location.

The other thing to watch out for, of course, is that you drop a directory tree where you intend to and not on a directory one up or one down from your intended target. Cross-eyed fatigue or too much coffee can make you miss the mark, and then you will have created a whole new copy of your mailbase directory tree (which can be very large) in an unrelated directory. If you don't notice the mistake when you make it, you may go looking for your backup copy at some point later on and not find it.

Manual drag and drop is bottom-feeder backup technique. It's much better to find or buy a good backup utility that allows you to load a backup profile and let the utility handle all the heavy lifting.

Use Backup Utility Software

There are many utilities for performing disk backups. For some of the major email clients, there are actually mailbase-backup utilities that can find your mailbase for you and handle all the details with a few clicks. Here are some suggestions:

√   Han-Soft's Auto Backup Software is a general-purpose backup system that allows you to create a backup profile and run it either on demand or on a scheduled basis. $28.95. **www.han-soft.com/habt.php**

√   AllNetSoft's 123 Outlook Express Backup performs either manual or scheduled automatic backups of your Outlook Express mailbase. $29.95. **www.allnetsoft.com**

√   Genie Soft's Genie Backup Manager performs both general Windows disk backups and specific backups of Outlook, Outlook Express, and Eudora mailbases, as well as IE bookmarks, the Windows Address Book and Registry, Outlook schedules, and many other things. The latest release (4.0) includes extensive CD and DVD copying features, though I haven't tested them. Very potent program. $49.95. **www.genie-soft.com**

I haven't tested all of them, and I'm sure I haven't even heard of many. Talk to your friends about what they use, and don't be afraid to browse the download archives at Tucows (**www.tucows.com**) and other similar sites.

Summing Up—The Habits of Highly Effective Emailers

As with degunking anything, the process of handling email in a low-gunk manner is one of psychology more than technology. The plan itself is simple. The hard part is simply forcing yourself to work smart and stay ahead of the email pile. The two prime directives are these:

√ Sort email as it comes in and process as much of it as possible the day you receive it; and

√ Budget yourself time to handle things like pending messages and mailbase backup.

If you can keep to those two general principles, your periodic mailbase degunking sessions (See Chapter 6) will fewer, farther between, and easier!

Read and Degunk Your Email from Anywhere

Degunking Checklist:

√ Make sure you have reliable Internet connectivity when you travel.

√ Establish a dialup account, tuck a network patch cable into your suitcase, and equip your laptop with a Wi-Fi adapter.

√ Find out if your ISP supports Web mail access to your POP account.

√ Learn how to solve the "port 25" problem.

√ Avoid creating two separate and non-identical copies of your mailbase—"forking" your mailbase.

√ Use an email account that supports IMAP because it can sync any number of copies of your mailbase to a centrally stored copy.

√ Use recent Web mail services such as Gmail that have expanded storage (up to 2 GB).

Email as most of us understand and use it is a lot like a traditional telephone. It's tied to one place and works easily and reliably from that one place. Making telephones travel involved dealing with problems that simple didn't arise with a phone that was screwed to the wall. Roaming, hand-off, caller ID, ability to locate 911 callers, and a scattering of smaller issues had to be solved before cellular phones could truly become a reality.

So it is with email. Reading email from your PC at home is simple and easy. Your mailbase lives on your desk PC, and you always connect to the Internet from that PC, though your Internet service provider (ISP). And as you've learned in the previous three chapters, degunking your stationary email and keeping your mailbase gunk-free and organized is a straightforward process.

Using email that travels and degunking it is another story. You'll need to deal with a number of issues that don't turn up if your email just stays at home. Because of the challenges, I've devoted an entire chapter to the types of issues that you can encounter while traveling with email, how these issues can cause gunk in your mailbase, and how you can get around them. Even if you don't travel much, or don't take your email with you when you do travel (I try to escape email entirely now and then!) I recommend reading this chapter. You never know when your boss may hand you a laptop and send you to Boise, telling you to "keep in touch."

Get Reliable Access to the Net and Your Mail Server

Your first challenge when traveling is figuring out how to reliably connect to the Internet. This is important so that you can keep up with your emails and perform the regular degunking tasks that you learned in previous chapters. If you're traveling regularly or if you take a long trip, you don't want to let your email get all gunked up.

Accessing email while on the road has gotten much easier than it was even a few years ago. Many hotels have installed broadband network jacks in their rooms or wireless broadband systems that allow you to connect to the Net from anywhere on the hotel premises. This service is not always free (though it sometimes is, where many hotels are competing). If you're in a strange city, connecting to the Net through a hotel jack or wireless system is straightforward. There is also wireless Internet access available at many restaurants and coffee shops, again, often for free. (I use Panera Bread's free Wi-Fi access a lot when I travel and it works beautifully.)

TIP: Take a Category 5 network patch cable with you when you travel. These cables are inexpensive and can be had in several lengths at computer, office supply, and appliance stores. Many new hotels have broadband network jacks in the walls, but the hotels will not always provide a cable to connect your laptop to the jack. There's nothing like being in a hotel room with a laptop, a network jack...and no cable!

Absent a public broadband connection, you're left with dialup access. The big dialup ISPs like AOL and AT&T Worldnet have "points of presence" in virtually every area code in the country. Each of these points of presence has one or more phone numbers, which you can dial from your hotel room or anywhere else you can connect a phone cable to your laptop. I've had an AT&T Worldnet account for years, and it's served me well when I travel. I can dial into the Internet via a local phone call from almost anywhere in the country.

GunkBuster's Notebook: Going Wireless on the Road

If you only have one PC at home, you probably haven't felt the need to install a wireless network. On the other hand, with more and more hotels, libraries, and coffee shops installing wireless Internet access systems, you might benefit from equipping your travel PC (generally your laptop) with wireless capability. The technology is called Wi-Fi (for Wireless Fidelity) and many adapters now cost less than $50. A typical Wi-Fi adapter for laptops is shown in Figure 5.1. It plugs into one of the add-in PC card slots present in virtually all laptops.

Figure 5.1
The Linksys WPC11 Wi-Fi adapter (Photo Courtesy of Linksys).

Adding a Wi-Fi adapter to your laptop is pretty simple: If you're running Windows XP, you buy a PC card Wi-Fi adapter for your laptop and plug it in. Versions of Windows older than XP will require that you first install drivers and utilities that come on a CD with the Wi-Fi adapter. Then you plug it in, and Windows Plug and Play will handle the rest.

Some cautions:

√ Before you buy anything, make sure your laptop didn't come with Wi-Fi built in. Many newer laptops do, and you won't see an antenna or anything sticking out. Check your documentation.

√ Some Wi-Fi adapters are high-speed *Cardbus* cards. These can be inserted *only* into laptops with Cardbus slots. Laptops older than 2000 often do not have Cardbus slots. If you have an older laptop, buy an adapter that does not require a Cardbus slot.

Once installed, a Wi-Fi adapter will generally connect automatically to the strongest Wi-Fi signal it can find. If you're traveling, that's fine, if you open it in a hotel or coffee shop with a Wi-Fi access point. On the other hand, if you're at home and don't need Wi-Fi, disable the adapter to avoid automatically connecting to one of your neighbors' wireless networks!

Wireless networking is a big subject, and I've written an entire book on it. If you'd like to learn more, look for *Jeff Duntemann's Wi-Fi Guide, 2nd Edition* (Paraglyph Press, 2004).

Alas, getting connected to the Net is the easy part. Getting access to your email is a little more complex. Here are some possible problems you may face:

√ Broadband ISP email accounts (like our fictional Andy Stanton's account at CrankyNet) are generally not accessible from outside the ISP's network, except via a crude Web mail interface. CrankyNet is local to Springfield, Illinois, where Andy lives. When Andy's in Boise, he can dial into the Internet from his AOL account, but he can't reach his CrankyNet email server to read and answer his CrankyNet email.

√ Similarly, dialup ISP email accounts are generally not accessible except through the ISP's points of presence. Some dialup ISPs have begun to implement Web mail interfaces to their dialup accounts, so you can read your dialup mail via a hotel broadband connection. AT&T Worldnet has already done this, and I predict that others will follow suit.

√ "Pure" Web mail services (whether free or not) are accessible from any Internet connection but make it difficult to add keeper messages to a permanent mailbase.

√ Registering your own Internet domain and getting an account with a Web hosting service that offers email addresses is generally your best bet for portable POP or IMAP email access, but under certain circumstances, you cannot send mail through your own server while traveling because the ISP through which you have connected to the Net blocks port 25. This is a new problem, and a fairly technical one, which I'll explain in detail a little later.

√ Finally, if you can get access to your POP server while on the road, there is the further question of how to take your mailbase with you while you travel without "forking" your mailbase into two separate versions, one living on your PC at home and the other living on your laptop, with no easy way to recombine them when you get back home.

Some of these points warrant detailed discussion. Let's take a closer look.

Understand the Port 25 Blocking Problem

When you get an account with an ISP, you're almost always given an email address somewhere on your ISP's domain, using your ISP's in-house email server. In other words, if you establish an account for Internet access at an ISP named CrankyNet, you might receive an email address like **astanton@crankynet.com**. As I've said earlier in this book, the email address you get from your ISP is not a good candidate for your primary email address, for this reason: If the spammers find it and make it unusable, you may not be able to get a different address from your ISP.

I always recommend buying your own Internet domain (especially if you're a Public Professional) and establishing an account with a Web hosting service. Our fictional Andy Stanton registered **stantonservices.com**, and his primary email address is **astanton@stantonservices.com**. His hosting service, **sooperdooperhosting.com**, is located in Costa Mesa, California, and is not associated in any way with his ISP, CrankyNet.

And this is a problem. Spammers have been planting "spam zombie" servers on PCs around the world, using viruses and worms. (I'll have more to say about spam zombies later in this book.) Some of these spam zombie servers were planted on PCs connected to the Internet through CrankyNet, and CrankyNet has found that immense quantities of spam were originating on its own network, coming from these infected PCs. (And you wonder why they're cranky!)

A spam zombie is a kind of "relay station" for spam. A shadowy black hat type sends a spam message and an address database to a spam zombie PC through a "back door" and the spam zombie server starts spraying spam at hundreds of thousands of email addresses worldwide. Shutting off individual infected PCs is difficult and upsets the customers. CrankyNet therefore tries something a little different, a technique pioneered in California by SBC Networks, a major cable broadband ISP. They disable port 25.

This may seem a little technical, but follow me here if you can. An Internet port can be thought of as a communications channel. (Think of channels on CB radios.) Multiple ports (there are thousands of possible ports) allow multiple types of communications to occur at once between two Internet servers. A spam zombie is actually a miniature, stripped-down email server, using the Simple Mail Transfer Protocol (SMTP) mail transmission mechanism. SMTP servers, when they need to send a message, must connect to the POP server that handles mail for the address to which the message is sent. SMTP servers use port 25 to establish their connections. Block port 25 and it becomes impossible for an SMTP server to connect to a POP server. The SMTP server thus cannot send any messages.

Because a spam zombie is an SMTP server, blocking port 25 basically shuts them all down. The only exception is the ISP's own SMTP servers. CrankyNet set it up so that the only SMTP servers that can operate from its network are its own SMTP servers, which CrankyNet's techies can monitor for spam.

In Andy Stanton's case, this means that his email client cannot connect to the SMTP server at **sooperdooperhosting.com** in California, which handles the outbound mail for Andy's domain **stantonservices.com**.

How would this affect you while traveling? It will probably be a problem *only* if you have your own Web and email domain but use a dialup account for sending and reading email while on the road. By blocking port 25, your dialup ISP may refuse to let you connect to the SMTP server at your Web and email hosting service. (If you just use the email address given to you by your dialup ISP, you won't have any problem at all.)

Using the Local Network for Outbound Mail

The fix in Andy's case—and your case, if you run into this problem—is fairly simple: You have to configure your email client to use your local ISP's SMTP server to send mail rather than the server at your Web and mail hosting service. When you signed up for an account at your ISP and got an email account from it (whether you use that email account or not), your ISP gave you a list of server names and other information pertaining to the account. Look for your SMTP server name. (This is for outgoing mail.) For example, for AT&T Worldnet (the dialup ISP that I use for travel), the SMTP server name is **mailhost.att.net**. The server name you received from your travel ISP must replace whatever server name is listed for outgoing mail in your email client.

Figure 5.2 shows where this is done for Outlook and Outlook Express. These are the steps required:

1. Select Tools|Accounts from the menu bar.

2. In the accounts dialog, select the account you want to change and click the Properties button.

3. By the field labeled Outgoing Mail (SMTP), type the name of your ISP's mail server. For Worldnet this would be mailhost.att.net; in Andy Stanton's case, it would be **mail.crankynet.com**.

The dialog shown in Figure 5.2 sets Outlook Express to receive mail from Andy's Web hosting service mail server at s**ooperdooperhosting.com** but send mail through CrankyNet's SMTP server. There's nothing the least bit odd about "splitting the ticket" like this. It doesn't matter at all which SMTP server actually sends an email message. You can use whatever SMTP server is "legal" from the ISP you use to access the Internet.

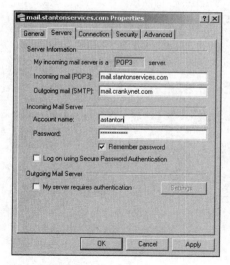

Figure 5.2
Setting the SMTP server for Outlook and Outlook Express.

The configuration for other email clients is similar; bring up the accounts setup dialog (typically on the Tools menu) and look for the server name field for outgoing mail. This is the field in which to enter the server name you received from your travel ISP.

GunkBuster's Notebook: Create a Travel Account to Solve Port 25 Problems

One way to keep all your email servers straight when you travel is to create separate accounts in your email client for travel and for work at home. All the popular email clients except Eudora make it easy to create and modify email accounts.

In email client jargon, an *account* is simply a separate, named setup for email. Typically, you have an account with your Web and mail hosting service and an account in your email client for email through your hosting service email address. However, you can have multiple accounts in your email client to serve a single account with your Web and mail hosting service.

For example, one of my own email addresses is **jd@junkbox.com**. This address is hosted at the same service that hosts all my Web sites, even though I don't have a Web site posted for **junkbox.com**. It's strictly an alternate email address. I have two accounts in Poco Mail to handle this one address, one for work at home and one for travel. The two accounts and the server names that I use are shown below:

	Home Account	Travel Account
Incoming Mail (POP):	**mail.junkbox.com**	**mail.junkbox.com**
Outgoing Mail (SMTP):	**mail.junkbox.com**	**mailhost.att.net**

When I'm at home, connecting through my broadband connection, I use the home account. When I travel and connect to the Net through AT&T Worldnet, I use the travel account. I set up travel accounts for any email addresses I intend to use when I'm on the road, and it works beautifully.

Don't Fork Your Mailbase!

Your mailbase is the collection of messages stored by your email client. If you've been using email for some time, you may have a lot of messages in your mailbase. (There are currently about 20,000 in mine.) Some of those messages may be important for future reference, and when you go on the road, especially for business travel, it can be extremely useful to take your mailbase with you.

One way to do this is what many people do: They install the same email client on their laptop as they have on their desktop PC and then copy their entire mailbase from their desktop PC into their laptop. This can be done by connecting the two PCs via a network or by burning a copy of the mailbase onto a CD-R and then reading it from CD-R into the laptop.

I don't recommend this approach because as you travel, you download your email onto your laptop, and when you get home, you have messages stored on your laptop's copy of your mailbase that are not present on your desktop PC. This may not matter, at least after a single trip during which no "keeper" messages come in. But over time, you'll begin to have important messages in your laptop's copy of the mailbase that are not present in your desktop copy of the mailbase and vise versa. The two copies will begin to diverge, as though there were a fork in the road. This is called "forking" your database. It's a species of gunk because there's confusion between the two copies. Which copy has that big spreadsheet I received from Roger at the office? Did it come in while I was in Boise? Or is it buried somewhere in my desktop PC?

To avoid forking, here are some solutions that involve physically taking your mailbase with you:

√   Configure your laptop email client to leave all messages on your email server all the time you're on the road. (I'll explain how to do this shortly.) When you get home you can download all the mail again to your desktop and sort what came in during your trip.

√   Accumulate and sort your email on your laptop during your trip, just as you would at home on your desktop. Then when you get home, copy your laptop's mailbase back to your desktop PC and overwrite the desktop's older version of your mailbase with the newer one from the laptop. Your mailbase thus "moved" from your desktop to your laptop while you were on the road and then "moved" back to your desktop PC once you returned to your desk. This works, but it's a fair bit of fooling around, especially if your mailbase is very large.

√   Use an email client that can "synchronize" two copies of the same mailbase. The only email client I know of with this feature is The Bat, from RIT Labs.

√   Use an IMAP mail server instead of POP. (I described both in Chapter 3.) With IMAP, your email remains in storage on your email server and whenever you log into your server, any messages on the server that have not yet been downloaded to your email client will come down.

√ Use a "deep storage" Web mail service, and simply leave your mailbase on the service's Web servers. This way, no matter where you are when you sign in to your Web mail account, your entire mailbase will be right there. As wityh IMAP, it can't fork because it exists in only one place. This concept may be problematic for several reasons, which I'll discuss later in this chapter, in the section on Google's new Gmail service.

Let's talk about a few of these options in more detail.

Leaving Mail on the Server

The simplest way to avoid forking your mailbase is to leave your email on the server while you're traveling. On returning home to your desktop PC, you download everything from the server that arrived while you were traveling and sort it into your mailbase. Then, before your next trip, copy your mailbase from your desktop PC back to your laptop again.

There are a couple of snags in doing this, but they may be acceptable, depending on your circumstances:

√ If you archive sent messages (copies of mail you sent to others while on the road), you may be out of luck. There's no easy way to move "Sent Items" messages from your laptop to your desktop. Only the mail that arrived from others will come down from your server. On the other hand, most people archive few if any of the messages they send to others, so this may not be a problem.

√ This trick works best for short trips, when you don't expect to get a lot of email. If you do get a great deal of mail, the burden of sorting it into your mailbase when you get back is yet another thing to do when you're already trying to catch up with all the stuff that stacked up while you were gone.

The key to leaving mail on the server is to make sure that *only* mail you want to keep remains on the server. Most pointedly, spam and those "read and toss" messages don't need to become a part of your mailbase and thus should be removed from the server while you're on the road. That way, you won't have to deal with them yet again when you return home.

How? Nearly all email clients have a "Leave mail on server" option that will delete mail from the server when you delete it from your inbox and then empty the trash or Deleted Items folder. In the following descriptions, I've included both options:

√ In Outlook and Outlook Express, select Tools | Accounts and click on the account you wish to modify. Click the Properties button. When the dialog appears, click the Advanced tab, and check the "Leave a copy of message on server" check box. Also check "Remove from server when deleted from deleted items." Click OK. See Figure 5.3.

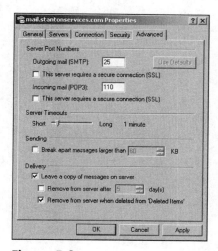

Figure 5.3

Configuring the Outlooks to leave mail on the server.

√   In Eudora, select Tools | Options. When the dialog appears, select the Incoming Mail section. Check the "leave mail on server" check box. Also check "Delete from server when emptied from Trash." Click OK. See Figure 5.4.

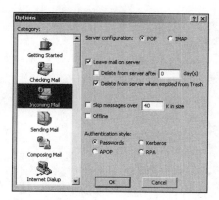

Figure 5.4

Configuring Eudora to leave mail on the server.

√ In Poco Mail, select Tools | Accounts Setup and click on the account you wish to modify. Click Edit. When the dialog appears, select the Incoming section, and check the "Leave Mail on Server" check box. Also check "Remove from server when emptied from Trash." Click OK. See Figure 5.5.

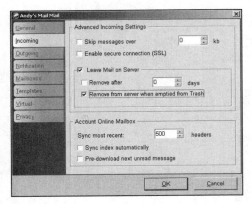

Figure 5.5

Configuring Poco Mail to leave mail on the server.

√ In Mozilla Thunderbird, select Tools | Account Settings. In the left margin of the dialog that appears, select the option Server Settings under the account that you wish to modify. Check the "Leave mail on server" check box. Also check "Until I delete or remove them from Inbox." Click OK. See Figure 5.6.

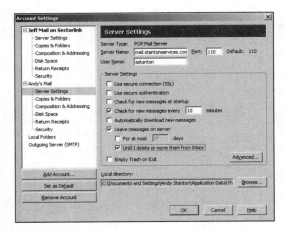

Figure 5.6

Configuring Thunderbird to leave mail on the server.

Synchronization and the "Holes Don't Travel" Problem

Very few email clients have a feature called *synchronization*. Synchronization between two copies of a mailbase ensures that both copies contain the same messages. (This is called *peer-to-peer* synchronization.) For the purpose of traveling with your mailbase, it works this way: Both your desktop PC and your laptop have a copy of the same email client, one that supports synchronization. Before you leave on your trip, you synchronize the two email clients. Any messages that are on either computer are migrated to the other. When synchronization is complete, *both* computers have all messages that had been present on *either* and the two copies of the mailbase are identical.

When you return from your trip, you synchronize again. Any messages that came down to your laptop while you were on the road are now migrated over to your desktop PC, so that after synchronization is complete, the two copies of your mailbase are again identical.

Synchronization thus prevents forking your database. However, the problem with synchronization is that "holes don't travel," meaning that *deletions are not synchronized*. If you delete a message from one copy of the mailbase but not from the other, synchronization will copy the deleted message back to the system from which it had been deleted. Since a goodly part of keeping your mailbase clean of gunk lies in deleting messages, this is counterproductive. To delete a message from both copies of the mailbase, you must delete it from both email clients, making deletions twice the work.

The "holes don't travel" problem is the reason I don't support this sort of simple peer-to-peer synchronization. There's another, better way to do mailbase synchronization, called IMAP.

Traveling with IMAP

Compared to the venerable POP protocol, Internet Message Access Protocol (IMAP) is much newer. It was developed at Stanford University in 1986. The idea behind IMAP is that your mailbase lives in one primary place: on your IMAP server. From that server, you can access it from any IMAP-capable email client, no matter where you are. The IMAP protocol allows you to create an "image" of the server-based mailbase on an IMAP email client. In other words, your mailbase remains on the server, but you can download a copy of the mailbase to any number of PCs and the copies will always reflect the current state of the centrally stored mailbase.

This is a form of synchronization, but in the case of IMAP, holes *do* travel. In other words, when you delete a message, you delete it from the central server, and then when the server downloads an image of the mailbase to an email client, that new image does not contain any of the deleted messages. It's synchronization, but one-way synchronization: always from the server to the clients.

In some respects, IMAP is an almost perfect solution to the problem of traveling with your mailbase. There are some problems to be aware of, however:

√   Because your mailbase is stored on the central server, you will have storage limits and your mailbase can only become so large without bumping into those limits. Most IMAP account providers limit you to between 50 and 250 MB of storage. This is a lot, but if you have a really large mailbase, it may not be enough!

√   Because of the large storage requirements, many ISPs and Web hosting services do not offer IMAP email services, or they offer them at additional cost.

√   Not all email clients implement IMAP completely, or exactly the same way that others do. Some IMAP features are simply missing, and other IMAP features may work in slightly different ways.

As much as I like IMAP, I will admit that it's given me a lot of trouble when I've tried to use it. The newer email clients are much better at implementing IMAP, and amazingly enough, the best IMAP client I've yet tested is the completely free Mozilla Thunderbird. If you want to use IMAP, get Thunderbird!

How you set up IMAP is dependent on both your email client and your email hosting service. Your hosting service should be able to provide setup instructions for the major email clients. Check your email client help file for additional information.

Traveling with Web Mail

People who don't receive a lot of email, and especially those who don't need to send or receive attachments while traveling, can often do very well using an ordinary Web mail account or a Web mail interface to a conventional POP or IMAP email account. With a Web mail interface, you can access your mail no matter where you are, as long as you can connect to the Internet and the Web.

That's the upside. The downsides may be these:

√   Many Web mail systems have clunky, slow interfaces.

√   Many free Web mail systems subject you to ads.

√   Some Web mail systems do not allow you to send or receive attachments.

√ Many Web mail services have no mechanism for downloading individual messages to your laptop or desktop PC. This makes it impossible to add messages received through Web mail to your mailbase.

Web mail is evolving quickly right now, spurred by Google's Gmail. (More on Gmail at the end of this chapter.) Web mail service providers are adding more storage, more interface options, and more features to remain competitive. If you're shopping for a Web mail service, shop hard and pay attention to the details. If you already have one, check with the service provider to see if there have been upgrades to your account that you may not even be aware of.

POP Interfaces to Web Mail

Some of the major Web mail providers also allow access to an account via Post Office Protocol 3 (POP3) and any standard email client; check with your Web mail provider to see if such an interface exists. You may be pleasantly surprised! It may not always be good news, however; Yahoo Mail had such an interface until April 2002; now there is no direct POP interface. Many clever programmers have put together interface programs that talk to a Web mail provider on one side and a POP3 email client on the other side. This allows you to use an email client like Mozilla Thunderbird or Poco Mail with a Web mail account when you're home and a Web browser when you're out and around. Table 5.1 summarizes the major POP–Web mail interface utilities and the Web mail systems that they support.

Table 5.1   POP3–Web Mail Utilities.

Utility	URL	Systems Supported	Cost
Hotmail Popper	www.boolean.ca/hotpop/	Hotmail	$17.50
Web2POP	www.jmasoftware.com	Hotmail, Yahoo, AOL, more	$26.00
Email2POP	www.email2pop.com	AOL, Gmail	$25.76
MrPostman	http://mrpostman.sourceforge.net	Hotmail, Yahoo	Free
IzyMail Online	http://izymail.com	Yahoo, MSN, Hotmail	$10.95/yr[1]

[1] Sold by subscription only. IzyMail is a Java app that runs on many platforms.

The big advantage to using a POP interface to a Web mail system is that it gives you the best of both worlds: the "read it anywhere" advantage of Web mail, and the "keep your keepers in a mailbase" advantage of a mailbase stored locally on your laptop. (You still have to deal with the issue of forking your database while traveling, which I covered a little earlier in this chapter.)

Web Mail Interfaces to POP Accounts

Just as it's possible to read your Web mail from a POP-based email client, you can access your POP email account from a Web browser when traveling. Many ISPs and Web hosting companies provide their own Web mail access to their POP-based email accounts. Not all do, and many that I've seen are clunky and difficult to use. There are several services that allow you to log in and read your POP email account from a Web browser while you're on the road. Table 5.2 lists my personal favorites.

Table 5.2   Sites Allowing Web Access to POP3 Accounts.

Site	URL	Comments
Mail2Web	www.mail2web.com	Free.
Mail Inspector	www.mail-inspector.de	Java browser plug-in. Site is in German!
NetMyMail	www.netmymail.com	Free, ad-supported. Ad-free, $4.50/month.
POP3Now	www.pop3now.com	Up to five accounts. Encrypts all traffic. $5/year.

Use a Client on a Key Chain: Poco EmailVoyager

If you need to travel with a significant mailbase, maintaining it while traveling becomes a problem. Integrating messages accumulated on the road with the master copy of your mailbase is a nuisance, as I've explained earlier in this chapter. IMAP is one solution, and Web mail is another, but neither is without its drawbacks.

Early in 2004, Poco Systems released a whole new approach to the problem: EmailVoyager, which is basically a way to put your entire mailbase—and your email client program—on a—"key chain" flash drive the size of your index finger. EmailVoyager is shown in Figure 5.7. It can be purchased in several different capacities, up to 256 MB, which would contain a *very* substantial mailbase! (Even at its very largest, mine was never more than 210 MB in size.)

The real magic of EmailVoyager doesn't lie in its ability to contain your mailbase. Any flash drive could do that. The problem is taking your email client along with you when you travel. Most Windows software cannot be installed on a removable medium like a Zip drive or a flash drive. EmailVoyager contains a version of Poco Mail (Poco Mail PE: Portable Edition) that was specially written to allow it to install and run on a removable device like a Zip drive or flash

Figure 5.7
Poco Systems's EmailVoyager.

drive. Thus, if you have access to a PC at a public library or a copy shop, you can plug EmailVoyager into a USB port, and you're ready to read and send email from your own mailbase and your familiar email client.

Having the email client software on the flash drive with your mailbase allows you to literally wear your email system around your neck. EmailVoyager comes with a lanyard allowing you to do exactly that, though doing so will send your geek index off the top of the charts and into the stratosphere. It's probably better to use the lanyard to hang EmailVoyager on a peg on the wall when you're not using it.

EmailVoyager is used by simply plugging it into a USB port on any PC running Windows 2000 or XP. Windows will automatically detect it as a USB drive; no driver installation is required. (However, drivers *do* need to be installed for use with Windows NT and 9.*x*.) Under Windows XP, Poco Mail PE will launch automatically when the EmailVoyager device is detected. Under Windows 2000, you will have to launch Poco Mail PE manually by navigating to the program on EmailVoyager and double-clicking on it.

Handing Off a Mailbase Between Poco Mail and EmailVoyager

EmailVoyager is a very new product, and the first release does not include a way to synchronize a Poco Mail mailbase between EmailVoyager and the desktop version of Poco Mail. If you use EmailVoyager as your sole email client, that's not a problem: You load your mailbase into EmailVoyager and then use it, both at home and on the road. To use Poco Mail at home and EmailVoyager on the road, you need to transfer your mailbase from one to the other. This is done with careful use of the Backup and Restore features present in both programs.

To transfer your mailbase back and forth between EmailVoyager and Poco Mail, you should use a technique like this:

1. Identify a folder accessible by both Poco Mail and EmailVoyager. Use the File|Backup and Restore|Backup menu item to create a backup copy of the mailbase in the common folder.

2. Select the File|Backup and Restore|Restore menu item to copy the mailbase from the common folder to the destination, whether Poco Mail or EmailVoyager. You will need to select the common folder to which you saved the mailbase in Step 1.

This works identically in both directions: From the PC with Poco Mail to EmailVoyager and from EmailVoyager to the PC copy of Poco Mail.

CAUTION! *Make sure that you don't get confused and transfer the mailbase in the wrong direction, which will eliminate any new messages that came in since the last time you transferred the mailbase. To protect against this possibility, always back up your mailbase to a separate location before you attempt a transfer between Poco and EmailVoyager.*

TIP: *Keep in mind that Flash memory is not nearly as fast in terms of access as a fast hard drive, and saving or restoring a large mailbase to EmailVoyager may take several minutes.*

Use Google's Gmail: "Deep Storage" Web Mail

In April 2004, Google announced that it would be creating a new free service: Gmail. It's a form of Web mail with a couple of interesting wrinkles:

√ Each user has *one gigabyte* of online storage for mail.

√ Organizing and managing mail is done through keyword labels and Google's sophisticated search machinery rather than through a folder hierarchy.

At this writing, Gmail is still being beta-tested, and it is not available to the general public. I did obtain a beta test account and have had a chance to use it. Like all Web mail services, it's available anywhere you have Web access, and if you're accessing the Web through a broadband connection, Gmail is quite fast. Figure 5.8 shows the beta-test version of Gmail displaying a message. The user interface is simple and self-explanatory.

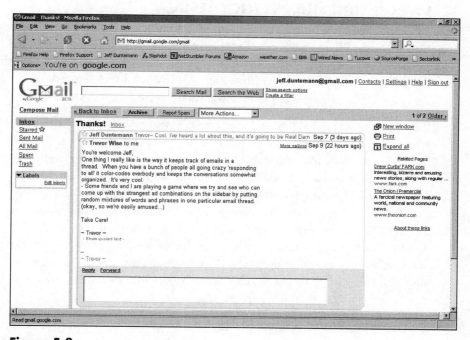

Figure 5.8

The Gmail user interface.

The beta test version of Gmail allows file attachments of up to 10 MB in size, but it will not deliver attachments with either a .exe or .vbs file extension, in the hope of reducing the potential of Gmail to spread attachment-based viruses.

Managing a mailbase in Gmail is done by applying keyword labels to messages and then searching for that label using Google's search machinery. One Gmail feature that isn't quite there yet is the ability to import existing messages from another email client into Gmail. It can be done, but it's very messy and not all clients cooperate. This is something that Google's developers will have to spend a little more time on because most serious email users have existing mailbases containing thousands—sometimes tens of thousands—of archived messages.

More work will also need to be done on the import feature for address books. With the beta test version, you have to create a Comma Separated Values (CSV) file containing your address book data, which is not a task for the nontechnical and is probably a stopgap measure until Google can write import code specific to individual email clients.

Gmail and the Privacy Issue

Although Web mail has been around for a long time, Gmail gives Web mail a new wrinkle: Your entire mailbase is stored on someone else's server. Most people shrug and say, "So?" Some people, on the other hand, find that this a very dicey proposition, especially since 9/11. What's to keep federal security agencies from forcing Google to allow them to troll for keywords?

There are nuances here. Email as a communications medium is protected by the Electronic Communications Privacy Act of 1986. However, the law only protects messages for 180 days. After that, the law ceases to consider them communications and considers them database records instead. Government agencies then can force access to any 181-day-old message using a subpoena rather than a search warrant. Privacy activists make the telling point that because Gmail will likely become an *immense* repository of thousands—or even millions—of people's email traffic, it will be extremely attractive to government investigators, especially given the search machinery that Google has at its disposal. The temptation to look in Gmail *first,* before doing any serious sleuthing in the physical world, will be strong.

Several people have pointed out in Web articles that there are data mining techniques that look at word frequency and distribution to create "profiles" that might suggest terrorist or child abuse potential. Not necessarily illegal *acts*—just people who talk about aircraft in one message and Islam in another or people who talk about children in one message and pornography in another.

The worst of it is that, given the federal government's current obsession with secrecy, such searches might never be disclosed, and no one outside government would know that they were going on.

Whether this matters is up to you. I already have a longstanding policy of not saying anything in an email that I wouldn't mind posting on the front page of the *New York Times,* but the potential for data mining statistics to cast suspicion on me because of my word choice across hundreds or thousands of unrelated messages does give me pause. There are some interesting discussions on the Web that you might check out if you're weighing the Gmail privacy issue:

www.templetons.com/brad/gmail.html
http://gmail-is-too-creepy.com
www.oreillynet.com/pub/wlg/4707

Pop Goes the Gmail

Third-party "helper" utilities have already begun appearing for Gmail, long before its full public release. One of them is POP Goes the Gmail (PGtGM), a POP proxy that sits between Gmail on the Web and your email client and provides POP access to Gmail from any POP-capable client. This allows you to keep your mailbase on your PC but still receive messages from Gmail and add them to your PC-based mailbase. PGtGM is free and can be found here:

http://jaybe.org/info.htm

Gmail Loader

Mark Lyons has created an interesting utility, GMail Loader, or GML for short, that takes some of the drudge work out of uploading large numbers of messages from your local PC email client to Gmail. This allows you to incorporate your existing mailbase into Gmail. Mark has expanded the program considerably from its modest origins and over time hopes to cover all popular email storage formats. At this writing, most of what GML handles is the "mailbox" (.mbx) format, which most modern email clients support for exports. Outlook and Outlook Express formats are not currently supported, though Mark intends to add them over time. GML is truly free and open source, and can be found here:

www.marklyon.org/gmail/

Competitive Pressures

It didn't take long for the rest of the Web mail world to respond to Gmail's stirring of the waters. Within a few months, several additional services began offering 1 GB Web mail, including Lycos, Spymac Hosting, and Walla.com. Yahoo and Hotmail, not to be outdone, upgraded their free accounts to 100 MB and 250 MB respectively, and both increased their paid accounts ($20/year) to 2 GB of storage. Although no one knows what Gmail's final feature list will be, Google's effect on Web mail is already clear: Storage is no longer a limitation. At its very largest, before I took degunking seriously, my mailbase contained about 35,000 messages—and even then, occupied only a little over 200 MB. A full GB is as much email storage as anyone is ever likely to need. The next frontier will be additional tools (notifiers, uploaders, bulk labelers, and so on) and integration with the desktop. Web mail will never be the same after Gmail!

Summing Up—Traveling Smart

Anyone can read email on the road. The trick is to do it from any Internet access point, and do it without making a mess of your mailbase. Having two mailbases, one on your desktop and one on your laptop, that grow further apart with each trip you take is a really, well, gunk-y idea. Work smart and avoid the mess—and if your mailbase begins getting messy, there's some degunking to do, and that's the subject of our next chapter.

Cleaning and Organizing Your Mailbase

Degunking Checklist:

√ Create a hierarchy of topic-based folders for messages that can be displayed on only one screen.

√ Keep time-delimited mail in specific, separate folders.

√ Sort your inbox into your folder hierarchy, remembering the 100-message rule.

√ If you have sender-oriented folders, create subfolders in them that are topic based.

√ Delete messages in your Sent Items folder that are more than 90 days old.

√ Scan your attachments folder for unnecessary files; make sure you have virus protection in place and up-to-date before examining attachment files.

√ Check your Drafts folder for draft messages that have been abandoned or should have been sent out.

√ Check for abandoned copies of your mailbase and delete them.

Believe it or not, there are actually people in this world who do not have a mailbase. Really! I've met a few of them, and they're happy, well-adjusted, and otherwise pretty normal folks. But for some reason, they have never received an email message that they judged to be worth keeping. A mailbase, as I've been discussing throughout this book, is that body of messages that you have received, and perhaps replied to, and wish to retain for future reference. It starts out small (everybody starts with no email messages at all!), but unless you're in that small and blessed group who keep *nothing,* it grows relentlessly over time. At last count, my personal mailbase occupied 200 megabytes of hard drive space, which is more hard drive space than I had on my PC until 1994.

22,000 messages. Wow.

One reason for the size of my mailbase is that I've been on Internet email since it became available to the general public. I am also a fearless Public Professional and an information pack rat. As my friends know all too well, my interests are broad, and I enjoy reading about nearly all fields of human endeavor except for sports and opera. That's a lot of territory, and my mailbase reflects it.

So consider me a good example of a worst-case email scenario. I have retained 22,000 messages on virtually every topic you can imagine, and yet somehow, I can zero in fairly quickly on anything I have in my mailbase. This wasn't always the case. This chapter summarizes what I had to learn to keep the mailbase monster on a short leash and all those thousands of saved messages at my fingertips.

Understand the Two Faces of Mailbase Gunk

There's something very important to understand right now: If your mailbase is large enough, it can be hideously gunked up, *even if every one of the messages it contains is worth keeping.* In a mailbase context, gunk can be either or both of two things:

1. Messages (and their attachments) that you don't need to have hanging around.

2. Messages stored randomly in one or two folders, with no effort made to sort them by topic.

Basically, mailbase gunk is measured by its bulk and its degree of chaos. This chapter is about reducing email gunk in both of its manifestations. It's best to learn this early in the game, when your mailbase is still small, because going through 22,000 messages shot through with garbage and lacking any master plan for organization is basically impossible. You might as well nuke till it glows and start over.

TIP: Mailbase chaos is real gunk and not simply a figure of speech. Think of it this way: If you can't find it, it isn't there! Don't think that message classification is an exercise for anal-retentive librarians. It's done to allow you to locate what you've retained, months or years down the road.

Degunking an existing mailbase is done in three steps:

1. Create a folder hierarchy. Examine your email situation carefully and create a folder hierarchy by topic that reflects what you do and the type of email that you send and receive. It's a little like creating your own private version of the Dewey decimal system.

2. File your messages. Go through your mailbase message by message. For keeper messages, drop each into the appropriate folder, creating additional folders as required. If a message isn't a keeper, nuke it or drop it in a "deep archive" folder. (More on this later.)

3. Check for unnecessary files. Perform a few additional checks on things like your attachments folder and whether there are unnecessary copies of your mailbase stored somewhere.

Yes, it's simple, but it may not be easy, especially if you've ignored your mailbase for a number of years and have lots of unorganized messages. The good news is that this is a project that can be done over a period of time; you could spend 15 minutes a day for a few weeks and get the job done in no time. Once you're done, this process will have made future "spring cleanings" of your mailbase a lot quicker and easier.

Create a Folder Hierarchy

The single biggest secret to keeping your mailbase manageable lies in creating a suitable hierarchy for folders in which to store your messages. Most email clients come with just a few built-in folders: Inbox, Outbox, Trash, Sent Items, and perhaps Drafts. These five folders are the ones through which your daily mail passes. They are *not* for storing mail over the long haul! For those "keep" and "hold" messages, you need to create folders.

Nearly all email clients allow you to create folders (which in some clients are called mailboxes) that are displayed in a window to the left of the message panes themselves. Most clients allow a folder *hierarchy*—that is, folders can contain other folders—and this makes organizing a very large mailbase much easier. It's not uncommon to find computer professionals with tens of thousands of messages in their mailbases (I'm a perfect example, and by no means alone). For people like that, a good many folders may be required to make sense of it all and allow individual messages to be found quickly when needed.

Apply the Single-Screen Rule

The key in creating a folder hierarchy is not to have so many folders in the left margin that you forget that you have them. The way to do this is to limit your folders to a single screen's worth. The rule of thumb is this: If you have to scroll a list of folders up and down, you have too many. If you feel you absolutely need more folders than will fit in a single screen, nest related folders together under a parent folder. I do this, and it works, as long as the nested folders are used often enough to not be forgotten.

Use Folders for Topics, not Senders

Deciding what folders to create (like deciding when to nuke a message) is more psychology than technology. Many people first attack mailbase gunk by creating folders for mail from individual senders: a folder for mail from the boss, a folder for mail from your spouse, from each of the kids, from close friends. While initially useful in helping you find individual messages within the growing throng, this is really the wrong way to go about it. Take a few steps back and think hard about how you use email, not so much in terms of who it comes from but rather what the messages are *about*. When you want to refer back to a message, you may recall who sent it, but primarily you'll be looking for the message's topic. Folders should thus be about topics and not people, as in the following examples:

√   Mail relating to your job (Sales, Manufacturing, Travel Planning)

√   Mail relating to your church or civic groups (Lions, Chamber of Commerce)

√   Mail relating to e-commerce and services that you use on the Internet (Amazon.com, Travelocity)

√   Mail relating to your hobbies and interests (Programming, Model Railroading, Kite Flying, Ham Radio)

√   Mail relating to projects or research you're undertaking, such as research on a medical condition or for an article you're writing.

Just to give you something to begin with, let's postulate a set of mail folders for a mythical Everyman, Andy Stanton, a computer consultant living down the street from the Andersons in Springfield:

In	
Out	These four come standard with most email clients
Sent	
Drafts	
Hanging Fire	Mail that can't be processed right now
Boy Scouts	Mail about Andy Jr.'s Boy Scout activities
Online Shopping	Mail about things Andy buys online
Chamber of Commerce	Mail relating to Andy's C of C activities
Church	Mail about events and other things at St. James
Consulting Practice	A folder containing other folders (see the section "Use Folders within Folders Carefully.")
Genealogy	Mail from relatives gathering family history data
Humor	For those funny messages Andy's brother sends out
Kitchen Remodel Project	Mail relating to Andy's remodel job on the kitchen
RC Airmodels	A hobby listserv Andy subscribes to
Dead Letter Office	For those messages that don't fit anywhere but that Andy can't bring himself to delete

This file structure is pretty straightforward, and it serves Andy well. It's a very nice folder list because it can be displayed on a single screen.

Andy uses the Hanging Fire folder for messages that can't be handled the moment they come in and must wait until Andy has some additional information or time to process them fully. (I described this concept in detail in Chapter 4, relating to the "hold" part of Keep, Pitch, or Hold.) Hanging Fire is a sort of alternate inbox, and it must be used with a certain amount of discipline to keep it from accumulating too many messages.

A "hanging fire" or "pending" folder is *not* your dead letter office! Create a separate folder for those messages that you simply don't know what to do with, and call it Dead Letter Office. Review it periodically, delete what you can, and every so often, burn its contents to disk and empty it completely.

Keep Your Time-Delimited Mail in Separate Folders

Note in the list Andy's Kitchen Remodel Project folder. It contains mail from the suppliers and contractor who are rebuilding the kitchen in Andy's house. The project is pretty intense, but it is definitely time delimited. After the project is done, the mail in the folder is no longer useful and certainly won't be referred to on a daily basis, as it was during the project's execution. Once his kitchen is completed, Andy can delete or (more likely) burn the folder's messages to a CD and then put them in a drawer somewhere. The folder itself can then be deleted from his folder hierarchy.

This process is what I call *deep archiving* and is actually a way of deleting messages with a measure of comfort that in some unlikely future circumstance you can retrieve them again, even though it might take some time and some digging.

Use Folders within Folders Carefully

Andy is a computer consultant, and he has a separate folder for all mail relating to his consulting practice. His consulting practice generates far more email than all of his other interests and activities combined. Is one folder enough to manage it all?

No, it isn't. However, the single folder Consulting Practice doesn't tell the whole story. It contains several subfolders that relate to his consulting practice:

Accounting	Mail from and to Andy's accountant
Clufre Realty	One of Andy's clients
Continuing Ed	Mail relating to night courses Andy takes
Dell Tech Support	Technical info about Andy's main PC
Gas Transport Inc	One of Andy's clients
Harvest Moo Dairy	One of Andy's clients
Insurance	Mail relating to Andy's business insurance
Network Tech Support	Technical info about Andy's network
Sergeant Ron's Army Surplus	One of Andy's clients
Tax Matters	Mail concerning tax returns and documentation

Andy actually has more folders within the folder Consulting Practice than on his main screen. That's OK, because Andy uses these folders on a daily basis and none of them is ever out of sight for very long. However, in general it's not a good idea to put folders within folders unless you refer to the subfolders often.

It's much too easy to forget a rarely used folder hiding under another rarely used folder in your hierarchy.

TIP: If you do create folders within folders, limit yourself to two folders deep. It's all too possible to create a hierarchy that splits hairs and nests folders too deeply for you to keep the whole scheme in your head at one time. Go three levels deep or more and eventually you will forget about one or more of those deeply buried folders!

Sort Your Email into Folders

Creating a folder hierarchy is the fun part of degunking your mailbase. Sorting messages into the folders you've created is a grind. There's not much to be done but start at the top, highlight a message, and make the decision: In which folder should it go? Drag it and drop it. Repeat until done. Heh.

Let me suggest a general plan for the Big Sort:

1. Get your inbox down to less than 100 messages (as I recommended in Chapter 4). Take a first pass through your inbox. Delete anything that isn't necessary, and sort as many messages as possible into the folders you've already created. There will inevitably be messages—probably a fair number of them—that won't classify easily into any of the existing folders. After your first pass, go back and see if you can spot any topics represented by groups of these "unsortable" messages. If so, create new folders for those topics and drop the appropriate messages into the new folders. Repeat this process until your inbox is down to a manageable size.

2. Purge and sort your Sent Items folder. Sent Items will likely require a whole different mindset to process correctly. The bulk of the messages in Sent Items have little or no value after a few months. The occasional message you write to others with lasting value *to you* should be sorted into an appropriate folder by topic, just as you sorted the messages in your inbox. The easiest way to handle Sent Items is to sort the messages by date sent, and either sort into folders or delete anything more than 90 days old. Be especially careful to eliminate any messages you sent to others containing large file attachments. These can eat a *huge* amount of space, usually needlessly. (The files are yours and are thus usually stored elsewhere, and any attachments in Sent Items are very likely duplicates of things you already have.)

3. Eliminate folders named after senders. If you have existing folders devoted to senders rather than topics, sort their messages into your new topics folders. Resist the temptation to leave any "unsortables" in the older sender-oriented folders. Put them all somewhere else and then delete the old folders. If necessary, create a "dead letter office" folder for messages that just

can't be sensibly sorted into a topic folder. Don't just put them back into your inbox!

GunkBuster's Notebook: What Should Live in Sent Items?

Every time you send a message to someone, a copy of it is saved in your Sent Items folder—and if you don't move it or delete it, it stays there forever. People who don't have much call to refer to their past messages are often surprised to find thousands of messages in their Sent Items folder. So what should be there, and what shouldn't?

The Sent Items folder is really short-term memory for messages you send to other people. It has the following three important uses:

√ Sent Items contains replies to recent messages and inquiries. These allow you to determine whether you responded to another person's message and, if so, what you said.

√ Messages in Sent Items are short-term insurance against failures of the Internet to deliver messages to others, as well as insurance against messages being eaten by spam filters. (This is a serious and growing problem.) If somebody comes back and says, "I never got that email," you have it sitting in cold-storage in Sent Items, ready to resend.

√ Messages you send to multiple recipients are stored in Sent Items against the possibility that you might later (though not *too* much later) need to send the same message to additional recipients.

See the common element here: All three uses are time delimited. In other words, Sent Items contains messages you have written that you may need to refer to or resend in the *near* future for some reason. After two or three months, the likelihood that you'll still need the messages drops precipitously.

Nothing should live in Sent Items forever. If you've written a long and carefully crafted message to someone that you feel may have some future value to you, sort it into a topic folder. If you have written messages—even short messages—pertaining to taxes or legal issues that you may need to produce in the future to stay out of trouble, sort them into a topic folder. Rule of thumb: Leave nothing in Sent Items that's more than 90 days old. If it needs to be kept longer than that, it belongs in a folder.

Clean Your Attachments Folder

Email attachments are separate files that "ride along" on an email message. Attachments can be any sort of file, but they are often content that cannot be expressed in text, like spreadsheets, images, or sound files. This means that they can be very large—sometimes megabytes in size—and if you accumulate enough of them, they can become a *huge* source of email gunk.

An associate of ours tells the story of a clueless employee at his firm who was sent a humorous animation of an alien singing a disco song and then decided to send it to every single person in the company. The animation was 4 MB in size, and when multiplied by the hundred-odd people in the company, it completely filled whatever space was left on the company's already-strapped mail server. (This was some years ago, before 100 GB hard drives were a commonplace.)   Lesson: Email attachments can quickly become gunk, and big email attachments can be the equivalent of electronic landfill. Show restraint when saving (or sending) attachments.

The Trouble with Attachments

How email clients handle attachments varies. Attachments begin as separate files but when mailed, they are encoded within the message so that the message and its attachments (there may be more than one) travel as a single data block. Most clients allow you to click a link or a button and "Save as…" to store the attachment on your hard drive. What you must remember is that even after you save an attachment somewhere else on disk, *it most likely still exists in your mailbase* until you delete the message it came in with. This is the fundamental problem with attachments.

Worse yet, some email clients automatically save attachments as separate files into a Windows directory somewhere, and by default the attachments remain in that directory even after you delete the message that carried the attachment. I touched briefly on this problem with attachments in Chapter 4, where I advised that you should configure your email client to delete message attachments with the message they came in on. This is almost never the default, so when you delete a message, its attachments may well stay behind.

Be sure to look in your email client's documentation to see where and how it stores attachments. There may be a separate directory in the Windows file system (often called Attach) where attachments live. Go to that directory and see what it contains—and be prepared to be surprised. You may be looking at a hundred megabytes or more of files you don't need and may already have stored elsewhere.

If you have a mail folder with a lot of messages in it and are looking for messages containing attachments, see if your email client has a column (most do) for an attachment icon. (This is typically a paper clip; see Figure 6.1.) If so, make sure that column is displayed because your client may not display that column by default. Another way to spot attachments is to sort messages in a folder by size: The larger messages will almost certainly be carrying attachments.

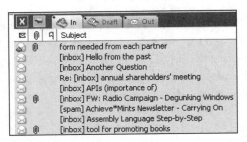

Figure 6.1
The paper clip icons for attachments.

TIP: *Before you begin working with the files in your attachments folder, run a virus check on your system (or on your attachments folder, if your antivirus software allows running checks on individual folders) to be sure there are no known viruses in any attachment file. (Most modern viruses ride in as attachments.) Make sure your virus definitions are up-to-date. New viruses appear regularly, and your virus checker needs to know what to look for!*

GunkBuster's Notebook: Displaying the Full File Name in Windows Explorer

Whether you have to go poking around in your attachments folder or not, be *sure* that you have enabled the full display of file extensions in Windows Explorer! Most Windows installations default to hiding the file extension, which is a *very* bad idea. Why? A Windows file name can legally have more than one period character in it. A virus can send a copy of itself with the name ParisHilton.jpg.exe. This looks peculiar, but it is completely legal. Its true nature is that of an EXE (executable) program file that could very well be a virus. If your Windows installation is hiding file extensions, the file name of the virus will appear as ParisHilton.jpg. If you double-click on it to view the "picture" of that famous vacuous blonde, then you may have just downloaded a virus. To disable hiding of file extensions, bring up Windows Explorer and select Tools|Folder Options. Click the View tab and uncheck the item marked "Hide file extensions for known file types." (See Figure 6.2; the option to uncheck is marked by an arrow.) Then click OK. With the option unchecked, all file extensions will be visible at all times.

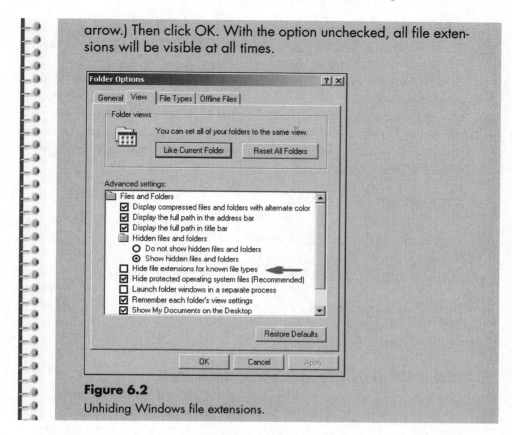

Figure 6.2
Unhiding Windows file extensions.

File Extensions and File Types

Once you've located where your email client keeps attachment files, you may be confronted with hundreds—or thousands!—of individual files, most of which will be unfamiliar to you. Some of them may be useful. Most will not. A handful may in fact be dangerous because they may contain viruses. Before you begin making decisions on which to keep and which to delete, become familiar with the common file types you'll encounter in email file attachments.

DOC

These are Microsoft Word document files and have the extension .doc. They may contain script viruses. If your antivirus program allows checking individual files (most do), check the file to see if any viruses are present.

EML

These are saved message files (the extension is .eml). They are in text format, and they generally show up when one message is forwarded to you from a third party. To view them drop them on Windows Notepad.

EXE, SCR, PIF, COM

These are executable files (.exe, .scr, .pif, .com). They are dangerous because they may contain viruses, worms, or other *malware*—software that damages your PC, spies on you, or does other Bad Things without your permission. *Do not simply double-click these files to see what they do.* One way to check on unknown executable files is to Google on the file name. Any executable file that comes in via email—even from someone that you know—should be treated with *great* suspicion. I'll have a lot more to say about this issue later in this book, when I address malware itself.

HTM, HTML

These are HTML-formatted files (.htm, .html), which typically land in your attachments folder when they are forwarded to you by a third party. HTML files are a species of text file, and they can be inspected by dropping them on Windows Notepad. They can contain scripting viruses and spam beacons (more on these later in this book), so I advise *against* loading them into a Web browser for viewing. A quick peek by dragging it and dropping it onto Notepad will be completely safe and should let you decide what the file is and whether it's worth keeping.

JPG, JPEG, TIF, TIFF, GIF, PNG, BMP, WMF

These are graphics image files (.jpg, .jpeg, .tif, .tiff, .gif, .png, .bmp, .wmf). They are generally safe to inspect by loading them into an image editor like Paint Shop Pro or one of many freeware image viewers available online. My favorite is DIMIN Image Viewer (**www.dimin.net**). The more common file types (.JPG, .GIF, .PNG) can often be viewed in a Web browser.

PDF

These files have a .pdf extension and are Adobe Acrobat documents. To read them, you must install the free Adobe Reader utility. This may be obtained from **www.adobe.com**.

TXT

These are text files (.txt) and are typically messages that are forwarded to you from third parties. They can be safely inspected by dropping them on Windows Notepad.

VCF

These files, with a .vcf extension, are v-cards, which are virtual business cards. Some email clients and Web directory systems (like Plaxo) can be configured to transmit a v-card with every message. They are text files and may be safely inspected by dropping them on Windows Notepad.

XLS

These are Microsoft Excel spreadsheet files (.xls). They may contain scripting viruses. If your antivirus program allows checking individual files, check the file to see if any viruses are present. Also, unless you desperately need them, disable macros in Excel, which prevents scripting viruses from running.

ZIP

These files, with the .zip extension, are compressed file archives created by PKZip, WinZip, and other archiver programs. They cannot themselves be malware, but they may contain malware. It is safe to open them with an archiver program like WinZip, but be *very* careful what you do with what's inside. Many email viruses now transmit themselves through email inside a ZIP archive. If you don't recognize the files inside a ZIP file, it's safest to delete it, especially if it contains executable files with .exe, .com, .scr, or .pif extensions.

ZL or ZM

When the ZoneAlarm personal firewall sees a file that it recognizes as malware, it "quarantines" the file by giving it one of many .zl★ and .zm★ extensions (the ★ represents a number or a letter). This makes it impossible to run the file by double-clicking it. Such files are almost always malware and should be deleted. The third character tells you what sort of file it was before it was renamed by ZoneAlarm. To see the list, go to **www.icdatamaster.com/harmful.html**. If you're not running ZoneAlarm, you won't have these files on your PC.

Keep in mind that these are only the most common file types. There are literally thousands of others, and (worse) some of them do double or triple duty and may have different roles and meanings depending on what application created them. There are several Web sites devoted to indexing file extensions. My favorite is **www.icdatamaster.com**.

Clean Up the Odds and Ends

There are a few additional email degunking tasks that you will need to perform from time to time, especially if you're a heavy user of email. These are things that you needn't worry about every day but should check occasionally or when you change email clients or move your mailbase around on your PC.

Watch Out for Abandoned Drafts

Most email clients have a folder for messages that you begin writing but can't finish in one session. This is generally called the Drafts folder, but some clients may call it the Outbox folder. (The term *outbox* is more commonly used for mail that has been sent or for a message that is completed and waiting for you to log on to the Internet so that it may be sent.) Some email clients will automatically save a message that you're writing to the Drafts folder after you've worked on it for more than a certain amount of time—and if you forget to send it, it will remain in the Drafts folder until you explicitly send or delete it. You may well have a half dozen or more incomplete and abandoned messages in your Drafts folder. Open the Drafts folder and take a look at what's in there. There may be nothing at all—or it may contain a lot of *really* moldy leftovers!

Poco Mail performs an additional operation that many of its users aren't even aware of: When you attempt to send a message and the send operation aborts with an error for some reason, a copy of the message you attempted to send is saved into Drafts. There is no announcement that this is being done; it just happens. The message itself remains in a window, but it's also now saved in Drafts—and if you click Send again and the message goes out successfully, it will still be in Drafts and it will remain there until you manually delete it.

These abandoned drafts rarely take a great deal of space unless you had attached a large file (say, an MP3 audio or image file) to one of the drafts. Still, it's a good idea to check on your Drafts folder (or whatever it might be called in your email client) to make sure there isn't a lot of unnecessary gunk there.

TIP: *If possible, check and see that a completed message stored in Drafts actually went out! Sometimes it may look like a message went out when it did not. This is another good use of your Sent Items folder: If a message is in Sent Items as well as in Drafts, it was successfully mailed and you can delete it from Drafts.*

Delete Obsolete or Duplicate Copies of Your Mailbase

All the major email clients have the ability to import an existing mailbase from the other major email clients. (If you're moving to or from a more obscure email client, you may have trouble bringing your mailbase over.) After your mailbase has been copied over to your new email client, there is still a copy of your entire mailbase stored with the old email client, and that copy of the mailbase will remain on your hard drive, *even if you uninstall the old email client.* If your mailbase is substantial, that can mean a *lot* of gunk. (My current mailbase occupies almost 200 MB.)

Of course, it's not a bad idea to keep the copy of your old mailbase on your hard disk for a couple of weeks while you become familiar with the new email client, just in case you decide you really don't like the new client. But at some point, you should delete the old mailbase—or at least deep-archive it to a CD. Deleting it is easy using Windows Explorer; the mailbase is nothing more than one or more files in a directory. Delete the directory containing the mailbase files and the mailbase is gone. Sometimes, however, the tricky part is just *finding* the mailbase on today's cavernous hard drives. (See Chapter 4, under the sub-head "Find Your Mailbase" to locate a mailbase for all the major email clients.)

Outlook's Mailbase and Windows Address Book

There is a very big warning to be heeded when you want to delete a mailbase for "big" Outlook. Outlook's PST files may contain your copy of the Windows Address Book! Delete a file with the .pst extension and you may delete your entire address book. This is a serious bummer because PST files are often very large and they do not compress very easily, even after you delete some or all of the email messages they contain.

The rule is this: If you use Outlook, your Windows Address Book will almost certainly be stored in a PST file. If you do not use Outlook, your Windows Address Book will be stored in a file with a .wab extension. Keep in mind that if you change from Outlook to some other email client, your Windows Address Book will remain in the PST file you used while you used Outlook as your email client. It's unfortunate, but exporting mailbase and address book information out of Outlook to another email client is extremely difficult. This is one of many reasons (security holes being the most important one) that I advise you to avoid using Outlook if you possibly can. If you have been using Outlook and your Windows Address Book is stored in its PST file, you must either export that address book data to another address book format for management by another application (which is virtually impossible for nontechnical people) or leave the PST file in place.

Outlook is a "tar baby" application of the highest order. Once you get your data into it, Microsoft does everything possible to keep you from getting it out again!

Remove Outlook Express Email Gunk from the Windows Registry

One of the supremely irritating things about Outlook Express is its habit of storing inappropriate things in the Windows Registry. The prime example is Outlook Express's blocked senders list, which is the list of addresses or domains whose mail should go directly to the Deleted Items folder. This list is stored in the Registry, and if you end up blocking hundreds of spam senders or spammer domains (as most people who use email a lot inevitably do), you will be gunking up the Windows Registry big time.

If you choose to use Outlook Express, you have no choice: Blocked senders will be stored in the Registry. However, if you stop using Outlook Express and even uninstall it, the blocked senders entries will remain in the Registry until they are manually removed.

The only really safe way to remove these blocked sender entries—which constitutes gunk, in my view—from the Registry is to do it from within Outlook Express. You remove them using the same dialog that you used to add them, and it's easy except for one thing: You cannot select more than one blocked sender at a time, and therefore you must remove them one at a time, selecting and deleting each one individually. If you have hundreds stored, this is a nuisance that may take some time.

But here's how it's done:

1. From within Outlook Express, select Tools | Message Rules | Blocked Senders.
2. In the Blocked Senders dialog box that appears, notice that each blocked sender entry is a separate line.
3. Highlight the first entry and click the Remove button.
4. Repeat that step on subsequent entries until they are all gone.

Editing the Registry with REGEDIT32

If Outlook Express no longer functions correctly, or if it cannot see the list of blocked senders stored in the Registry, you have no choice but to edit the Registry directly to remove the entries. This is not tremendously difficult, but it's something that you do *not* want to get wrong! Damage the wrong items in the Registry and your Windows installation won't work correctly—and perhaps not at all. You should not attempt it without a solid understanding of what the Registry is and how it works.

It can be useful to examine the Registry to see if any blocked sender entries are stored there. This is done using the Windows RegEdit32 utility. Follow these steps:

1. Run REGEDIT32.exe.
2. Expand My Computer and highlight HKEY_CURRENT_USER.
3. Using View | Find Key, search for the string "Block Senders."
4. Expand Block Senders, and expand Mail beneath it. If there's nothing to expand under Block Senders, then you have no blocked senders stored in the Registry.
5. Expand Criteria under Mail. You'll see a long list of Registry entries with hexadecimal numeric names like 001, 002, and so on. Each of these represents a blocked sender. If you click on one of the entries, you will see it expanded in the right pane and the address or domain of the blocked sender will be visible.

Again, if you do find blocked senders in your Registry and are no longer using Outlook Express, you should run Outlook Express (and install it if you uninstalled it) and remove all the blocked senders manually.

Email Spring Cleaning

People who depend heavily on email will accumulate gunk over time. As hard as I try to take my own advice and follow the recommendations that I laid out in Chapter 4 and in this chapter, I find that the gunk piles up. It doesn't pile up as quickly as it used to, but it piles up nonetheless. This being the case, I've found it useful to budget one full day a year for "spring cleaning" in the email realm.

Note well that this annual spring cleaning does not mean you can slack off on all of the other good email habits I've been describing. This is especially true if you're a Public Professional and (as I and many others do) you receive 40 or 50 "real" messages (not counting spam) every day. Things slip past you; gunk slides "under the fold" and is forgotten. Sooner or later you have to go in and review it all over again.

Here's a checklist for your annual email spring cleaning:

1. Schedule a couple hours for it. This might sounds like a lot of time, but if you let your mailbase get away from you and gunk up, you will lose a lot more time than that searching for lost messages in the morass.

2. Count the messages in your mailbase. No email client will simply present you with a single number representing every message you have in every folder, but many clients will tell you how many messages are in each folder. Just take a pocket calculator, go down your list of folders, and add all the messages up. Prepare to be surprised! (And if you're a good record keeper, try to keep a record of the size of your mailbase over time, perhaps taking the count once a month. If it's significantly bigger each time you check, you may need to recalibrate your sense for what to keep and what to get rid of!)

3. Begin with your Sent Items folder. It keeps a copy of every single message you send, and few of them are worth keeping longer than 60 or 90 days. Older messages should be deleted or deep-archived, unless they need to be retained for tax or legal purposes. Those should be filed in an appropriate folder.

4. Next, go through your inbox and either delete or classify anything you can until you get the total number of messages to 100 or fewer. Pay particular attention to the area "below the fold" (that is, out of sight beyond your most recent message arrivals) where messages can be easily forgotten. Start with the oldest messages in your inbox. If something's been there since your last spring cleaning, get a clue! Classify it, nuke it, or put it in a Dead Letter Office folder for eventual deep archiving. Force yourself to deal with anything difficult or unpleasant that's been sitting there awaiting action. If you end the scan convinced that you can't possibly get your inbox down under 100 messages, you're fooling yourself. You may need a new folder or two for recent interests or topics that don't fit in any other folder. You may need another cup of coffee, or a walk around the block. Whatever you do, just come back and get it down to 100!

5. Check your attachments folder. Things will tend to stack up there, but if you're good about filing and deleting messages, getting rid of the attachments residue is actually pretty easy. (Remember to be careful before double-clicking on unknown attachment files! Have your virus checker on and up-to-date before you start fooling around with attachment files!)

6. Cull the collection. Pour yourself another cup of strong coffee, start at the top of your folder list, and start scanning the messages you've retained in

your mailbase. Look at each message and, for each folder, see what you no longer need to keep. No longer interested in radio-controlled models, sold your plane, and haven't flown since last April? Deep-archive or delete the entire RC Models folder. Sometimes a message that looked liked a keeper last year—or last month—doesn't look quite as essential now. Let it go. Sometimes messages you thought would be valuable forever are really time delimited. Be ruthless. It's the only way to stay ahead of your mailbase.

7. Keep records of what you've done. This is pure psychology, but it works: When you're finished nuking and deep-archiving, count up the messages that remain in your mailbase to see how many you've eliminated. Keep a record somewhere (a short text file in your mailbase folder will do fine) indicating how large your mailbase is this time. Better still, make it an ongoing log file and add entries periodically. It helps make all the work seem worthwhile to remind yourself that you really are staying ahead of things. You don't necessarily have to *shrink* your mailbase (unless it had gotten out of control to begin with), but you sure don't want to let it grow like a fungus!

Summing Up—Clean Me Now... or Clean Me Later!

Most of what's in this chapter came out own my own personal experience. Even with what I thought was regular housecleaning, my own 10-year-old mailbase swelled to 41,000 messages at its peak. It took a good long while (most of a week's time, distributed over a month or so) to get it down to about 20,000 messages, but with regular attention and a little gumption, I'm staying ahead of it. You can too. You simply have to summon the will to *do* it!

Avoid Becoming a Spam Magnet!

Degunking Checklist:

√ Don't patronize spammers—responding to them keeps them in business and adds your email address to more spammer mailing lists.

√ Don't respond to "survey" or "dating service" spams, which only exist to verify your email address and will lead to even more spam.

√ Choose an email address that is not vulnerable to dictionary attacks.

√ Don't post your email address on your Web site as a live link.

√ Never attempt to unsubscribe from a spammer's mailing list.

√ Before joining an email list, make sure it isn't archived (along with your email address) on the Web, where address-harvesting spambots will find it.

√ Omit or obfuscate your email address when posting to Usenet newsgroups.

√ Use a disposable email address (see Chapter 2) when dealing with all but the biggest and most reputable online commerce sites.

As I sit down to begin this chapter, I just came in from outside, where (in heavy leather gloves and high leather boots) I have been pulling thistles. I do this every spring and early summer, and during that period I fill our 60-gallon trash can as full as I dare with thistles, every week without fail. Why do I do this? Easy: *Unless you pull thistles remorselessly, they take over.* I try to get them before they bloom and release their seeds, which will merely become next year's crop of thistles.

What's so bad about thistles? My list:

√ They're ugly. I don't care if they're the national flower of Scotland. (And no, this does not mean I have some subconscious animus against the Scots. C'mon, guys. Sometimes a cigar is just a cigar.)

√ They bite. They bite sometimes even through the heaviest leather gloves I can find.

√ They crowd out the flowers that Carol and I try to maintain.

√ And although this may be a circular reference, they take time in the pulling that I would rather spend doing something else, like writing more books.

It's a little scary how much thistles are like spam.

Understand the Prime Directive Against Spam

Anytime an email message arrives in your inbox from somebody you don't know trying to sell you something or elicit some other response, well, that's spam. It's a horrendous problem. At this writing, spam represents over 60 percent of all email transmitted over the Internet. Almost two thirds!

It's enough to make you crazy. This and the next several chapters of this book are focused on avoiding spam as much as possible, and getting rid of what (inevitably) arrives in your inbox. As with the war against thistles, there's no easy or lasting victory in the war against spam. No matter how careful you are, it will begin to arrive eventually, and however hard you try to filter it directly to your trash folder, some of it will get through.

Still, we have to start somewhere. I like to begin by encouraging my readers to adopt what I call the Prime Directive Against Spam, which is really a three-point program for destroying the economic roots of the spam industry:

√   Never buy anything offered through a spam message. Never ever *ever*.

√   Never respond to a spam message that asks you some sort of question.

√   Educate your family, friends, and co-workers about the crucial importance of points 1 and 2.

Basically, the harder we make it for spammers to make money, the fewer people will enter the spamming business and the fewer spam messages will be bouncing around the Internet. Let's look at the three points of the Prime Directive a little more closely.

Don't Buy from Spammers!

Quite apart from reducing the obvious incentive for people to continue spamming (and for new spammers to join them), there are good reasons not to buy things offered through a spam message. Let me cite a few here:

√   **Prices aren't competitive**. Goods offered via spam are not necessarily a better deal than you can get in retail stores. I recall a Christmas season when I was peppered constantly with pitches for these little radio-controlled cars the size of my thumb. While shopping at Walgreens, I saw the same radio-controlled cars for considerably less than what the spammers were asking.

√   **It can be illegal**. Ordering prescription drugs without a prescription (or through a person who is pretending to be a physician, as often happens in spam-driven "pharmacies") is illegal and can net you stiff fines, a criminal record, or even jail time. The U.S. government is *extremely* twitchy about illegal drugs, especially painkillers.

√   **Many of the goods offered are fraudulent**. To keep their sellers out of trouble, the "pain pills" you order may be sugar pills. Ditto the "herbal supplements," like those idiotic penis enlargement pills. I asked a urologist. *The pills don't work.* (What you have is what you will always have. Live with it.) And if they don't work, what recourse do you have? You probably have no idea where the spammer or the Internet retailer is in the physical world, and they may be beyond the reach of U.S. law. Finally, imagine yourself on the phone with the nice young woman at the Federal Trade Commission, entering your complaint: "You see, I, um, ordered these pills to enlarge my, um, you know…"

√   **The goods may never arrive**. Suppose you never receive that bottle of Vicodin painkillers ordered (illegally) without a prescription. What are you going to do? Call the cops?

√ **Spammer Web sites aren't secure**. Generally, to buy things from spammers you have to go to a Web site somewhere and enter your credit card number. You have no idea who's behind the Web site, nor where it's located (probably overseas), nor how pure its owners' intentions are. You may be handing your credit card information to a gang of identity thieves.

The rate of fraud seen in spam-related retailing is awesome. Reports I've seen indicate that as many as 50 percent of customer transactions initiated by spam messages are fraudulent. Flip a coin. Feeling lucky today?

Don't Respond to Sneaky Spam Messages

Many people have asked me why they receive so many messages that don't appear to be selling anything. A lot of these have subject lines reading "Who do you support? Bush or Kerry?" or "Should we withdraw from Iraq?" What are they selling? What's going on here?

It's simple: They're trying to get you to verify that your email address is "live" and (worse still, from your standpoint) is owned by someone who pays attention to spam. What they're selling is *your email address*—to other spammers.

Keep in mind that when a spam message arrives at your PC, the spammer who sent it does not necessarily know that your email address is valid. It may be an old address that you abandoned years ago. The spammer may be "guessing" that **andy@stantonservices.com** is a valid email address. (This is called a dictionary attack, more on which shortly.) Either way, the message is sent "on spec," just in case the email address is in fact live.

What you do *not* want to do is *prove* that your email address is live! That makes you a "verified recipient," meaning your address is known to belong to a real person. Spammers constantly build special lists of such verified recipients and sell them—at a high price—to other spammers, who will then send you even more spam. A spammer who asks you to complete a survey or answer a question is simply trying to get you to demonstrate that your email address is real and active. The same is true of these supposed online dating sites, which pepper you with messages indicating that—"Someone you know has set you up on a date! Click here to get the details…." These sites are phony. There are no other people setting you up on dates. There are no people trying to get dates with you. Their sole purpose is to get you to hit the Reply button, or click on an embedded link and go to their Web site. (The link is encoded with your email address. Click to their Web site and you verify your email address.) A few of the sites ask for money before revealing who your "secret admirer" is. There is no secret admirer. If you send them money, you have basically *paid* to get your email address on a multitude of spammer mailing lists. As these sites are generally not in the United States, good luck trying to get your money back.

The most treasured email address list of all, of course, is the list of people who have actually ordered goods offered in a spam message and sent the spammer money. After that, it's *le deluge,* baby!

Friends Don't Let Friends Buy from Spammers!

None of this should be news to you, but if it is, take it upon yourself to educate your friends and family about the dangers of responding to spam messages—especially if they are nontechnical and just getting their first computers or first Internet connection and email accounts. (Think your grandparents.) Older people have a tendency to be trusting, and in the email world, trust is something to be offered with great care and hesitation.

Teach them well:—*Consider anything you read in an email message from someone you don't know to be a lie, and consider anything offered to you in an email message to be a fraud.*

It's actually worse than that: Spammers have ways of pretending to be people you know, so a message that looks like it may be coming from a friend or a family member may be from a spammer who simply forged the email address. (The term for this is *address spoofing.*) If you ever get an email message that isn't in any way "personalized" or that simply doesn't sound like something the sender would say, be suspicious.

Why Is Stopping Spam So Hard?

The war against spam has been going on almost since the Internet was opened to the general public. The notion of spam first surfaced in 1994 when a pair of lawyers sent a message advertising their services to illegal immigrants to every single newsgroup on Usenet. From there it jumped quickly to email, and newsgroups and email have been beset by spam ever since.

Why is fighting the spam battle so hard? There is at least one federal law and numerous state laws against certain kinds of spam. Why can't we make more progress?

There are many reasons:

√ People continue to buy things from spammers, and the profit margins are quite high. The lure of easy money keeps bringing in new blood—and new spam.

√ Many spammers are in other countries (especially China) and are beyond the reach of U.S. law.

√ Having seen the telephone telemarketing industry gutted by the National Do Not Call Registry, the direct marketing lobby has been trying very hard to derail any enforceable laws against spam and has tried to be as invisible as possible while doing so. So far they've been very successful.

√ The U.S. government has more important things to do (think fighting terrorism) than enforce CAN-SPAM, a vague and badly drafted anti-spam law that was mostly declawed by the direct marketing lobby.

√ More and more spam is being transmitted through thousands of "spam zombie" PCs that act as anonymous "relay stations" for spam mailings. These spam zombie PCs become zombies after being infected by a spam zombie virus like SoBig. The identity of the spammer is lost when email is sent through a spam zombie, making the true origin of much spam virtually impossible to determine. Sending fraudulent spam through spam zombies is basically the perfect crime. I'll have much more to say about spam zombie viruses and the PCs they infect booking Chapters 11 and 12, when I take up the subject of viruses in general.

It's not like people aren't trying, and I hear whispers that many old-time spammers are leaving the field because it's now much harder to make money spamming than it was in the golden years of 2000–2003. There are technologies on the horizon that will make spamming more difficult. In the meantime, the best way to fight spam is to make sure that everyone you know understands that nothing should ever be purchased from spammers and that "real" companies that advertise through spammers (Ancestry.com is an excellent example) should be utterly shunned and constantly slandered.

Choose a Spam-Resistant Email Address

Many people who register their own personal or business names do the simple and obvious thing and create an associated email address by using their first name and the domain name. A consultant like our mythical Andy Stanton might register the domain **stantonservices.com** and create an email account **andy@stantonservices.com**. You'd have to forgive poor Andy for not suspecting how much spam gunk such an address would attract.

Avoid Dictionary Attacks

The biggest problem with Andy's email address is something called a *dictionary attack*. Because spammers pay nothing per message to send out spam, and with broadband access you can send literally millions of messages per day, a dictionary attack is a way to gather email addresses as spam targets. Spammers (using custom mailer utilities intended for spamming) choose a domain, like **stantonservices.com**, and start cranking out email to addresses in a sequence that might look like this:

Abe@stantonservices.com

Abby@stantonservices.com

Al@stantonservices.com

Alan@stantonservices.com

Albert@stantonservices.com

Andrew@stantonservices.com

Andy@stantonservices.com

Ann@stantonservices.com

Anna@stantonservices.com

These names come from a dictionary of names and common words that spammers compile from online dictionaries and email addresses that they find on the Web. They use automatic mailer software, which generates small test messages, many of which have no body text at all. The mailer software keeps track of bounces—messages that come back because an email address does not exist—and purge the address of any bounced message from the list of addresses mailed to. If a generated address receives a message that doesn't bounce, that address is considered "live," and spam will soon begin to be sent to it—*even if the address has never actually been used!*

This is legal and costs nothing per address, so spammers send literally billions of such test messages daily, looking for new addresses to mail to. Avoiding dictionary attacks is simple, if not foolproof: Choose your email address carefully, and choose a name or word that is not in any dictionary. In other words, don't use **andy@stantonservices.com** but something not easily guessed by a program. This could be your first initial and last name like **astanton@stantonservices.com** or something you make up yourself, like **rugster@stantonservices.com**, where *rugster* is a word you make up from whole cloth. Don't use ordinary words that are in the dictionary (even peculiar words like *hellion* or *symbiont*) or words and names from popular culture, like *Gandalf* or *muggle*. String words together, or make up new ones. An artist friend of mine hit upon a magnificent email address, which is **gonzoforcats@stantonservices.com**. (I used Andy's mythical domain here—and changed the first part slightly—to protect her privacy.) She will never be hit in a dictionary attack, that's for sure.

More Advice on Choosing an Email Address

On the other hand, *don't* use random strings of letters, like **jkwts@stantonservices.com**. This looks like a "from" address generated randomly by spammer utilities, and there are now filters that look for random-looking "from" addresses and treat them as spam.

It used to be effective to add a middle initial after a common first name, in an address like **AndyR@stantonservices.com**, but in recent years spammers have been cycling through first names and middle/last initials as well. If you have an unusual first name it might be effective (is anyone named Butherus E. McCorquodale anymore?), but nothing beats a totally made-up word!

Don't Hand Your Email Address to Spammers!

It may surprise a lot of people to discover that most of the time, spammers get your email address…*when you hand it to them!* Dictionary attacks are one time-honored method for building a spammer mailing list, but only one. Most of the others depend completely on your carelessness or even your trust. Spam being the scourge it is, you must be *extremely* careful about how you use your email address and where you post it or allow it to appear. Once you get onto a spammer's list, it's virtually impossible to get off, and after your address has been traded around the spammer underworld for awhile, you'll have no recourse but to abandon that address for a new one.

What all this means is that if you attempt to unsubscribe from a spammer's mailing list, you will get even more spam, and lots of it.

Never Post Your Email Address on the Web

Getting new addresses to spam is one of a spammer's highest priorities, and they go to great technological lengths to snag them. In the late 1990s, spammers took a hint from Web search engines and created *Web crawlers,* or *spiders,* that simply pulled down Web page after Web page, 24/7, and searched for that telltale @ symbol. If your email address (all of which contain one of those @ symbols) happened to be in one of those Web pages, well, you were hosed, er, spammed.

The lesson is plain: Do *not* post your email address in "naked" form on your Web page. The spamspiders are still out there, crawling day and night. Furthermore, make it clear to your friends and other contacts that they cannot post your email address on the Web. This is a problem for people who are publicly known for some reason and for people who serve on nonprofit boards and other things for which Web contacts are useful. (I have this problem a great deal, and it's the primary reason I get almost 600 spams every day!)

TIP: *If you create or serve as an officer or other significant figure in an organization with a Web page, use a disposable address for the "contacts" section of that Web page.*

Put Your Email Address in a Graphic

The only unbreakable (so far, at least) workaround for the spamspiders is to render your email address in a graphic image and post the graphic image on the Web. The spamspiders are searching for text, so if there is no text associated with the image, there's nothing for them to grab. The downside to this is that people cannot simply click the image and bring up an email edit window, but that may be the price you have to pay.

Obfuscate Your Email Address on Your Web Page

Many people have written and used clever JavaScript functions that obfuscate (obscure) an email address in the JavaScript source code, which then assembles it on the fly into a cleartext (readable) email address when someone clicks the link. This may reduce the number of spamspider hits, but it has two disadvantages:

1. No such system is unbreakable, and there are spammers who brag about their efforts to break JavaScript obfuscation code. Web spiders have been written that parse and execute JavaScript code copied from Web pages, and if the code can turn an obfuscated address into cleartext, the spider can too. Because systems like this are an affront to spammers' intelligence, they are willing to spend enormous efforts to break them—and once broken, they're broken forever.

2. The number is uncertain, but somewhere from 10 to 15 percent of all Web browsers disable JavaScript completely, and people using those browsers will not be able to click on your JavaScript obfuscated address link anyway.

Never Unsubscribe from a Spammer Mailing List

Ever find it funny that a spam message rarely gives any crisp information concerning who and where the spammer is but almost *always* includes a link to "unsubscribe"? That's because unsubscribing from a spammer's mailing list is *always* a hoax and a lie. (This should surprise you? *Everything* about spam is a hoax and a lie!) The whole purpose of that unsubscribe link is to verify that your email address is live and functional, and that whoever it belongs to pays enough attention to their email to attempt to get off of a spammer's list. That tags you not only as a live address but as a good prospect, one that the spammer can sell to other spammers for a good deal of money.

Basically, if you unsubscribe from a spammer's list, you may not get any further messages from that particular spammer domain. However, most of the larger spammer shops have dozens or even hundreds of Internet domains, and it's never entirely clear what domains belong to what spammer. So the best you can hope for is to be dropped from one of those dozens or hundreds of domains—and once you verify that your address is live, you will be added to all the others that you aren't already on. Furthermore, within a few weeks, your address will be sold to other spammers. There is no such thing as unsubscribing from a spammer's mailing list. The reality is that you will be dropped from one and added to 50 more.

Remember the mantra, and chant it often: *Everything about spam is a hoax and a lie!*

Check to See if Listservs Are Archived to the Web

There are a great many email list servers (called *listservs* for short) on the Internet, focused on every conceivable topic. A listserv is a sort of "group echo" for an email message. You send a message to a single email address (for example, rc-airmodels@grbhobbies.net) and the message is sent to all those individuals who have subscribed to the listserv. It's an excellent medium for group discussion, and very popular.

You should check one thing before joining a listserv, however: See if the archived discussions are made publicly available on the Web. If they are, your email address is likely to be present in any message in the archive, and if the archive is posted on the Web, the spambots will eventually find it.

Even if no one says that a particular listserv is archived to the Web, it's probably a good idea to use a disposable email address for listserv discussions, just in case, at some time down the road, the list owner changes their listserv policy.

Obfuscate Your Email Address on Newsgroups and Discussion Boards

Just as there are spamspiders that crawl the Web, searching for email addresses to spam, there are spiders that download and scan Usenet newsgroups and Web discussion board postings for email addresses. Postings to newsgroups and discussion boards usually require the entry of an email address of some kind. Some newsreaders do not require the entry of an email address at all, and I advise you to avoid posting an address if you feel you don't need "private" communication apart from the newsgroup or message board itself. Some people who prefer to post anonymously simply make up a phony address, but if you want people to be able to reach you apart from the newsgroup or discussion board, obfuscating an address is necessary. (Making up a phony address is dicey, because you can never be quite sure that the address you "make up" isn't actually being used by some unsuspecting person somewhere!)

The idea with address obfuscation is to create an address that is "broken" in a way that a spider cannot fix but that any reasonably intelligent human being can. For example, here are a couple of obfuscated forms of Andy Stanton's email address: **rugster@stantonservices.com**

rugster@stantonNOSPAMservices.com

rugster@stantonPULLTHISservices.com

As given, these addresses will bounce unless you delete the *NOSPAM* or *PULLTHIS* text.

This system worked well for many years, but spammers (to whom such mechanisms are a terrible affront) have created ever more sophisticated spiders. These days, spiders are regularly searching for blocks of uppercase letters within an address that is otherwise completely in lowercase and stripping out anything in uppercase.

The current solution (current for how long, we're not sure) is to mix case in an obfuscation, like this:

rugster@stantonPuLLThISservices.com

It takes a little more thought to remove the obfuscation, but most people (especially those used to the conventions of newsgroups and discussion boards) will catch on quickly.

By the way, it's now unwise to use the word *spam* in an obfuscation, whether in upper- or lowercase. Some have tried to spell it backwards, but *MAPS* has other meanings and can be confusing to newcomers.

As anyone who has read Usenet newsgroups for a while already knows, the discussions on newsgroups can get vicious. I've heard tales of newsgroup combatants who have taken revenge on their online enemies by signing them up for spammer mailing lists or posting their email addresses on their Web sites, thus subjecting those addresses to huge amounts of spam. As my father told me once: *Enemies are a cost center; allies are a revenue center.* Keep your temper in check on newsgroups and discussion boards. Venting spleen online rarely does any good for anyone, and it can seriously boomerang back on you!

One final note about discussion groups: Many people have reported that signing up for a Yahoo Groups account opened the gates to huge quantities of spam, even though Yahoo insists it does not sell lists of email addresses to spammers. This has happened to many people in our immediate acquaintance, so in light of that experience we strongly recommend *against* creating a Yahoo Groups account.

Use Disposable Email Addresses for E-Commerce

Although the largest and best-known e-commerce retailers like Amazon.com can probably be trusted not to sell your email address to spammers (they have too much to lose if it ever came out, for way too small a financial gain), midsize and especially smaller retailers are another matter. When creating an account with online retailers, always use a disposable email address. These are email addresses obtained from one of the many free email services that are everywhere on the Web. They cost nothing, and when an address inevitably becomes a spam magnet, it can be discarded and another one obtained.

Nearly all email clients of any consequence can support multiple email accounts, with one email address per account. Simply set up a separate account for each address you use, and then when you click the check mail button, the client will read them all and deposit all the mail from any of the several accounts into your inbox. It's sometimes useful to create a filter that will deposit all the mail sent to a disposable address (say, one devoted to use with a single e-commerce retailer) into a specific mail folder. Creating filters can be an advanced topic, and it's always very specific to a particular mail client. Whatever mail client you use, read your documentation and give it a try. Filtering can be very useful, even though it takes some practice to get it right.

If you limit the use of a disposable address to a single vendor, you'll be able to tell quickly if that vendor is selling your address to spammers, especially if you direct all mail sent to that address to a single folder. If they do, write them an angry letter indicating that you'll never buy from them again. It's the only way we'll ever break them of that habit!

Don't Complain to a Spammer's ISP

Finally, many people have hit upon the idea to complain about spammers to the ISP (Internet service provider) of the party that sent you the spam message.

Don't do it.

First of all, the ISP community has gotten much more sensitive to the issue of their customers spamming, and by the time you get a spam from someone originating at an ISP, the ISP has probably already cut off the account. But more important, *the spam may not have come from that ISP at all.* Spammers are consummate forgers, and the majority of spam messages have forged From fields. Some of the addresses in the From field of a spam message are completely bogus and made up, but many are actually the addresses of real people who have been hit by an address harvester virus or whose addresses have been harvested from someone else's address book by an address harvester virus.

That being the case, there has arisen a subindustry of ISPs who specifically cater to spammers and won't cut them off for pursuing their trade. It's not hard to set up an ISP business, and given the money that spammers are still raking in from the heedless masses who either don't know or don't care about the damage they're doing by patronizing spammers, the spammer ISPs don't need a lot of customers to make a tidy living. They won't care if you complain about spam coming from one of their customers. Worse, they may take your address and give it to one or their customers. Or all of them.

Don't complain. Fighting spam can only be done through education and through filtering. Attacking the spammers themselves is pointless, at least for people who do not have boatloads of money to launch continuous lawsuits.

GunkBuster's Notebook: Watch Out for Spam Beacons!

Depending on which email client you use, even *opening* a spam message may verify your email address to the spammer who sent the message. This diabolically clever hack is called a *spam beacon,* and here's how it works: The spammer has a PC with a custom database program used to generate spam email messages and transmit them. Your email address (and millions of others) is in the database. The program generates HTML-formatted messages for a mailing run, and every message contains graphics in the form of separate image files, which are downloaded from the spammer's Web server. The HTML formatting code sent to you in a spam message contains special statements (called *IMG tags*) that specify which image file is to be downloaded and where to find it. When the database application grinds out millions of messages to send to people like you, it encodes each message a little bit differently in those IMG tags. It inserts a code number linked to your email address in the spammer database.

When the message arrives in your inbox and you open it to see what it is, the HTML code executes in order to draw the message on your screen, and in the process those IMG tags "phone home" to get their specified graphics images. The spammer's Web server logs those special code numbers embedded in the IMG tags just before it transmits the images down to your PC. Later on, the spammer can compare those logged code numbers against the code numbers in his database. Bang! You're nailed. You opened the message, and you brought down the encoded graphic image, and the spammer literally has your number. Your address has been verified, and the spammer can now sell your email address to other spammers as a "verified recipient."

Avoiding sending that "spam beacon" back to the spammer means that you have to be very careful about viewing messages that may be spam. This not only includes opening the message in a separate window (usually done by double-clicking the message header in the header list) but even previewing the message in the preview pane.

You can only avoid spam beacons by choosing email clients that allow you to disable the downloading of images to HTML messages. The great abuser here is Outlook Express. You cannot disable image downloading to the Outlook Express preview pane. Preview a spam message and you've automatically confirmed your address to the spammer. If you must use Outlook Express, turn off the preview pane. This is done by selecting View|Layout and unchecking the Show Preview Pane box in the lower half of the window. (See Figure 7.1.) Better still, use a more powerful client that gives you control over image downloading. These include Poco Mail, The Bat, Pegasus Mail, and Mozilla Thunderbird. (See Chapter 3 for a more detailed discussion of email clients, including a matrix showing which clients offer this feature.)

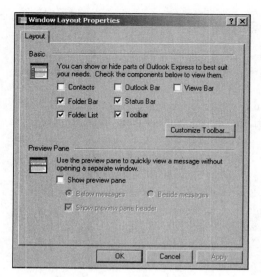

Figure 7.1
Disabling the Outlook Express preview pane.

Avoid Triggering Other People's Spam Filters

While keeping spam out of your own inbox is probably much on your mind these days, keeping the messages that you send out of other people's spam filters is something you should also be thinking about. Here are a few tips to help you keep your mail from "looking like" spam when it gets to its recipient:

√ Avoid putting certain words in the subject header. These include *free, insurance, dating, mortgage, penis, enlargement*, and the names of many popular drugs, including Viagra, Xanax, Vicodin, Hydrocodone, Lortabs, Valium, Levitra, and so on. In general, watch the spam that comes into your own inbox and avoid the distinctive words they use in their subject headers. If you work in a field that uses certain spam-favored terms like *mortgage, refinance,* or *meds,* try to keep them out of your subject line if possible.

√ Avoid using certain words in the body of your message. The big offender here is *unsubscribe,* which many people filter on as a sure-fire spam telltale. But in general, don't write things that sound like a sales pitch. Terms like *limited time, great deals,* and so on will trigger a lot of spam filters, as will any verbiage that comes from the gutter or can be mistaken for gutter talk by a spam filter. (The sad poster child here is *summa cum laude.*)

√ Avoid including images in your email. Many people have become so desperate to filter spam (most of which uses images) that they filter on the HTML IMG tag and consign any message containing an IMG tag to the Trash folder. If you have a need to send an image to someone, it might make more sense to direct them to a file on your FTP site (if you have one) or at least tell them in a separate email that you're sending an image so that they can watch their spam folder. Forgoing images means you'll have to give up graphical backgrounds for your messages, but it's a small price to pay to help your message get through!

√ If at all possible, beyond merely excluding images, send your email as plain text rather than HTML. About 80 percent of spam is sent as text formatted with HTML because many spammer tricks depend on HTML tags and comments. If you send plain text rather than HTML, many Bayesian filters (see Chapter 9) will be more inclined to consider your note as legitimate.

Summing Up—From Prevention to Cure

As in the realm of real-world illnesses, prevention is good but everyone gets sick now and then. Spam prevention is no better in that no matter what you do, you will eventually get a certain amount of spam, and the amount that you get will grow over time as you use a given email address. (This is why a lot of people—especially Public Professionals—have resigned themselves to changing their primary email address every couple of years, or even once a year.)

After you've done whatever you can to prevent spam, you'll have to begin thinking about how to filter out whatever spam begins to arrive. This is a big and complex (and unavoidably technical) subject, and the one I'll be taking up in the next few chapters.

Understand the Spam Filtering Conundrum

Degunking Checklist:

√ Set your email client to use your address book as a "sender whitelist."

√ Don't put your own email address in your address book.

√ Don't allow your email client to automatically add v-cards to your address book.

√ Carefully consider each filter term you select to be sure it won't trigger false positives.

√ In filtering spam, filter order is crucial: your whitelist filter should run *first,* and the most time-consuming spam filter should run last.

√ If you get a lot of spam, POPTray can "thin" your inbox by deleting your regular spammers from your mail server automatically.

Way back in 1886, John Wanamaker (who invented the modern department store) said, "I know that half of my advertising budget is wasted. I just don't know which half." Now, put your PC in John Wanamaker's place, and task it to figure out which half of the email landing in your inbox is spam.

Actually, consider yourself *extremely* lucky if only *half* of your email is spam. At this writing, my own statistics tell me that 91.38 percent of my email is spam. I have been hammering on the spam problem for several years now, and I have tried almost every filtering system known to man. Some work better than others; some barely work at all. A thin few seemed to be the silver bullet when they first appeared, but the First Law of Spam Filtering soon asserted itself: *No spam filtering mechanism works forever.*

It's an arms race. As new filtering techniques appear, spammers adjust their approaches to beat them. If you do not continually adjust your filters to take new spammer tricks into account, you'll begin losing the race and the spammers will take over more and more of your inbox. Spam filtering takes a certain amount of time and effort on your part. There is no such thing as "set it and forget it" spam control. If a vendor claims its filtering product is that good, they're lying. Trust me.

In this chapter I'll explain the various approaches to spam filtering, with the upside and downside for each. It's important that you've already read Chapter 7, in which I explain preventive measures that will keep you from being a spam magnet. If you violate any of the principles I laid out in Chapter 7, all the filtering in the world won't help you.

Understand Spam Filtering Jargon

To speak meaningfully of the tangled world of spam filtering, you'll have to understand certain terms. The list that follows is not in alphabetical order because the definitions refer to the other terms and reading them in the order given will allow this section to make the most sense.

Blacklist. A list of email addresses and Internet domains from which all mail is to be considered spam and discarded. No further analysis is done. If a message's sender or the sender's domain is on the blacklist, it's spam. Some email clients call this a blocked senders list or banned senders list. There may also be lists of banned subjects or text to be found in the message body.

Whitelist. A list of email addresses or Internet domains from which you will *always* accept email as legitimate. Your whitelist would thus contain the email addresses of people and organizations that you trust: your spouse, friends, children, and co-workers or newsletters and email lists that you subscribe to. A whitelist is the reverse of a blacklist. Many spam filtering products allow you to import your Windows Address Book as a ready-made whitelist, under the reasonable assumption that your address book does *not* contain the addresses of spammers!

False negative. When a spam message is mistakenly identified as a legitimate message, this is a false negative. A false negative will show up in your inbox with all your legitimate email and you will have to delete it manually. It is very difficult to eliminate false negatives entirely, and if you try, you may increase the rate of false positives (see the next entry), which are *much* worse.

False positive. When a legitimate email message is tagged as spam (and, worse, automatically discarded with the rest of the trash), it's called a false positive. These are the bane of spam filters, and your main job will be to tweak your spam filter technology so that your false positive rate goes as close to zero as possible. Doing so may increase your rate of false negatives, but those are easier to deal with.

Content filtering. In this ancient technique, a filtering program looks at something in an email message—the From field, the Subject field, or something in the body of the message itself—and compares it to a list of words or Internet domains known to be used by spammers. If a message is from **sleazyspammer.com** and you've placed **sleazyspammer.com** in your email client's blacklist, the filter treats it as spam. If the Subject field contains "Get cheap Xanax now!" and *Xanax* is in the filter's database of spammer terms, the message is tagged as spam. If the body of the message directs you to **www.cheapillegaldrugs.org** and that Web URL is in the filter's blacklist of spammer Web sites, the message is treated as spam.

Bayesian filtering. This is a fascinating technology that allows a spam filter to "learn" how to spot spam by using statistical analysis of message length and the distribution of words present in a message. Basically, you pass a certain number (at least 100) messages through a Bayesian filter and somehow indicate to the filter (generally by clicking a button) whether each message is spam or legitimate email. The filter analyses what words tend to be in spam versus real email and then uses that analysis to "guess" whether a message is spam or not. If you're persistent about training a Bayesian filter, the filter gets better with each message it analyses, and after a week or so its "guesses" will be accurate to better than 90 percent—and probably closer to 95 percent. (Chapter 9 is all about Bayesian filters.)

Magnet. This is a term used primarily by the Bayesian filter called POPFile (see Chapter 9), but other filtering technologies are beginning to adopt it. A magnet is a user-defined term or address that "pulls" a message toward a spam classification or a non-spam classification. In POPFile, for example, if you create a magnet based on seeing your boss's email address in the From field, that magnet will "pull" all messages from your boss into your inbox as real email. On the flip side, you can define a magnet based on the word *Viagra* that will "pull" any messages with *Viagra* in the subject line to the Trash folder, or wherever else you banish spam to. Magnets can be problematic and must be used with care. I'll have much more to say about them in Chapter 9, which is devoted to Bayesian filtering with POPFile.

Mail retrieval proxy. Nearly all modern email clients allow some sort of spam filtering. However, many of the best spam filtering products are not email clients at all but mail retrieval proxies, or programs that insert themselves between your email client and the mail server from which your email is delivered. All your email passes through the mail retrieval proxy, which then filters for spam and either deletes the spam or marks it so that your email client can delete it after you inspect it. POPFile, Norton Anti-Spam, and McAfee SpamKiller are all mail retrieval proxies. Most are currently limited to use with Post Office Protocol (POP) servers, but in the near future I expect most will also support IMAP and Exchange email servers. (POPFile has already declared this a near-term goal.)

Spoofing. This is what spammers do when they forge the From field of a message that they send. The address may be a real address belonging to someone else or a completely fake address generated randomly by a spammer utility. There is currently nothing in the email protocols to prevent or detect this, so it's very common. The From address in spam is spoofed about 60 percent of the time.

Spam zombie. A recent class of computer viruses (pioneered by one called SoBig) takes care not to damage its host system or announce its presence in any way. Instead, they plant a piece of software called an *open email proxy,* which is a kind of email relay station. (This is no relation to a POP proxy, though the similarity causes a lot of confusion.) The presence of an operating open email proxy turns the infected PC into a spam zombie that is used to relay spam from a spammer and thus conceal the spammer's identity.

Develop a Good Spam-Fighting Philosophy

To be successful in combating spam, you'll need to develop a sound spam-fighting philosophy. I'll help you by explaining how I see the spam wars and what my priorities are in fighting them. All the advice I'll give in this chapter and the next are based on these points:

√ Prevention is better than cure. You don't have to filter spam if you're not getting any, so do whatever you can to avoid becoming a spam magnet. (See Chapter 7.)

√ Don't get angry and don't take spam attacks personally. Some people get so nuts when spam clogs their inboxes that they do stupid things that end up increasing their false positives or (worse) letting the spammers know that they're out there with a live address and care enough about spam to look at it. That's exactly what the rotters want you to do. So keep your cool and *never* try to contact a spammer for *any* reason.

√ Set up filters to reduce the spam in your inbox without generating any false positives. Getting zero spam is impossible unless you're willing to accept a significant number of false positives. This means you're losing real messages, which subverts the whole purpose of email.

√ Maximize the control you have over your filtering mechanism. There is no "one size fits all" spam filtering system. Let somebody else make the decisions and you will have many false positives without necessarily eliminating all spam.

√ Fighting spam takes real work. We have made spamming *much* more difficult than it was a few years ago. The spammers have become desperate, and out of their desperation has come a diabolical cleverness that they have brought to bear on defeating our spam filters. There is no "set it and forget it" solution to spam filtering. Any system that blocks all spam without effort on your part will block a significant portion of your real email.

Why do I take time to lay all this out? As we go on, I will be pretty blunt about what sorts of spam filters I recommend and what sorts I don't. Some anti-spam product vendors will doubtless be annoyed at what I say.

That said, let's get started.

Love Your Address Book—and Use It!

Your single most powerful weapon against spam isn't a filter at all: It's your address book. It's where you keep the email addresses of people you contact on a regular basis. If you choose, it can also contain street addresses, phone numbers, fax numbers, cell numbers, ham radio callsigns, names of spouses and children, anniversaries, and so on. It's where you store data about the people you communicate with.

A lot of people don't use any sort of address book, even though an excellent one is provided with Windows and all email clients of consequence come with one built in. (An amazing number of people I know still keep all this information on paper in a memo book!) My first advice on spam filtering is simple: Learn to use a software address book—and then use it religiously. Some point-by-point explication:

√ Use the address book that integrates with your chosen email client. If that's Outlook or Outlook Express, the address book will be the Windows Address Book. Major email clients like Poco Mail, The Bat, and Mozilla Thunderbird all come with a highly integrated address book of their own. This tighter integration allows you to do certain things with the "internal" address book that you could not with the Windows Address Book.

√ Don't try to use both the Windows Address Book and the address book that's part of your email client. All the major email clients can import data from the Windows Address Book, so if you're not using one of the Outlooks, import Windows Address Book data into the address book in your email client and *use the address book in the email client*. If you've divided your data between two address books, the two address books will eventually get out of sync with one another and old, obsolete data will be lurking in one or the other, ready to trip you up and waste your time at the worst possible moment.

√ Set your email client to add to its internal address book the email address of every sender to whom you send a reply message. This is how you build your whitelist of email senders.

√ Make sure that the From address of all of the email newsletters you subscribe to are present in your address book. Spammers often try to make their messages look like newsletters, and newsletters become false positives far more often than messages from ordinary people.

GunkBuster's Notebook: Don't Automatically Add V-Cards to Your Address Book!

A *v-card* is a small file that contains contact information, a virtual business card. Some email clients allow you to send a v-card automatically as an attachment to every message you send. Some email clients also allow you to automatically add a v-card contact to your address book as soon as one comes in.

Don't.

I have seen spam come in with v-cards attached. The idea is to get into your address book, which in most email clients also acts as your whitelist. Once a spammer's address is in your whitelist, anything they send will go direct to your inbox.

Make sure you configure your email client so that you must explicitly save a v-card to your address book rather than having it added automatically. Your whitelist must be under *your* control, not the control of the spammers!

Use Your Address Book as Your Whitelist

Address books are important in the spam wars for this reason: Most email clients either treat the address book as their whitelist or allow you to easily specify the address book as a whitelist. A *whitelist* is the list of email senders who will always reach your inbox, no matter what else your filters may decide about the messages that they send. If a message comes from someone in your whitelist, it goes to your inbox. Unless you go to great lengths to make it otherwise, whitelists trump blacklists.

If everyone with whom you regularly communicate is in your address book (and thus on your whitelist), you will have far fewer false positives. This is absolutely crucial when using statistical technologies like Bayesian filters, which "trip up" every so often for reasons that can't be explained. (I'll have much more to say about this in Chapter 9.)

TIP: *The flip side is worth considering, too: If you find that certain spam messages inexplicably make it to your inbox in defiance of your spam filters, check to be sure that the spammer's email address isn't in your address book somewhere. This can be a problem if you've had dealings with some less scrupulous e-commerce Web sites. These can spam you for years, often with pitches that have no relation to what you originally bought from them. Get them out of your address book and your filters will do the rest!*

GunkBuster's Notebook: Don't Put Your Own Email Address in Your Address Book!

A favorite spammer trick is to replace the spammer's own address in the From field with *yours* so that it looks like you sent the spam message to yourself. (Email header fields are absurdly easy for spammers to forge.) Obviously, they don't want you to know where the spam is coming from, but there's another reason to do this: Many people place their own email addresses in their email address book, and most email clients consider the address book a whitelist. With most email clients, any message carrying a From address present in the address book will get into your inbox, even if the message would otherwise fail one of your spam filters.

Remember: In email filtering, *whitelists trump blacklists.*

There's very little reason to have your own email addresses in your address book. If you must send yourself a test message, type your address manually rather than selecting it from the address book.

Aside from the occasional test messages you send to yourself, any message with your email address in both the From and To fields is almost certainly spam, and if your email client allows a filter that triggers on the same address in From and To, a significant number of spams can be caught that way.

Use Content Filtering

In a spam-fighting context, a filter is a sort of logical proposition. You're telling your email client, "If you find a message in which the From field contains the text *sleazyspammer.com,* send it to the Trash folder." Creating filters sounds forbidding to nontechnical people, but they're not hard to create and use once you get a sense for how your email client handles them. Filters are generally created by filling in Windows dialogs, and much of the work is done by selecting items from pull-down lists, so it's hard to make mistakes. I can't show you how every email client creates filters, but I'll provide an example later in this section.

Automatic or Manual Filtering?

Some of the better email clients have automatic spam or "junk mail" filtering. You click a check box somewhere and then the client will run each incoming message through a gamut of tests and make a decision as to whether it's spam or real mail. It sounds easy, but there are two problems, one minor and one major:

√   Minor Problem: You typically have to add spammer domains and key words to a file or a set of rules somewhere to make the system effective. This takes some decision making and a little work.

√   Major Problem: You aren't always told on what basis the client makes its decisions. Even where you're told how the client decides what's spam and what's not, you generally can't change the way the decisions are made if you find the client making bad calls on some of your mail.

Poco Mail is probably the best example of an email client with automatic junk mail filtering. Once you click a check box, it applies a complex system of tests to your mail (see Figure 8.1). It gives each message a numerical score, and if the score is greater than a certain threshold number, the message is called spam. You control what the threshold value is, and you can add and remove terms from several blacklists and whitelists. Many of the tests, however, simply aren't explained anywhere. I found the system obscure, inflexible, and prone to both false positives and false negatives. My own custom filters served me reasonably well, as long as I ran them before I let Poco's automatic spam testing run. (See "Run Your Spam Filters in the Correct Order" later in this chapter.)

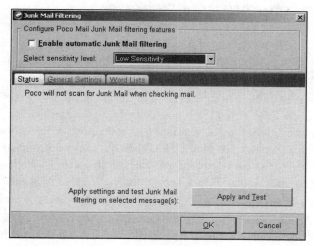

Figure 8.1

Poco Mail's junk mail filtering dialog.

Filtering on Sender Addresses and Domains

The most obvious sort of content filtering is to filter on the sender identity in the From field. Banning a sender or an entire domain is fairly easy: When you get a spam message, copy the address of its sender into a filter blacklist. Adding an address or a domain to a blacklist is easy to do in most email clients, and it's where most people begin their experience in spam filtering. Unfortunately, in more than half of the spam messages coming in (based on my own studies here), *the From field does not carry the email address of the spammer.*

It's important that you understand this. Spammers don't want to be blocked, and many of them (those sending scams, porn pitches, illegal drug pitches, and viruses) *really* don't want to be found. Therefore, many spammers forge the

From field, replacing their own address with either a completely fictional email address generated from a random list of words and domains or (worse) an address of some unfortunate person somewhere in the world. Forging email header fields like From is called *spoofing,* and it's extremely easy to do. No checking of the From field is ever done, and whatever is there (even nothing at all) is fine by the world's countless email servers.

In order to filter on the From field, you therefore have to exercise a little judgment and look closely at whatever address you find there.

TIP: *If your email client allows you to test for a blank From field, that's a good thing to do because virtually all messages with blank From fields are spam.*

Most email clients do their message filtering in roughly the same way. You create a *rule,* also called a *filter,* which has two parts:

1. *A match statement.* This is where you specify what part of the message to examine, what sort of comparison to make, and what to look for. It says, in essence, "Look in the Subject field. If it contains *Viagra,* this statement is true." You can select different parts of a message to examine, different sorts of logical comparisons (present, not present, begins with, ends with, and so on), and a value (or in some clients, a file full of values) to look for. Your choices will vary wildly by email client. Read your documentation or help files!

2. *An action.* If a match statement comes up true, the rule will take some specified action. This might be moving the message to the trash or marking it somehow as spam, moving a message to another folder, deleting it from the server, marking it as read or as high priority, and so on.

That's all there is to it! Rules are much less mysterious than most people think, and most are defined by selecting values from pull-down lists. As an example, here's how to create a simple rule in Mozilla Firebird:

1. Select Tools | Message Filters. The window that appears is a summary window for message filters. As you create filters, they will be listed here and will run in order from top to bottom.

2. To create a new filter, click the New button toward the upper-right portion of the Message Filters window. The window that appears is where you create new filters (see Figure 8.2).

3. Give the filter a title. If you don't, you won't be able to tell one from another in the summary window! For this example, title it "Sender Whitelist." The filter will tell Thunderbird to compare the From field to your address book and move any message for which that matchstatement is true to your inbox. This is a crucial filter that you should create before anything else!

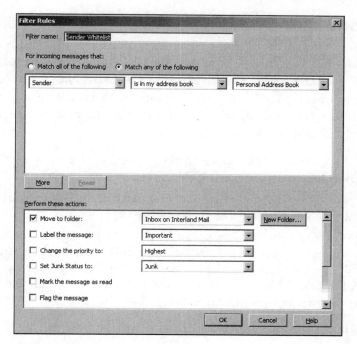

Figure 8.2

Mozilla Thunderbird's Rules Definition window.

4. Create one or more match statements. In the upper list pane, you can create any reasonable number of match statements. For this example, we only need one. Pull down the leftmost pull-down list and select Sender. From the center pull-down list, select "is in my address book." From the rightmost pull-down list, select Personal Address Book. If a rule must contain several match statements (say, if you want to search for the names of several drugs), you would click the More button to create another. Use the Fewer button to delete the highlighted match statement if you need to.

5. Choose an action. In the lower pane, check the box marked "Move to folder." From the pull-down list, select Inbox.

6. Click OK. You have created the filter! This filter will move messages from anyone in your address book to your inbox, making your address book a sender whitelist.

Mozilla Thunderbird has a very simple filtering system. Other email clients allow you to create much more powerful filtering rules. Poco Mail, in particular, gives you an enormous number of options, including the ability to run a script written in Poco Mail's scripting language. If the simple logic of rulemaking doesn't quite give you what you want, you can write a script that will do almost anything you might want to do.

Is It a Spammer Domain?

Blacklisting a spammer domain is easy. However, sometimes it's hard to tell whether an Internet domain present in the From field of a spam message belongs to a spammer or whether it's been forged and is actually the address of an innocent person or company. Some spam domains are obvious: If the domains contain words like *deals, free,* or other similar marketing-flavored text, they're almost certainly spam domains.

You can also check for further evidence of spamminess by looking to see if the questionable domain has an associated Web site. Here's how:

1. Highlight the domain portion of the address in the From field. Press Ctrl-C to lift it into the Windows Clipboard.

2. Bring up your Web browser. Click on the URL field where you normally enter Web addresses. Type "www." (include the period but not the quotation marks) and press Ctrl-V to drop the domain from the Clipboard into the browser URL field. Check to see that you have a "proper" URL (in the form **www.sleazyspammer.com**) and press Enter.

At this point, you'll get one of several things in your browser:

√   Error message, including the classic 404, Page Not Found. This often means that the domain is one of many "bulk" domains purchased by a spammer for which no Web page is ever created. On the other hand, it may also be owned by an innocent party. Error messages aren't proof of spammer-hood.

√   A "test pattern" Web page. These are default pages that an installed Web server sends out to Web browsers when no other page has been defined. This is generally a sign of a spammer-owned domain, but it's not a sure thing.

√   A blank page. This is generally a sign of a spammer domain.

√   An actual Web page of a person or company having nothing to do with marketing or email. This means that the spammer has forged the domain address of an innocent party in the From field, so the domain tells you nothing about where the spam came from. Don't blacklist the domain! Look to the Subject field or the message body for other possible terms to filter on.

√   A mostly blank screen with one significant feature: A link or button marked Unsubscribe. It's a spammer, and they want you to click the link and thus verify that you're a live address so they can sell your address to other spammers. Don't click! Instead, add that domain to your blacklist (see Figure 8.3).

√   A professional-looking Web page from a company that engages in "targeted direct marketing" or some such nonsense. Bingo! There's your spammer. Blacklist that domain *now!*

Figure 8.3
A typical spammer "unsubscribe" page.

TIP: Be particularly careful to avoid blocking the free Web mail sites, which are legion. They often have mail in the domain somewhere, just as spammers often do. For example, pandamail.net is a well-known free Web mail provider. On the other hand, beccamail.com is one of many domains owned by one spammer. (Look for that "unsubscribe" link. Any domain that takes you to an "unsubscribe" link is almost certainly a spammer!)

Cautious that I am of false positives, I'm conservative with blacklisting domains. Unless I'm *sure* it's a spammer domain, I leave it be and look for other elements in the message to filter on.

Filtering on Key Words in the Subject

Filtering on key words in the subject line can work well, as long as you keep in mind that spammers are aware of key word filters and try various tricks to defeat them. I got a great deal of spam for awhile with the cryptic legend *skuper vigraga* in the Subject field, and filtering on both those terms eliminate all of those messages. However, the spammer in question soon changed the spelling to *sugper virgara,* which I then had to add to my "banned subjects" file in Poco Mail.

There are a few spammers still willing to use the correct spelling of *Viagra* in the subject line, and assuming you're unlikely to ever engage in conversation with anyone about Viagra, you can filter on it and kill a few spams. Most of the time, spammers will attempt to obfuscate provocative subjects by misspelling them just enough to throw off spam filters but not enough to make them incomprehensible to potential customers. This is a good news/bad news thing: Creative misspellings are unlikely to be used in the Subject field of real mail...but creative misspellings must be blacklisted individually, and spammers only use them for a little while before changing them.

Mostly I use Subject filtering for the titles of recurring spam "newsletters," like "Sappy Inspirations" and "Dumb Joke of the Day." These keep their titles (generally) but switch sender addresses every so often, so filtering on the title is better than filtering on the sender address. These are becoming less common as more and more people filter spam. If you spot recurring Subject values in your spam, Subject filtering will take care of them.

Filtering on Key Words or Domains in the Message Body

About half of all spam is now delivered via *spam zombies* or *spam proxies,* which are virus-planted spam relay stations used to obscure the real origin of spam mail. This means that for half of your spam, you'll be unable to filter on the From field because it will contain either an imaginary email address or the address of an unfortunate virus victim, whose machine has been infected and is now a spam zombie.

Spammers like to use spam zombies because it makes filtering their messages a lot tougher. Bogus From addresses and vague subject lines will force you to filter on text in the message body. This is more difficult, and some email clients do not make it easy. Message body filtering takes more computer time because a message body may be large, with perhaps hundreds or even thousands of words, and searching it is not as quickly done as searching a 50-character Subject field.

Spammers make it harder by obfuscating the text within the message body, especially where the message is sent in HTML format. Spammers insert random HTML comments in the middle of key words like *Viagra* and make them unsearchable by most mail clients. Inserting a comment would make the word look like this in the HTML source code that defines the message:

```
Via<!-hjyrv->gra
```

Comments are not shown on the screen, so when this little bit of HTML is displayed by your email client, it just looks like *Viagra.* Your filter sees the whole thing and won't recognize the split word, so you won't catch it. The text in the comment is generated randomly in the spammer's mailer software and is never used twice. You can't filter on it.

Tricks like this will make you crazy, and if most of your spam carries such obfuscation in the message body, you may be better off using a Bayesian filter, like POPFile (see Chapter 9).

If you're going to filter on the message body, the one thing you can generally do is filter on what I call the "payload" URL or phone number. The payload is what the spammer wants to show you or a Web site they want to send you to. URLs cannot contain HTML comments, so if you can pick out a reliable spammer domain from the payload URL, these make dandy filter terms. URLs can be obfuscated to some extent (see the GunkBuster's Notebook on the topic), but the obfuscations sometimes serve as wonderfully unique filter terms themselves. This is why URL obfuscation is not very common any more.

Some spam is sent as plain text and you won't see the comments trick. The payload may be a phone number or a URL. Phone numbers are also reliable filter terms, though as with spammer domains, they change regularly.

GunkBuster's Notebook: Dealing with Obfuscated Spammer URLs

Some spammers make it *very* tricky to find the real domain within a URL, especially if you're not a tech geek who plays with servers and Web pages all the time. Obscuring a URL with technical tricks is called *obfuscation*. Here are some guidelines to help while you're digging inside spammer URLs looking for blacklist terms. Sometimes you don't even need to find the URL.

Most Web URLs are fairly simple:

http://www.duntemann.com/Diary.htm

Here, *http://* is a protocol specifier (for Hypertext Transfer Protocol), *www* is the local name of a server (for World Wide Web), and *Diary.htm* is an HTML file containing the body of the Web page that the URL points to. The domain is *duntemann.com*. The domain and the target file within the domain are separated by a forward slash.

Let's now look at a spammer URL. This one is a real URL from a spam that I received but with a phony spammer domain that I made up. It's very long, and spans three lines, but it's really a single URL. Which is the "real" spammer domain?

http://g.msn.com/0USls5.94556_377727/HP.1001?http://
g.msn.com/0USls5.94556_377727/HP.1001?http://
www.skladgrue.biz/form.asp?sid=3D150

Hint: It's certainly not msn.com. This is an interesting spammer trick. Notice the question marks. When a question mark appears in a URL, it indicates that the destination address after the question mark is where the browser will be taken if the first destination fails with an error. The technique thus provides a sort of "fail-safe" for legitimate Web sites and can send a browser to an information page telling readers how to report the error. In the URL above, there are two question marks, just to make things trickier. Both of the MSN addresses are bogus and will fail with an error. The first bogus address sends the browser to the second, which also fails and sends the browser to the third, at **skladgrue.biz**, which is the spammer's domain. Filter on **skladgrue.biz**.

Now, consider this one:

http:/%77%77%77%2E%69%74%73%74%6F%70%73%68%65%72%65%6E%6F%77%2E%62%69%7A/%63/

Yikes! This looks totally bogus, but in fact it's completely functional—and also easy to filter on. The spammer has taken each individual character in the URL and expressed it as its ASCII numeric equivalent.—%77 is w, for example, and %2E is the period character. Don't even bother translating it, or attempting to find the domain inside it. Only spammers use tricks like this. Filter on *http://%* and you'll catch nothing but spammers.

The next URL is something of a spammer work of art. It's fully functional (I changed the domain itself a little) but very difficult for the nontechnical to understand. You're expected to assume that *yahoo.com* is the domain, but that's bogus. In a URL, *anything to the left of a * character can be thrown away.* This is a legitimate technique used by spammers and consists of two URLs glued together with an asterisk. If the first URL (in this case, a bogus one at yahoo.com) cannot be found, the browser will redirect the user to the second URL, which is the spammer's Web site.

3Dhttp://drs.yahoo.com/blond_guayule/greenflycleveland/*%68ttp://commission_exportablehomoerotic_expiration.monkfish.%6Fblooboon.%62iz/0/p/?exocentric_unanimouspreemptive_listedancon_clientshiptudor-brad target=3D_blank

Once that first bogus URL is gone, the second remains inscrutable, but that's OK: The spammer outsmarted himself here. The %68ttp:// (http://) is a good search term, and so is %62.iz (biz). When the spammer obfuscates http:// or one of the standard top-level domains like com, org, or biz, you don't need to know the domain. Just filter on the obfuscation!

Most of the weird text in the URL is random gibberish inserted by the spammer's database utility for one mailing only. In other words, don't try to filter on *greenflycleveland*. It appears in only one mailing (or perhaps even one *message*) and you'll never see it again.

Finally, here's one you'll see fairly frequently:

http://192.168.148.225/images/gorp_pic.gif

Don't look for a domain here; there is none. That funny number is a "raw" Internet Protocol (IP) address. It takes the place of a domain, however, and is completely unique to the Web site of the spammer that owns it. Pull *http://192.168.148.225* out and drop it in your blacklist.

There's a lot more about obfuscated spammer URLs that I can't explain in this book. If you want to learn more, here are some Web links to follow:

www.rain.org/~mkummel/stumpers/08dec00a.html

www.pc-help.org/obscure.htm

Watch Out for False Positives When Creating Filters!

Whenever you're working on filters to catch those spammers who still manage to sneak into your inbox, remember that catching spammers is only half the challenge. *Not* catching genuine mail is the other half. Think hard as you select content filtering terms, and try to anticipate whether those terms might trigger false positives.

It's easy to forget, when confronted by endless spam messages, that some words have multiple meanings, and (worse) that some words are found "inside" other words. If you're not careful how you craft your content filters, you may begin losing real messages and (depending on whether or not you spot-check your

Trash folder) never even know it. Here are some pointers to keep in mind while crafting filters:

√   If your match statement is looking at the beginning of, the end of, or inside a Subject field, think about what innocent words may contain the filter term. *Sex* is inside a lot of words, like *Middlesex, sextant, sextuplets,* and quite a few more. *Ambien* (a popular sleeping pill) is inside *ambient*. *Anal* is inside *analysis*. *Rape* is inside *scrape, trapezoid,* and many others

√   Blacklist correctly spelled words with great care. After you've manually nuked two dozen messages telling you to "supersize your johnson," it's natural to want to blacklist *johnson*. Resist—especially if there are people in your circle of family, friends, or co-workers named Johnson.

√   Message bodies are hazardous territory for blacklisting anything but domains and phone numbers. *Unsubscribe* is present in a lot of spam, but in a lot of legitimate mail as well, especially newsletters and list server traffic like that generated by Yahoo Groups. It's very difficult to anticipate all the different contexts in which a word or phrase may be found in the body of a message compared to the more limited context you would find in a Subject field.

√   Finally, *don't forget what filters you have active.* Review them now and then. If in a fever you blacklist the word *mortgage* and later on forget that it's black-listed, you may someday wonder why all the loan companies you've contacted are ignoring you.

It's ugly work, but ya gotta do it: Scan your Trash folder now and then, just to make sure your filters aren't handing you a significant number of false positives. Unless you're getting many hundreds of spams per day, it only takes a minute or so, and you may not realize that one of your filters is overzealous until you actually catch it fingering the wrong messages.

GunkBuster's Notebook: Filtering on the IMG Tag

A very effective but slightly desperate filtering technique is to look for the HTML image tag IMG in the body of a message. Spammers use image tags extensively to bring down bitmapped images containing product pitches, and most ordinary mail does not contain them at all.

Note as well that some "real" email can and will contain IMG tags:

√   Some "free" Web-based bulletin board and forum sites append graphical image files containing ads to the ends of the messages you send from them. Yahoo Groups is famous for this.

√ Some "free" Web mail sites append graphical image files containing ads to the ends of the messages you send from them. If you filter on IMG tags, you will not see messages from real people who use such sites for their email.

√ Some email clients create messages in HTML format that use images for artwork, smilies, and other decorative bitmapped content. Messages like this, even though legitimate, will trip your spam filtering and be lost in your trash.

Filtering on image tags is easy: Just place the text <IMG in a filter. Don't forget the < or you may generate false positives by finding the characters IMG in the middle of text in non-spam messages. Don't filter on the IMG tag unless you have whitelisted your address book and especially the "real" newsletters that you subscribe to! (Most email newsletters these days are HTML formatted and make extensive use of IMG tags.)

Virtually all spam used to use bitmapped images to evade spam filters that were limited to searching for key words. Today, a great many spam filtering systems look for IMG tags, and spammers have begun using other methods that do not rely on HTML images at all. Still, you will catch a *lot* of spam by filtering on the IMG tag, and if you're comfortable with a certain number of false positives (and if you're *very* good about maintaining your whitelist!), it can be pretty effective.

Run Your Spam Filters in the Correct Order

Once you have more than one filter active on an email account, you also have to think about the order in which your filters run. In most email clients, filters that you create are run in the order that you created them. Sometimes that's not an issue, but other times it can cause trouble. The most important principle in defining your own filters is *apply your whitelist filter first*. That is, get "good" mail into your inbox before any of the other filters get a crack at it.

If you're like most people, *mortgage* is a dirty word when dealing with email. Mortgage spam is #3 for me, right after drugs and porn. However, if you're working on getting a mortgage, you *don't* want email from your banker to get tossed in the spam pile and incinerated. Your banker should be on your sender whitelist, and your sender whitelist needs to be applied to your mail before your spam filters get it. That puts mail from your banker in your inbox right away, while still allowing your spam filters to nab all the phony pitches for mortgages.

Here is a simple guide for how to arrange filter order in your email client. The general rules are these: Whitelist first, then blacklist—and after you whitelist, do the easy blacklist filtering first.

1. Filter the From field on your address book. Move any message from anyone in your address book to your inbox.

2. If you have an "allowed senders" list, filter From on that list next, with matches going to your inbox. "Allowed senders" are those entities that you want to receive mail from but aren't usually in your address book. Some clients call this list "collected addresses."

3. If you have an "allowed subjects" list, filter Subject on that next, with matches going to your inbox. Allowed subject text can be useful for getting "good" newsletters (as opposed to phony newsletters sent by spammers) into your inbox. Allowed subjects are used mostly to take action on classification tags added to the message Subject field by mail-sorting utilities like POPFile. (See Chapter 9, where I cover POPFile in detail.)

4. If you have any other whitelist filters (filters that look for "wanted" mail to move to your inbox), execute them before you begin your blacklist filtering.

5. Blacklist filters don't generally need to be run in any particular order, but *run the easy filters first,* namely the filters that don't have to search a lot of text. If you have a filter that searches the entire message body, run that filter *last* so that only those "hard-case" spams that defy all your other filters are sub-jected to a full-body search. Some spams are quite long, and filtering them can take a noticeable amount of time, so you want to use that filter as little as you can.

Changing the order of user-defined filters is usually done from the list of filters that the client keeps. Look for buttons marked Move Up and Move Down or with up or down arrows. Highlight a filter and click one of the buttons; the highlighted filter will move up (meaning toward first in run order) or down (toward last in run order). The filter list for Mozilla Thunderbird is shown in Figure 8.4. Filter order is changed with the Move Up and Move Down buttons.

In some email clients, there are no buttons for controlling filter order. Instead, you highlight a filter and drag it either up or down the list with the mouse. Poco Mail and Eudora both work this way. Poco Mail provides a graphical arrow (not a control; clicking it does nothing) to indicate the order of filter operation. See Figure 8.5.

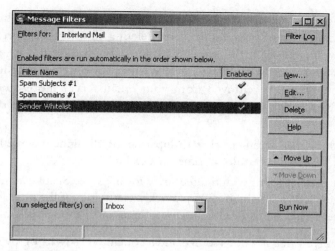

Figure 8.4

Setting the order of Mozilla Thunderbird filters.

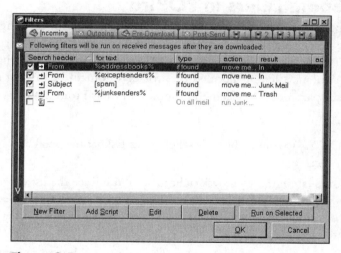

Figure 8.5

Poco Mail's filter order display.

"Inbox Thinning" with POPTray

As I described in Chapter 4, POPTray is a free email notifier that runs in the background and periodically checks your email inbox for messages from a list of priority senders that you define. This list might include your boss, your spouse, your key clients, your kids, your best friends. POPTray's notification mechanism allows you to bring down email using your email client only a few times a day (rather than every five minutes) without fear of missing an important message and failing to respond quickly.

POPTray has another trick that can be very valuable: It can "thin" your inbox by quietly checking a list of spam senders and deleting all messages from that list of spammers directly from the server without downloading the message bodies at all. Spam caught by POPTray never wastes your time coming down to your email client and is removed from your email server more quickly than it would if you had to download it first. This is especially useful in these situations:

√ You access your email through a slow dialup account. Bringing down 200 spams in the morning takes a lot of time on a dialup!

√ You have an email account with limited space for messages. Spam can make a limited-space server-side inbox fill up quickly. Getting it off the server ASAP can keep your inbox from filling to its limits and refusing real email.

POPTray is completely free and open source, and it contains no adware or spyware. For more details on obtaining and installing it, refer back to Chapter 4.

Defining Spam Filters in POPTray

First of all, keep in mind what I said earlier in this chapter about filtering on senders. Be sure you're filtering on an address or domain that sends you spam repeatedly and consistently. Don't waste a POPTray rule on a domain that is used a time or two and then abandoned or (worse) a domain belonging to a real person that a spammer has stolen and spoofed in their From field.

Follow these steps:

1. Bring up POPTray's window by right-clicking its taskbar tray icon and selecting Options.

2. Click the Rules tab in the window's right margin. You'll see the list of your previously defined rules in the left margin. These may have been rules set to prioritize mail, as I explained in Chapter 4. Rules used to filter spam are created in precisely the same way.

3. Click Add Rule at the top of the window. The various fields used to define rules will appear in the window. A blank rule will be created, with a default name like Rule45 (see Figure 8.6).

4. Give the new rule a name, and specify which of your mail accounts it is to be applied to. I recommend building the name of the spammer into the rule so you can tell the rules apart once you get as many as I have!

5. This is the heart of the process: There are two pull-down lists of criteria that you have to select from. The first list specifies where POPTray will look for its search term. Most of the time you'll select *From*. The second pull-down list defaults to Contains, which is what you want most of the time, so leave it as is (see Figure 8.7).

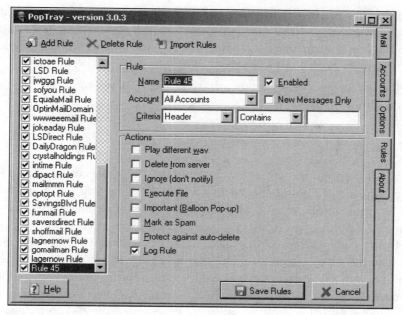

Figure 8.6
Creating a new rule in POPTray.

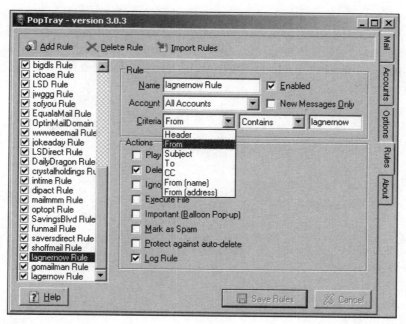

Figure 8.7
Filling out fields in a POPTray blank rule.

6. Enter the search term itself in the blank field to the right of Contains. Most of the time this will be a domain name, like **ukkyspammer.com**. As always with search terms, think *hard* about possible circumstances in which your rule might catch a real message.

7. Under Actions, check the box marked Delete from server.

8. Click Save Rules. You're done!

Summing Up

In this chapter you learned about the important processes of setting up spam filters. You learned about the various approaches that you can take and the upside and downside to each one. Setting up filters is definitely a worthwhile measure for fighting spam, but you should keep in mind that filters won't solve all of your spam problems. From the studies that I have done, I have determined that spammers have gotten so crafty that they are difficult to stop. As an email degunker, you always have to be on your guard. Some spammers are now buying domain names "in bulk," literally dozens or even hundreds at a time, and using a domain name only a handful of times—perhaps even once!—before abandoning it entirely and pulling another from the bag. This domain name turnover is happening at an awesome rate—5 percent to 8 percent per *day*.

If you receive 50 spams per day or fewer, content filtering is likely to be worth the trouble. If you receive *over* 50 spams per day, it will drive you crazy, and Bayesian filters like POPFile are likely to be much less work and aggravation for you. In the next chapter you'll learn how to degunk spam even more using Bayesian filters.

Deep-Clean Your Spam Using Bayesian Spam Filtering

Degunking Checklist:

√ Download and install POPFile, the best Bayesian spam filter.

√ Learn how to scan your inbox and spam or trash folder to make sure POPFile classified messages correctly.

√ Train POPFile by reclassifying any messages that it misclassifies.

√ Create filters in your email client to move both mail tagged as spam to your trash or spam folder and legitimate mail to your inbox.

√ Use POPFile magnets *only* to allow "spam-like" mail that you want to receive to come to your inbox as ordinary mail would.

√ Learn how to use the free Outclass utility for Microsoft Outlook.

In many people's minds, the war on gunk *is* the war on spam. Careful people who work smart and use appropriate technology to keep order on their PCs can win the war on most gunk, and with a little regular effort, keep it won. The war on spam is different. Spam gunk doesn't just pile up. It mutates, ducks, dodges, and always attempts to fly under the radar. As soon as you figure you have it licked, it starts trickling back in again.

For most of the Internet era, spam gunk has been fought with content filtering. In the previous chapter I explained why content filtering is less and less effective every year. How well it works depends less on how much spam you get and more on what kind of spam it is and from how many different spammers it comes. Ironically, as content filtering tools have improved, they haven't worked as well because spammers have gotten smarter about dodging them. Their increasingly vague, randomized subject lines and heavily obfuscated message bodies and payload domains require ever more effort to block.

Just as we thought we might be losing the gunk wars on the spam front, a new weapon appeared: Bayesian filtering. Unlike content filtering, which works best when you have a small or modest amount of spam with only a handful of spammers sending it, a Bayesian filter works better and better the more spam you throw at it—and the more spammers are sending it, the better it will recognize the gunk we will eventually receive from spammers who have not yet joined the game.

Unlike content filters, Bayesian filters *learn*. That's a gulf as wide as the one between conventional and nuclear weapons. Although only time will tell, a lot of Internet experts are starting to think that if there's a magic bullet against spam gunk anywhere, it's here.

Degunk Your Spam with Statistics

Using the methods of eighteenth century statistician Thomas Bayes, a man named Paul Graham devised a category of spam filter that looks at the statistical likelihood that a message is spam or genuine mail based on the words in the message. Bayesian statistical filtering works something like this:

1. You identify a group of messages as spam.

2. The filter picks apart the messages, counting individual words, and builds a statistical model that specifies the likelihood that a future incoming message is spam, given the words that it contains. For example, the word *sluts* rarely comes up in ordinary conversation (at least within my own social circle, heh), but it comes up quite a bit in spam.

The flip side is also true: Words like *irrespective, coerce,* and *anachronistic* rarely turn up in spam but will turn up eventually in genuine email. You can analyze the frequency of words in messages known to be genuine and build a statistical model predicting the likelihood that a message is legitimate based on the words that it contains—not just one or two or five words, but *all* of them.

A Bayesian filter builds a sort of fingerprint of the spam you receive and another, completely distinct fingerprint of your legitimate mail. It then uses those two fingerprints to predict whether future messages are spam or real email. These fingerprints are *extremely* specific to your own individual mail, which gives them tremendous precision as a filtering tool. Every time you get a new message, the fingerprints get sharper and clearer and better. In my own case, after a period of three months or so, a Bayesian filter named POPFile achieved an astonishing 99.76 percent accuracy at separating the wheat from the chaff— or the spam from the ham, as some say!

TIP: *If you're on too many spammer mailing lists, and if the spammers who bombard you are doing so through virus-hijacked "spam zombie" PCs (or if you just get several hundred spams per day), content filtering may be too much work for the benefits received. Bayesian filtering, on the other hand, can take over where content filtering leaves off and help knock out the spam That content filtering misses.*

The Bayesian Regimen

The regimen for maintaining a set of ordinary content filters is complex and time consuming. The daily regimen for maintaining a Bayesian spam filter is easy by comparison:

1. Download your email from your email server.
2. Scan your inbox looking for spam. If you find spam in your inbox, you mark it as spam and tell your Bayesian filter to recalculate its statistical model.
3. Scan your spam folder. If you find real mail in your spam folder, you tag it as real mail and, again, tell your filter to recalculate its model.

Day by day, you identify the filter's mistakes and train it to be a better spam recognizer. Over time, the filter gets increasingly accurate at predicting what's spam and what's not. In combination with an address book whitelist and a little other tweaking, a Bayesian spam filter will do a better job for you than anything else I've ever tested.

The Bayesian Downside

You might wonder if there's a catch, and there is. Bayesian filters need to be trained, and it takes a *lot* of messages to train them well. If you are a Casual Communicator and you don't get a lot of mail (lucky you!), training a Bayesian filter to acceptable accuracy could take a long time—perhaps as much as a year. Some people have "borrowed a corpus" (basically, taken a statistical model developed by another person from their email) and installed it as a basis for Bayesian filtering. This works to an extent, but because the borrowed statistical model was developed using someone else's email, it cannot be as accurate as one developed from *your* email. I'll discuss this more in the GunkBuster's Notebook "Tips on Borrowing Spam from Friends to Train POPFile" later in this chapter.

Another downside of the Bayesian filtering technique is that this approach is fairly new. Paul Graham published his paper in August 2002, and finished filter products usable by nontechnical people did not become commonplace before 2003. New Bayesian filter products are appearing regularly, and email client vendors are now beginning to build Bayesian filters right into their client programs. I've tested many of them, and they all suffer from the roughness that comes of something that was just poured from the crucible. The oldest are the best and most polished, and I'll cover the best of the breed, POPFile, in this chapter.

If you receive fewer than 15 or 20 spams per day, it will be a long, slow climb up the filter's learning curve. On the other hand, if you're a Public Professional and receive hundreds of spams per day, the filter can get *very* good *very* quickly. And there's even better news: The best Bayesian filter out there is absolutely free and relatively easy to install and use. If after three months it's still making an unacceptable number of bad calls, you can always uninstall it and go back to your old method of spam control.

Further Reading

In this chapter, I'll tell you everything you'll need to know to get POPFile up and running. If you're curious about Bayesian filtering and want to learn more, the following Web links should be helpful:

√   "A Plan for Spam" by Paul Graham: **www.paulgraham.com/spam.html**

√   "The Spammer's Compendium" by John Graham-Cumming: **http:// popfile.sourceforge.net/SpamConference011703.pdf**

Learn about POPFile

POPFile is completely free and open source (without adware or spyware or any other gotchas) and may be downloaded from its SourceForge home page:

http://popfile.sourceforge.net/

You have to be diligent about training it, but it's not a lot of work, and the results are nothing short of magical.

Why Is POPFile So Good?

POPFile isn't the only Bayesian spam filter utility out there, but it is the best. It is *strikingly* better than the brand-new Bayesian filter modules built into Mozilla Thunderbird and Poco Mail, which theoretically implement the same technology.

In Chapter 8, I wrote about obfuscation and described several of the tricks that spammers use to defeat content filters. Some of these same tricks can be used against Bayesian filters. For example, dropping HTML comments into the middle of words in an HTML message body can defeat both content filters and statistical filters—unless those filters know how to strip out or ignore HTML comments. POPFile strips out HTML comments and—"garbage tags" (like <ggh7th>) before it analyses a message.

Recognizing the power of Bayesian filters, many spammers now add lists of random words or snippets of text culled from unrelated Web documents to their spam messages, making this extra text invisible or nearly so by putting it in 1-point type or white-on-white color. They add more "invisible" text to extraneous email headers that the email client simply ignores and doesn't display. They place punctuation marks between characters, making *mortgage* look like *m,o.r*t;g'a,g:e*. They encode URLs in numeric form.

All of these tricks are in vain. POPFile "parses" HTML-encoded spam messages in great detail, tossing out comments, bogus tags, and invisible text. It removes interspersed punctuation from words (as in *mortgage*) and sees them as they really are. John Graham-Cumming has evolved POPFile's message parser according to the following dictum: *If the (human) reader of a message can't see it, POPFile shouldn't either.* This effort must be ongoing because spammers will be compelled to devise new workarounds, but POPFile has been amazingly good at staying ahead of them.

GunkBuster's Notebook: How Mail Proxies Like POPFile Work

Like nearly all standalone spam filtering utilities, POPFile is a mail proxy, and unless you have some experience in the server world, the term *mail proxy* is probably new to you. In the simplest possible terms, a mail proxy is a software utility that you insert between your mail client and your mail server to process your email before it is delivered to your inbox.

Mail proxies can be used for various purposes, but nearly all are used to filter spam. This filtering can be done in several ways, and many filtering utilities use several different methods to separate spam from legitimate email, including whitelists, blacklists, keyword and key phrase filters, and Bayesian statistical analysis. Typically, a mail proxy will look at a message in the light of its various filtering technologies and then decide whether it's spam or legitimate. The mail proxy will then mark the message, often by inserting a short text tag like *[spam]* at the beginning of the subject line, and then send it down to the email client.

The email client still has a part in the filtering task: It looks at the tags added by the mail proxy and routes anything marked as spam to its trash folder. This process is shown in Figure 9.1. The mail server is somewhere off on the Internet, typically owned

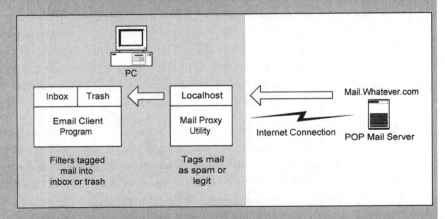

Figure 9.1

Email downloaded through a mail proxy.

and operated by your Internet service provider (ISP) or Web hosting service. The mail proxy and email client are both programs that run on your PC, which is represented by the shaded box. When your email client sends out its request for new mail, this request (which usually goes directly to the server) passes through the mail proxy. The mail proxy passes on the request for new email to the server, which delivers new email to the proxy.

The proxy inspects and marks the new email, and then passes it on down to the email client.

The mail proxy has two different "faces." From the perspective of the email client, the proxy looks like an email server. The proxy accepts requests for new mail and sends mail back to the client. From the perspective of the email server, the proxy looks like an email client. The proxy sends the server a username and password and accepts the mail that the server sends back. This allows both the client and the server to operate pretty much as they always did. A mail proxy must be configured with your email account information since it acts as an email client "by proxy" when communicating with your email server.

Install POPFile

POPFile is downloaded as a ZIP file containing a single setup.exe file from the following page:

http://popfile.sourceforge.net/

Once you download and unzip it, run setup.exe. It installs just as any Windows application installs, using a wizard that asks you questions until it knows enough to complete and configure the installed program. You can safely accept all of the install wizard's default values until you get to the Buckets screen.

Selecting POPFile's Install-Time Buckets

Most of the way through the POPFile install, you'll be shown a dialog that asks you to choose the buckets that you'll need when using POPFile. A bucket is simply POPFile's name for a category into which email may be classified. By default, POPFile creates four buckets on install: Inbox, Spam, Personal, and Work. Unless you intend to do more with POPFile than simply separate spam from real mail, you only need the Inbox and Spam buckets. To eliminate the other two, check Remove for them before clicking Continue, as shown in Figure 9.2. (If you change your mind later on, you can add additional buckets at any time.)

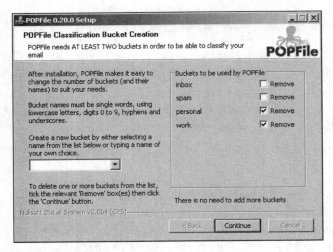

Figure 9.2
Removing unnecessary POPFile buckets.

With the Inbox and Spam buckets defined, POPFile's install can go to completion, after which it will begin working. No conventional program window will appear, but you'll see POPFile's trademark yellow octopus icon in the taskbar tray. By default, POPFile will be run automatically when Windows starts. Anytime you see the octopus icon, it's right there running in the background.

Configuring Your Email Client to Use POPFile

The only real subtlety in configuring POPFile for simple spam filtering lies in setting up the mail server addresses in your email client. POPFile itself requires almost no configuration at all. It doesn't even need to know your mail server's address. It gets that from your email client.

Find the place in your email client where addresses for mail servers are displayed and edited, and change them in the following fashion:

1. Change the address of the POP email server that delivers your email to 127.0.0.1. This is a "naked" local IP address, the address at which POPFile "listens" for commands and from which it delivers mail. From the perspective of your email client, POPFile *is* your POP mail server.

2. This is tricky: Change the value in the username field to the real name of your POP mail server, followed by a colon and the username you use to log into that server. For example, if the name of Andy Stanton's POP server is **mail.stantonservices.com** and his username is **astanton**, the value he would need to enter here is **mail.stantonservices.com:astanton**. Note

that some mail servers require that the entire email address be used as the username; in other words, you may have to enter **mail.stantonservices.com:astanton@stantonservices.com** as the username. Check with your ISP or hosting service provider for the details!

3. POPFile works with incoming mail only. No changes have to be made to your outbound mail (SMTP) configuration at all.

Figures 9.3 through 9.6 show how several major email clients handle POPFile account setup. Eudora 6.1 has configuration information on two tabs in its configuration dialog, and both are shown in Figure 9.6.

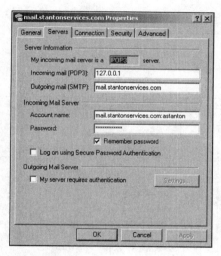

Figure 9.3

POPFile account setup in Outlook Express.

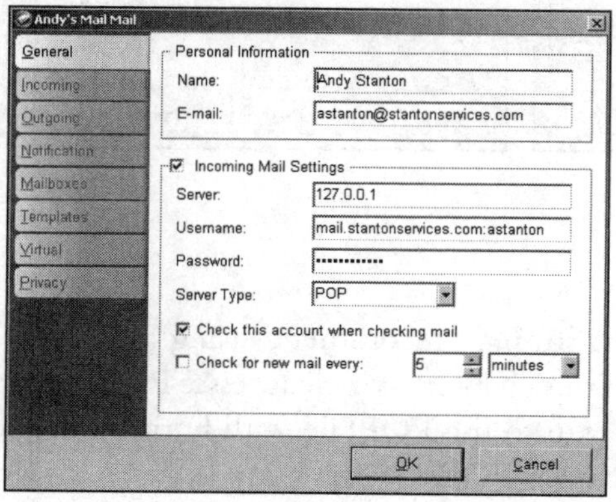

Figure 9.4

POPFile account setup in Poco Mail.

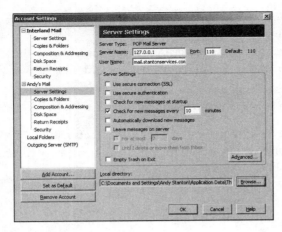

Figure 9.5
POPFile account setup in Mozilla Thunderbird.

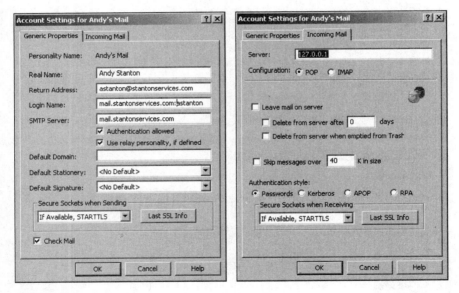

Figure 9.6
POPFile account setup in Eudora.

If you're using "Big Outlook," I strongly recommend using a product called Outclass (discussed at the end of this chapter), which accesses POPFile through an Outlook plug-in and allows you to use POPFile with both the IMAP and Exchange Native protocols as well as POP.

What Happens When POPFile Checks Mail

Once you modify the account settings in your email client according to the instructions in the previous section, POPFile is basically installed. Here's how the whole system works: When Andy Stanton clicks the "check mail" button, his email client will send the text string **mail.stantonservices.com:astanton** to POPFile at the local IP address 127.0.0.1. (Note that this is a *local* IP address, inaccessible outside your PC; nothing is going out on the Internet, even though your mail client communicates with POPFile by way of an IP address.)

POPFile separates the mail server name (**mail.stantonservices.com**) and the username (**astanton**) and uses those two separate strings to log into Andy's remote POP server. Once the connection has been established, the email client sends its password to POPFile, which POPFile simply passes along without modification to the remote POP server. After that, the conversation between the mail client and the mail server continues normally until the connection opens for the downloading of new mail from the POP server.

Each time a message is downloaded from the remote POP server, it passes *through* POPFile on its way to Andy's email client. POPFile parses the message into a list of distinct words, undoing numerous spammer obfuscation tricks as it goes. It compares the list of words to the statistical model it has stored on disk and makes one of three determinations:

1. The message "looks like" spam.
2. The message "looks like" real email.
3. It's too close to call and the message is declared "unclassified."

Once the decision is made, POPFile adds one of three tags to the very beginning of the Subject field in the message. These tags are enclosed in square brackets: [spam], [inbox], and [unclassified]. With the tag added to the message, POPFile then passes the tagged message on to the email client itself.

When the message reaches the email client, one more step occurs: At minimum, the email client has a filter set up to look for the text string "[spam]" in the Subject field. If the string "[spam]" is found, the message is moved directly to the junk mail or trash folder, or some other place to which spam is exiled. In most cases, messages tagged with [inbox] or [unclassified] simply go to your inbox by default. However, you can insure against certain (rare) false positives by creating a second filter that looks for the tag [inbox] and moves any message with that tag in the Subject field to your inbox.

This is useful in certain clients like Poco Mail that have an entirely separate spam filtering mechanism. On rare occasions, Poco Mail may declare something to be spam even though POPFile has decided it's real mail. My own experience has shown that POPFile is usually right, so a Poco Mail filter enforcing POPFile's [inbox] tag is a good idea, and cheap insurance.

Train and Use POPFile

When you first install POPFile, it has no corpus (a disk-based statistical model). It builds the corpus over time as messages pass through its hands. The first time you check mail after installing POPFile, *every single message* will come through as "unclassified." Some of these will be spam and some will be real mail. You'll have to delete the spam manually from that first batch, but more important, you'll have to *train* POPFile to recognize spam by reclassifying messages using the POPFile user interface.

Training POPFile

If you set up POPFile using its defaults, the POPFile user interface is brought up in one of two ways:

1. Double-click the yellow octopus icon in the taskbar tray
2. Select Run|Programs|POPFile|POPFile User Interface.

POPFile is a browser-based program, and the POPFile user interface appears in your default Web browser. The History screen is the one that appears by default when you bring POPFile up. This is the screen that lists all the messages that have passed through it and shows you how POPFile classified them (see Figure 9.7).

In the record for each message is a pull-down list of all the POPFile buckets that you have defined. Most people simply define Inbox and Spam, but you're not limited to those two, and whatever buckets you have defined will be in each list. You reclassify a message by pulling down the list of buckets and selecting the bucket to which you want a message classified (see Figure 9.8). Once you have "marked" each message that needs reclassification with its new bucket, you must click the Reclassify button at either the top or the bottom of the history list. (The two Reclassify buttons do precisely the same thing.)

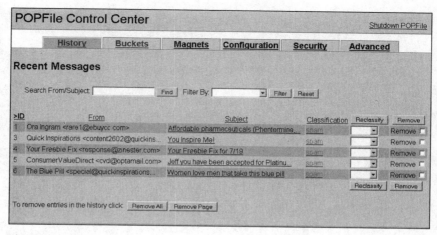

Figure 9.7
POPFile's History screen.

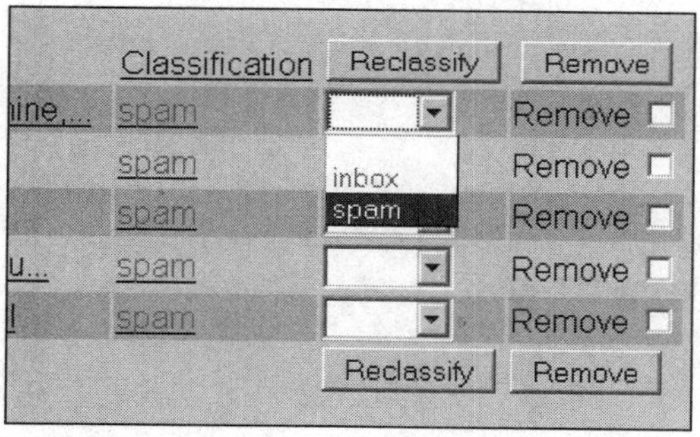

Figure 9.8
Reclassifying a message in POPFile.

TIP: *For best results with POPFile, click Reclassify each time you mark a message with a new bucket name. If you don't, you may forget to click the Reclassify button at all and therefore POPFile will learn nothing from the changes that you've marked!*

Once all messages needing to be reclassified have been reclassified, you can click the Remove Page button to clear them from history. If you have more than one screen of messages waiting action, the next screen will appear, ready for either approval or reclassification.

GunkBuster's Notebook: Increasing POPFile's Certainty

POPFile classifies most messages with a great deal of certainty. A few messages, however, could fall into a fuzzy middle zone. These are the messages on which POPFile makes its occasional mistake: either false negatives (spam in your inbox, bad) or false positives (real mail in your trash folder, *way* bad!). Sometimes, when a message is so close to a coin toss that POPFile refuses to make the call at all, the message comes through to your inbox marked [unclassified]. Unless you specifically filter these messages to a different location in your mail client, they will end up in your inbox.

This is not a completely bad thing. I'd rather have an unclassified message in my inbox than a real message in my trash folder. If this is your perspective as well, you can require POPFile to be more certain before classifying a message. You will get more unclassified messages in your inbox but fewer genuine messages in your trash folder.

Hidden in the POPFile Control Center Advanced screen is a configurable parameter called bayes_unclassified_weight. (see Figure 9.9). This is a number that installs with a value of 100. The higher the number is, the more certain POPFile must be before classifying a message into any bucket.

Parameter	Value
bayes_corpus	corpus
bayes_database	popfile.db
bayes_dbauth	
bayes_dbconnect	dbi:SQLite:dbname=$d
bayes_dbuser	
bayes_hostname	ariel
bayes_subject_mod_left	[
bayes_subject_mod_right	]
bayes_unclassified_weight	1000

Figure 9.9
Locating the bayes_unclassified_weight parameter.

This applies to spam as well as real mail. How high you can raise it without hugely increasing the number of unclassified messages depends on the nature of your spam. If it's all blatantly "spammy" spam, you can jack it up very high and POPFile will still be very certain of its classifications. However, if you get a lot of those normal-sounding loan pitches that begin "Dear sir: We have received your mortgage application and you are tentatively approved. We need more information before closing...," you may see more of them in your inbox as unclassified. I recommend 1000 as a first attempt. If you get too many unclassifieds, you can lower the value again. If you don't get any additional unclassifieds, you can raise it even more.

Setting Up a Spam Category Filter in Your Email Client

In Chapter 8 I showed you how to degunk your spam using content filters. Creating filters to look for the tags that POPFile adds to your messages is no different. The logic is simple: When a message comes into your client with the tag [spam] in the Subject field, the filter should move the message to your spam or trash folder. Some people move spam directly to the trash folder. More cautious people move spam to a spam folder that they create and empty the folder periodically after checking it for false positives.

All mail clients create filters in slightly different ways, but the logic of the filter will be the same and can be expressed this way:

IF Subject: CONTAINS "[spam]" THEN MOVE MESSAGE TO Trash.

Key here is the term *contains*. You don't want to use *equals* or *is*. The [spam] tag is present in the Subject field, but it's not the only thing there; the message subject text is there as well. An example from Mozilla Thunderbird is shown in Figure 9.10.

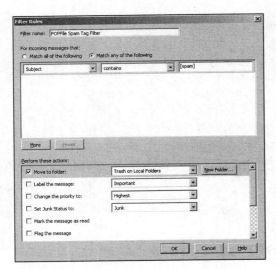

Figure 9.10

A POPFile spam tag filter in Mozilla Thunderbird.

GunkBuster's Notebook: Filter on Both [spam] and [inbox]!

Because incoming messages go to your inbox by default, some people create a mail client filter for only the [spam] tag that POPFile places in the subject line of spam messages. This is a (minor) mistake. Create a separate filter for [inbox], or whatever tag you use to identify "real mail," and make sure it runs *before* the filter that looks for the [spam] tag!

Here's why: Every so often you will get a false positive; that is, a real message tagged as spam. If you spot one, you can reclassify it and then move the message from the trash or other spam folder back to your inbox. However, if you reply to the misclassified message, the reply will carry the [spam] tag as well. If the person from whom the message originally came replies to your reply, here's what the subject line may look like:

Re:[inbox]Re:[spam]We'll be there Saturday night

If you have a filter looking only for [spam], the reply will go to your trash folder, even if the [inbox] tag is present! Don't forget that POPFile simply tags messages after classifying them. Where they go when they reach your mail client is governed entirely by how your client filters work.

To prevent losing messages in this admittedly uncommon situation, a filter that moves messages marked with [inbox] to your inbox is essential. Create it, and check the filter order to be sure it runs *before* the filter that looks for the [spam] tag.

Use POPFile's Magnets

Most of the time, the difference between spam and non-spam is obvious, but sometimes it's a little more subtle. Spammers often try to make their messages look like email newsletters. This can cause POPFile to think that all email newsletters are spam. In truth, the difference between certain types of spam and certain types of real email is simply that you want one and don't want the other. Messages containing discounted book offers from Amazon.com are welcome in my inbox, but messages offering discounts on mortgages, lawn furniture, dog food, drugs, or porn are *not*.

This is why POPFile has a feature called *magnets*. A magnet is a kind of override. If you create a magnet on Amazon.com, messages from Amazon will be "pulled" to your inbox. A group of magnets can be thought of as a built-in whitelist, but there's an important distinction: *POPFile learns nothing from messages classified by magnets.*

Magnets should be used only to prevent "real" messages that strongly resemble spam from being classified as spam. Product pitches and announcements that you want to receive should be covered by magnets. You don't want POPFile to have to dance on a razor and attempt to differentiate between nearly identical product pitches that are basically the same except that you want to read one but not the other.

Use magnets to keep POPFile from learning the wrong things. Real email that looks like spam will confuse POPFile. The reverse may also be true: Spam that looks like real email can confuse POPFile as well, but it's much harder to create a magnet for those slippery spammers who forge headers and change the Subject field on every mailing. Reserve magnets for any genuine mail you get that looks like spam:

√ Email newsletters, especially those that contain ads offering discounts on products or services.

√ Communications from trusted e-commerce sites like Amazon.com and Half.com, or any person or site from which you buy things on a regular basis.

√ Communications from companies or people with whom you're discussing things popular with spammers: mortgages, pharmaceuticals, and so on. The magnet can be temporary: If you're negotiating a mortgage via email, put the bank's address on a magnet until the loan closes and then delete the magnet.

Creating Magnets in POPFile

A POPFile magnet is created from the Magnets screen in the POPFile Control Center, as shown in Figure 9.11. There is some helpful explanation right on the Magnets screen, but the process is really very simple:

1. Specify the type of magnet, which cooks down to which email message field to look in. You can choose the From field, the To field, the CC field, and the Subject field.

2. Specify the value that the magnet is to match. The value is the word, phrase, email address, or domain to look for in that field. A partial match is still a match; in other words, the email address **tjkqv@sleazyspammer.com** will match **sleazyspammer.com**.

3. Specify the bucket into which a matching message will always go. POPFile can be used to classify legitimate email into any number of buckets, but most users simply specify two buckets: Spam and the legitimate mail bucket, usually called Inbox.

4. When you have all three fields filled out, simply click the Create button to create the magnet.

One caution: Be careful of partial matches that can accidentally match unrelated items. Fortunately, on a magnet that "pulls" mail to your inbox, any of these will be easily spotted. On POPFile's History screen, a message that satisfies a magnet's conditions will be specially tagged in the Classification column.

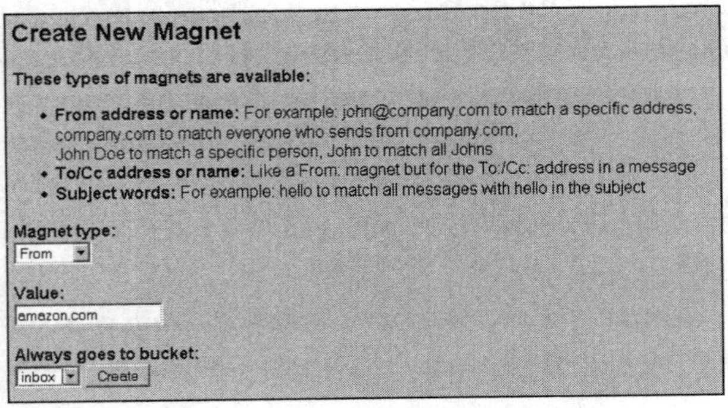

Create New Magnet

These types of magnets are available:

- **From address or name:** For example: john@company.com to match a specific address, company.com to match everyone who sends from company.com, John Doe to match a specific person, John to match all Johns
- **To/Cc address or name:** Like a From: magnet but for the To:/Cc: address in a message
- **Subject words:** For example: hello to match all messages with hello in the subject

Magnet type:
From

Value:
amazon.com

Always goes to bucket:
inbox   Create

Figure 9.11

Creating a POPFile magnet.

If an unrelated message satisfies a magnet, you may need to rethink and adjust the magnet.

Back Up and Share POPFile's Corpus Data

POPFile builds a statistical model of your email over time. This model is called the *corpus,* and it's a database of words associated with the categories that you define in POPFile. The corpus is what POPFile "knows," and if a virus, worm, or PC failure of some sort destroys the corpus, you will have to start from scratch and train POPFile all over again. It can take months of classifying mail to bring POPFile up to its full potential accuracy, so backing up the POPFile corpus is very important, and should be done regularly.

Finding the Corpus

As with your mailbase, the big trick in backing up POPFile's corpus files is simply finding them. Starting with version 0.21.0, POPFile began to support multiple users, each with a separate corpus. This means that each user's corpus files are stored in a separate directory, usually under the Documents and Settings folder on C:. The path is usually something like this:

C:\Documents and Settings\<user name>\Application Data\POPFile\

Another way to find the POPFile corpus or corpuses (if there are multiple users) is to search for the file popfile.db. Once you find the directory where that file lives, you should back up the entire directory. There are several other files containing configuration options and other important data, so grab 'em all.

"Borrowing" a Corpus

It's possible to transfer another person's POPFile corpus from their PC to yours so that you can begin sorting mail with a considerable degree of accuracy. This may be worth trying if you get relatively little email. If you get only three or four real messages and eight or nine spams per week, training POPFile will take what seems like forever. In a case like that, you might want to see if one of your friends has a "mature" (thoroughly trained) corpus that they might be willing to give you.

Borrowing a corpus is basically a process of backing up someone else's corpus to a CD or other removable disk and then restoring it to your PC. The best process to use is this one:

1. Have your friend clear POPFile's history list and then back up the corpus directly to removable media. If you don't clear history, whatever messages are

pending in the History display will be transferred over, and they're of no use to you!

2. Install POPFile on your PC. During installation, POPFile's installer will create the directory where the corpus resides.

3. Find the corpus directory. Search for popfile.db; where that file is, the corpus is.

4. Copy the borrowed corpus into the corpus directory.

5. Uninstall POPFile and then reinstall it.

Step 5 may seem to be optional, but it's a good idea to do it, to be sure that POPFile recognizes the newly transplanted corpus.

Now, having said all that, there are a couple of issues involved with borrowing a corpus:

√   A certain amount of information about your friend's mailbase comes with their corpus. You can look up certain words and see how frequently they appear in real messages. This may not be an issue, depending on how close you and your friend are, and how much of a privacy freak your friend may be.

√   There is some question as to how much better having a borrowed corpus is than building your own from scratch. My experiments were ambiguous: Using a mature but borrowed corpus gave me more false positives than a mature corpus I had built myself…but it was more accurate sooner than building a corpus from a slow mail stream.

Basically, if you're on good terms with the owner of the borrowed corpus, and if you're the type who doesn't mind some experimentation, it's worth a try. Don't forget that a POPFile corpus is *extremely* specific to your own mail stream, and no one else's mail stream completely matches yours. Over time, you can train a borrowed corpus to recognize your own mail better by passing your own mail through it, but if your mail stream is very thin, this could take a long time.

GunkBuster's Notebook: Tips on Borrowing Spam from Friends to Train POPFile

If you have any computer enthusiasts or Public Professionals among your circle of friends, you'll probably hear them groaning about their spam burden. Ask them to save a few days' worth of spam in a folder for you and then forward or redirect the spam to you. POPFile will classify the borrowed spam and build its corpus more quickly than on the few spams you may be getting.

My own experiments have shown that using borrowed spam makes POPFile slightly less accurate at predicting your own future spam, but it gets to a better place more quickly, and over a longer time period, your own spam will "fine-tune" the corpus to your own needs.

Some pointers:

√ Have your friend or friends configure their email clients to leave the spam messages as close to their original form as possible. This primarily means not prefixing every line with a lead-in character like >, but some clients may make other changes to the message.

√ Don't have them forward the spam to you as attachments. POPFile ignores text in attachments.

√ After you receive all the spam, you may have to go into the POPFile Control Center's Advanced screen and remove your friends' email addresses from its database because it probably now thinks that they're spammers! (Hint: Add them to your address book/whitelist if you haven't already.)

Use Outclass to Access POPFile from Outlook

As its name implies, POPFile is used with Post Office Protocol (POP) mail servers only. People who must use other mail server protocols—for example, Internet Message Access Protocol (IMAP), Exchange Native, Lotus Notes—are out of luck.

Almost.

If you're using Microsoft's Outlook application, you have another option: A freeware utility called Outclass, which installs as an Outlook plug-in. Outclass gives you access to POPFile from inside Outlook. It installs a new toolbar in Outlook, allowing you to create and delete POPFile buckets and classify mail, all without leaving Outlook.

Security hole after security hole has been found in Outlook, and it is inextricably tangled up with Internet Explorer, which comes with its own set of security risks. On the other hand, people who use Outlook often have no choice, as it may be required by their employers. Outlook's security issues are important, but you can mitigate them by keeping both a virus protection program and personal firewall running and current on your PC. I'll have more to say about virus protection and firewalls later in this book.

For all of its security concerns, Outlook is a powerful application that allows you to access mail through several different protocols: POP3 (the current version of POP), IMAP, and Exchange Native. Outclass allows you to send and receive mail with Outlook using any protocol that Outlook supports and still spot spam with POPFile. Using Outclass is extremely easy because everything is done right there inside Outlook itself. You don't have to bounce back and forth between your mail client and POPFile to classify mail. If you're already an Outlook user, Outclass is a no-brainer: It's free, it's easy to install and configure, and it gives you all the benefits of POPFile.

Installing Outclass

Although Outclass has been tested with Outlook 2000, it works best with the newer Outlook 2002 and Outlook 2003. Don't even try it with versions of Outlook before 2000. The older Outlook versions lack certain interface features that Outclass requires to "talk" to POPFile behind the scenes. I tested Outclass with Outlook 2000 and Outlook 2003. Although Outclass worked acceptably with Outlook 2000, setting it up was more trouble and I had some mysterious crashes here and there. Outlook 2003 integrated with Outclass easily and without incident.

You can download Outclass without charge from its vendor's site:

www.vargonsoft.com/Outclass/

It's a conventional Windows installer. Before you install it, please read these notes:

√ Important: The version of Outclass that you use is specific to the version of Outlook that you have. The two are very closely tied, so read the fine print and only install the version of Outclass that works with your version of Outlook. Furthermore, if you upgrade Outlook, upgrade Outclass at the same time.

√ If you're not already a POPFile user, install POPFile *before* you install Outclass! Outclass configures POPFile, and unless POPFile is already installed when you install Outclass, that configuration won't happen and things won't work correctly. On the flip side, don't bother configuring POPFile to act as a POP proxy for your POP server. Outclass invokes

POPFile as a plug–in so that POPFile no longer needs to insert itself between your mail client and your server. Just install POPFile. Outclass will do all the configuring that POPFile needs.

√ *Don't configure POPFile to run automatically!* Outclass loads and runs an instance (that is, a memory copy) of POPFile when Outclass runs. If you configure POPFile to run on Windows startup, the copy that Windows launches is a second, unrelated copy, and things will not work correctly.

Once you complete the Outclass installer, run Outlook. Outclass will be visible as a new toolbar under Outlook's own toolbars (see Figure 9.12).

Figure 9.12

The Outclass toolbar within Outlook.

Configuring and Using Outclass

Outclass runs as part of Outlook. You don't have to run anything separately. Anytime you bring up Outlook, Outclass is there, ready to roll. To configure Outclass, do the following:

√ Define what POPFile buckets you want to use, beyond the two that are created by default.

√ Define what Outlook folder a message should be moved to after Outclass decides (with POPFile's help) what bucket the message belongs in. I call this a "folder transfer rule."

By default, Outclass defines two buckets for POPFile: Spam and Inbox. (Some versions use *Allowed* instead of *Inbox*.) If all you're doing is separating spam from real mail, those are all the buckets you need. POPFile can be used to further classify real mail into multiple categories, and if you're going to do that, you will need to define additional buckets.

Defining a folder transfer rule allows Outclass to automatically move messages out of your inbox and into designated folders, thus reducing inbox gunk. To define a folder transfer rule, click Outclass Options on the toolbar. The Options window is shown in Figure 9.13.

Figure 9.13
The Outclass options window.

Although you're allowed to define multiple inboxes in Outlook (in case you want each of your several email accounts to have its own inbox), I won't explain that further here because it contributes to email gunk. The single inbox that Outlook creates by default will be listed in the Inboxes pane. Highlight that inbox and click the Edit button. The window that appears is shown in Figure 9.14.

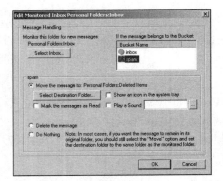

Figure 9.14
Editing inbox message handling.

What you have here is a way to define simple message rules for your inbox. All the buckets that you have defined are shown in a list in the upper-right corner of the window. You define a message transfer rule by highlighting a bucket (for example, Spam) and indicating the folder to which you want messages moved when they are classified into that bucket.

In Figure 9.14, the Spam bucket is highlighted, and below the list of buckets, an action has been selected by clicking the radio button marked "Move the message to." You select a destination folder by clicking the button marked "Select Destination Folder…" and choosing a folder from the Outlook folder hierarchy. In the figure, the destination has already been selected, and in this configuration, all message classified as Spam are moved immediately to the Deleted Items folder.

You can choose any folder, and if you like, you can create a folder called Spam or Junk Mail so that spam is not deleted along with everything else in Deleted Items. This is a good idea early in your training of POPFile, when the occasional real message will be tagged as spam and exiled to the spam folder. You want to be able to audit POPFile's decisions and retrieve the occasional false positive before it's deleted.

GunkBuster's Notebook: Define an Outclass Transfer Rule for Real Mail and Spam

Note the message at the bottom of the window shown in Figure 9.14, beside the Do Nothing radio button. Even though you want legitimate mail to stay in your inbox, it's a good idea to specify explicitly that mail marked [inbox] (or [allowed] if you prefer) be sent to your inbox. Why, if all mail not marked as spam goes to your inbox anyway? Simply this: If a real message is tagged accidentally as spam and goes to your spam folder, you can reclassify it as legitimate mail using the Reclassify button on the Outclass toolbar. If you have a transfer rule in effect for legitimate email, the moment you reclassify a false positive from [spam] to [inbox], the message will vanish from your spam folder and automagically appear in your inbox!

The key here is that transfer rules are not invoked only when email first arrives on your PC. *Every* time Outclass invokes POPFile to classify a message, it applies your transfer rules to that message. This includes reclassifying messages that have already been moved somewhere by a transfer rule.

A transfer rule moving legitimate mail to your inbox is created the same way a transfer rule for spam is created. Simply highlight the Inbox bucket (see Figure 9.14) and then click the Select Destination Folder button to select your inbox as the transfer rule's destination.

More Outclass Training Tips

Some people may find it useful to place Outclass in "training mode," which overrides any folder transfer rules you have defined and leaves all messages in your inbox, where you can scan them for errors all at once rather than having to inspect several different Outlook folders for new mail that may have been misclassified. To place Outclass in training mode, click Outclass Options and then select the Settings tab. Check the Enable Training Mode check box and click OK.

If you have older messages already in folders and want them classified, highlight them and then click the Classify Now button in the Outclass toolbar. Note that if you have automatic folder transfers defined, Outclass will immediately move messages to their intended folders as soon as it classifies them.

Using Safe View to Inspect Message Source Text

One minor but sometimes very useful Outclass feature is a toolbar button marked "Safe View." Clicking on Safe View opens a window showing the source text of the highlighted message. No attempt is made to render an HTML message. No images are downloaded for display (avoiding spam beacons), and no scripts are run. If you're curious about spam machinery, it's a fine way to see some spammer tricks in their naked form without worrying about accidentally playing into spammer hands.

Safe View is especially useful in Outlook 2000 and Outlook 2002, which do not have any good way to keep images (including spam beacons) from being downloaded in the preview pane. (Outlook 2003 finally disabled message download by default.) To some extent, Safe View can replace the preview pane in Outlook 2000 and 2002, especially for those messages you're not quite sure of.

Summing Up

This is the longest chapter in this book for a good reason: Nothing I have tested so far comes even close to Bayesian filtering in fighting spam, which is arguably the most troublesome species of gunk to be found on anyone's computer. Bayesian filtering requires a little work and some thought on your part, but much less work (and thought) than content filtering or, heaven knows, identifying and nuking spam manually. For those email users who get dozens or hundreds of spams a day, this type of filter is a really good idea to eliminate email gunk. Among Bayesian filters, POPFile stands out as the master because of the deep understanding that its creator, John Graham-Cumming, has of the spammer mindset and spammer techniques. A utility to invoke POPFile from inside Microsoft Outlook has already appeared, and I'm sure that more of these "helper" utilities will appear over time, making POPFile easier to apply to all sorts of mail.

Avoid Spam Control Methods That Don't Work

Degunking Checklist:

√ Learn how antispam technologies fail.

√ Discover why server-side spam filtering isn't always the answer.

√ Find out about peer-to-peer collaborative spam filtering.

√ Assess whether challenge-response spam blocking really works.

√ Learn why whitelists are so important.

Spammers have been clever these past several years, but the good guys in the spam wars have been just as clever. Many *extremely* innovative spam-fighting systems have come online since 2000. I discussed a few of them earlier in this book, the best example being Bayesian statistical filtering (see Chapter 9). Some of these systems work better than others. And like any treatment for a serious disease, many of these antispam systems have serious side effects. How serious these side effects are depends on who you are and what you use email for. What might never even be noticed by a Casual Communicator might be completely unacceptable to a Public Professional.

In this chapter, I'm going to be blunt and very honest and present the several antispam technologies that I do not like, and explain why. Of course, the ultimate decision as to how to continue to fight your spam problem is yours to make, but I recommend that you avoid using the technologies that are not as effective others. In the spam wars—as in the wars on termites, squirrels, politicians, and other pests that beset the general public—the key phrase is—*whatever works.*

Understand How Antispam Technologies Fail

Antispam technologies all have a pretty simple goal: to prevent spam from arriving in your inbox. But no victory in the spam wars is ever free. Blocking spam costs time and effort, and it may also cause collateral damage.

What sorts of failure modes happen in the spam wars? Here are the most important:

√ *Spam comes in anyway.* Most people understand that there are cracks in any system, and as the spam wars have progressed, spammers have become surprisingly clever. A few spam messages are inevitable, and most people are willing to nuke a couple every day—especially if they're used to getting hundreds.

√ *More traffic clogs the Internet.* Some antispam systems rely on passing spam messages or hash values (more on this later) around a peer-to-peer network. Others rely on challenge-response dialogs that require several messages passing back and forth before a single one goes through. When such systems work, this additional Internet traffic is considered the necessary cost of reducing spam. When they don't work, the additional data packets are simply a burden on the global Internet and the spam gets through anyway.

√ *"Rude" systems alienate people and inhibit communication.* Some antispam systems make people jump through hoops to get their legitimate email to a recipient. This "guilty until proven innocent" attitude upsets some folks, and, when confronted by such a system, they will often walk away, muttering, without concluding the transaction and getting a message through. Especially for Public Professionals who need to be accessible to the general public, this is a very serious failure.

√ *Genuine messages are blocked and never seen.* False positives are the bane of any spam filtering mechanism. It's very difficult to prevent them completely, and some server-side systems make it impossible to audit filter results or even know that you're getting false positives. The goal in the spam wars is to bring the rate of false positives as close to zero as possible, even if it means letting a few spams through. A few antispam systems get it backwards: They insist on zero spam, even if it means a certain number of false positives must be allowed to happen. I consider this a failure mode.

√ *People who are not spammers are blacklisted.* This is a very serious problem, especially in automated systems that add Internet addresses or domains to blacklists without any sort of human judgment. Blacklisting should never be done without absolute certainty of the guilt of the blacklisted address. False positives on a blacklist are completely unacceptable.

With all that understood, let's take a closer look at some antispam technologies that fail in one of these ways.

Be Careful with Server-Side Spam Filtering

For those weary of tweaking filters and weeding defiant spam messages from their inboxes, the idea sounds wonderful: *Make the mail server do the work.* Most of the filtering techniques on the client side can be done on the server side as well. When spam arrives at the mail server, where your POP or IMAP mailbox resides, the server performs its various checks and nukes the spam it finds right there on the spot. The spam never travels the rest of the way to your mail client, and you never see it. Less work for you, less unnecessary traffic on the Internet.

Well, maybe.

The *big* problem with server-side spam filtering is auditing the system for false positives. A few of the systems don't delete spam immediately but hold it in a buffer at the server site for a period of time to allow you to go to a Web-based screen and scan what spam was blocked from your system, making sure no genuine mail was blocked as well. Alas, a lot server-side filters just kill spam without holding it anywhere for you to spot-check. There's no way to recapture the real messages that are falsely accused, tried, and executed. Worst of all, there's no way for you to tell that those false positives ever even happened.

If you're considering using a server-side spam filtering system, here are some very serious questions to ask of the system vendor before you flip that fateful switch:

√ Are spam filtering parameters published somewhere for you to see? Don't count on this; some server-side systems shroud their algorithms in secrecy so that spammers can't devise system-specific workarounds.

√ Is there a way for you to adjust the parameters or the sensitivity of the server-side filters as they apply to your own mail? People in certain industries (pharmaceuticals, finance) may want to exclude certain key words or phrases used in their daily correspondence. (If you're a salesman for a drug company, you don't want to be reduced to saying, "This month's orders for you-know-what are way down due to price competition from that other you-know-what, and we need to respond…")

√ Is there a server-side whitelist feature? In other words, can you upload the addresses of people, newsletters, and organizations whose mail you *must* receive, irrespective of any other checks made by the server? (Email newsletters are famously vulnerable to server-side spam filters.)

√ Is an "IP black hole" blacklist used to filter mail? If so, will they tell you which one? Some black holes are more aggressive than others. A few are insanely aggressive and should be avoided at all costs. (More on IP black holes shortly.)

√ Is spam held in a buffer before deletion so you can spot-check filtered spam for false positives?

√ If spam is held in a buffer, can you download a message from the buffer if it turns out to have been a false positive?

Many people like server-side spam control because it's so effortless. This is fine if false positives are not an issue for them. My view is that false positives are *always* an issue and a completely and utterly pivotal one.

TIP: It's possible to research any spam-filtering technology on the Web. Just do a Google search on "**spamtech** effectiveness" or "**spamtech** accuracy" where **spamtech** is the name of the technology in question.

Here is an interesting Web site summarizing some of the problems with server-side spam filtering:

http://spamlinks.openrbl.org/filter-server-anti.htm

Watch Out for IP Black Holes

One filtering technique is widely used on servers: *IP black holes.* These are also called realtime black holes as well as realtime blacklists and realtime block lists, both abbreviated as RBLs.

Every Internet domain (like **stantonservices.com**) cooks down to a numeric value called an Internet Protocol (IP) address. A "raw" IP address looks something like this: 264.148.0.4. It's a group of four numeric values from 0 to 255, separated by periods. (My example is deliberately invalid, to avoid citing somebody's real IP address here.) The Internet runs on these raw IP addresses. The routers that guide data packets around the Internet use raw IP addresses to determine where packets have to be sent. Because remembering strings of numbers is difficult, a system called Domain Name Service (DNS) relates familiar alphanumeric domains to IP addresses. DNS is a database of domain names, and each name is associated with an IP address. When you look up a domain name (like **stantonservices.com**) in the DNS database, it will return a raw IP address. This IP address is the address of the host (a host is simply Internet-speak for a computer) where the **stantonservices.com** domain servers live. These can be Web servers, email servers, or servers for any other protocol that the Internet understands. Every email address resolves to an IP address. Every Web server (like **www.stantonservices.com**) resolves to an IP address.

Internet domains are cheap, and can be bought in bulk, used a few times, and then thrown away. IP addresses, however, are much scarcer and comparatively expensive. Many ambitious spammers who have registered dozens or hundreds of domains have only a handful of IP addresses. (By some reports, the vast majority of spam originating in the United States—billions of messages annually—comes from only 200 IP addresses.) Each one of their IP addresses may be associated with a hundred domains or more. Clearly, blocking raw IP addresses is likely to be *much* more effective than blocking individual Internet domains.

This is what an IP black hole is: a list of raw IP addresses known to belong to spammers. When an antispam technology makes use of an IP black hole, what it does is this:

1. It looks up a sender email address or "payload" Web domain in DNS to resolve the email address or domain to a raw IP address.

2. It looks up the raw IP address in the IP black hole's list. If the IP address is present in the black hole, the antispam system tags the message as spam or deletes it altogether.

This sounds terrific, and when handled carefully, IP black holes can be useful tools. There are some serious gotchas, however:

√ More and more spam is coming from "spam zombie" relays that were planted on innocent PCs by viruses. A spam zombie, as explained earlier in this book, is a one-way relay station for spam. A spammer sends a message to a spam zombie, and the spam zombie then changes the From address and resends it to the unfortunate recipient. Spam sent out in this way by a spam zombie PC is not traceable back to the real spammer. The IP address associated with relayed messages is that of the infected PC, not the spammer. Blocking the IP address only hurts the person whose PC is infected with the spam zombie virus.

√ More important is the way that IP addresses are placed on black hole lists. Some black holes are run by careful people who verify that a suspected spammer IP address really is owned by a spammer and deliberately used for spamming. On the other hand, many black holes are run by people I can only characterize as crackpot antispam vigilantes, who will black-hole not just individual IP addresses but whole ranges of IP addresses belonging to Internet hosting services that have not been sufficiently vigilant (in the vigilantes' opinion) in the war on spam. This causes collateral damage to people whose only crime is being hosted by a service that the vigilantes don't like.

√ IP black holes are used mostly on the server side. In most cases, you have no way to know if a message was "eaten" by an IP black hole. False positives do happen, and when they do, you have no way to tell and no way to retrieve a falsely black-holed message.

You may be using a black hole and not even know it. Black holes can be used on the client side of an email setup, but it's a fair bit of trouble for nontechnical folks, and mostly they're used at the server. Your ISP or mail provider may not even tell you that your mail is being filtered past a black hole, and there's probably nothing you can do about it either way. Before you sign up for a mail hosting service, always ask about IP black holes!

Malicious Spam Reporting and "Joe Jobs"

Perhaps the biggest single problem with IP black holes is the potential for deliberate, malicious abuse. Think about it: Request information from one of your online competitors, and when the requested email arrives, report it as spam to one or more IP black hole services like MAPS, SPEWS, or SpamCop. Boom! Your competitor is blacklisted and will have to spend a significant amount of time and energy persuading the various black hole services to unlist him.

This is called a "joe job," and it has definitely been done, especially against sites that sell the sorts of things that spammers sell (drugs, OEM software CDs, porn).

The black hole services claim to have mechanisms in place to prevent this kind of abuse, but as best I can tell, these mechanisms are all limits on the time period that a reported site spends on the black hole IP list. A listing may expire after 48 hours, but if you keep reporting your competitor (from different disposable email addresses, to hide your identity), the harassment may be able to continue for some time until you're caught out.

As you can tell, I don't much like IP black holes. Part of this is my general dislike for server-side spam filtering, and the rest is the checkered reputation that black holes have gotten over the past couple of years. Sure, good ones can be useful, but...hey, show me a reliable way to tell the good ones from the vigilantes.

SpamCop

SpamCop is a server-side spam filtering service. Both individuals and server administrators can make use of it:

√ Individuals can use SpamCop's filtering system for $30/year. Setup is a little awkward, but it works and involves either forwarding your mail from your ISP to SpamCop's server or letting SpamCop act as a server-side mail proxy, reading mail directly from your POP account and then allowing your mail client to download real mail from SpamCop's server.

√ Mail server administrators can use SpamCop's IP black hole without charge. Most major email server programs can scan mail as it comes in for the presence of a blocked IP address either in the From field or embedded in the message body.

I know quite a few people who use SpamCop's individual filtering service and are happy with it, even though it's an extra out-of-pocket cost. Spam is held in a buffer for two weeks, and messages may be moved out of this buffer and downloaded at any time. People typically check the spam buffer once a week or more often if they get a great deal of mail. SpamCop does generate false positives, but if you're willing to scan the spam buffer, the loss is not necessarily permanent. (You *do* have to check the buffer or you *will* lose real messages!)

SpamCop's IP black hole service is much more problematic because how much it impacts your genuine mail depends entirely on how a third party (typically your ISP or mail hosting service) makes use of it. In this case, all SpamCop provides is access to a list of spammer IP addresses. If your ISP or mail hosting service does not buffer mail tagged as spam through SpamCop's black hole, you won't be able to spot-check it or recover false positives, and in this case it's not SpamCop's fault.

SpamCop has made public the rules it uses for listing IP addresses on its black hole, and these are worth reading if you're considering using SpamCop or a mail server that uses SpamCop's black hole:

www.spamcop.net/fom-serve/cache/297.html

SpamCop is for people who hate spam so much that they don't mind false positives. That strikes me as odd (in my view, false positives are *never* to be blindly accepted as a cost of fighting the spam wars), but that's a choice that the SpamCop organization has made. There is opinion on the Web on both sides; here's an interesting counter-argument:

http://jhoward.fastmail.fm/spamcop.html

Peer-to-Peer Collaborative Spam Filtering

Most people remember the furor that Napster caused in the late 1990s by allowing people to share MP3 music files. What fewer remember is the hysteria that followed involving Napster's underlying technology: direct connections between end-user computers, called peer-to-peer (P2P) connections. Technologists were screaming that P2P networks were the Next Big Thing and would make all kinds of new things possible and all kinds of old things easier.

After a couple of years of furious searching, technologists discovered that what P2P networks do best is…share music files. Everything else they've tried has been a decidedly mixed bag.

Probably P2P's biggest failure, in my view, is collaborative spam filtering. In the abstract, it sounds good, and the idea works like this: A special email client or plug-in creates a P2P network focused on identifying messages as spam. When a message comes in that a user decides is spam, the user clicks a Mark as Spam button.

Once a message is marked as spam, it is subjected to a mathematical process called *hashing*. Hashing basically looks at a message using a mathematical algorithm and derives a numeric fingerprint from it. The same message will always produce the same hash value fingerprint, and these fingerprints are much shorter than the messages themselves. The fingerprints are then shared with a central server or sometimes directly with other network members. Once a given fingerprint gets a certain number of "votes" that it is spam, the network considers it spam and moves it to a spam folder or otherwise marks it for deletion.

Collaborative spam filtering is basically an un-popularity contest for individual email messages. Everybody on the network gets one vote, and after a few votes, a given messages goes down in flames. The idea has been implemented several times in slightly different ways, but mostly they work as I described. Table 10.1 lists the most notable and widely used.

Table 10.1   P2P Spam Filtering Products.

Cloudmark SpamNet	www.cloudmark.com	Outlook and OE only
Spamfighter	www.spamfighter.com	Outlook and OE only
Spam Inspector	www.giantcompany.com	Outlook/OE/Eudora/Hotmail/Proxy

My own testing is limited to SpamNet, which is Cloudmark's client-side filtering product. (Cloudmark caters primarily to enterprise-scale server-side filtering.) Most of the problems I identified in SpamNet appear to exist in the other products as well.

The issues I have with peer-to-peer collaborative spam filtering are these:

√   They depend on a relatively complex architecture of central servers and connections to many other people using the same software. If any element gets out of joint, the system doesn't work well.

√   They're not very accurate. I was never able to get SpamNet to capture more than about 88 percent of my spam, and this performance degraded over time without explanation. (I think spammers got wise to the hash-based fingerprint system; see the next item.) POPFile, by contrast, captures 99.7 percent of my spam and seems to get better as time goes on.

√   All hash-based systems depend on spam messages being identical as received by all members of the spam-identifying network. If the spammer software that generates the messages inserts random words or junk characters (often invisible) into each instance of a spam message, the fingerprints derived for all the various instances of the message will be different and the system will fail. For example, here is the Subject field of a spam message I received recently:

Fireworks MX 2004 esoteric

The message is selling OEM copies of Fireworks MX 2004; the word *esoteric* has nothing to do with the message and was pulled from a random word list and inserted only in the copy of the message sent to me. Someone down the street might have gotten the word *bratwurst* or *disheveled* where *esoteric* was in my copy. There is an arms race between the spammers inserting these "hashbusters" in messages and P2P systems identifying and removing them. Alas, computer software is only so clever, and it's difficult for software to tell the hashbuster words inserted in a message from the words making up the message itself. I don't think the P2P products can ever really win this one.

√ This is the kicker: You're trusting other people to tell you what spam is, and there are going to be differences of opinion in the margins. For penis-enlargement pitches, well, we all pretty much agree. However, as I've mentioned elsewhere in this book, a newsletter may be considered spam by some and useful and wanted by others. That's why you need magnets in POPFile: To "pull" messages to your inbox that POPFile might in all innocence tag as spam. I had a lot of trouble with this; SpamNet's whitelist works badly for reasons I could never pin down.

Before you try a P2P antispam system, spend an hour googling for other people's reactions. Pay particular attention to what they report as its accuracy. It seems as if P2P systems work better for some classes of users than others, and my intuition is that Private Professionals and Casual Communicators may do better with P2P than Public Professionals. Email newsletters and communications from e-commerce sites generally seem to suffer in P2P systems, probably because some people read these messages whereas others ignore them and consider them spam. In my view, only *you* should be able to decide which messages in your own mail stream are spam and which are not.

In summary, peer-to-peer collaborative spam filtering is a great deal of messing around and a lot of moving parts for something that can't get you within 5 percent of what a simple client-side utility like POPFile can do.

Challenge-Response Spam Blocking

Word is out on the street (oft-repeated by technology-naïve reporters) that the only way to completely block 100 percent of your spam is to use a *challenge-response (C-R)* email system. Whether this is true is open to debate. I will certainly grant that C-R email systems block more spam than any other antispam mechanism we currently have. However, it is not effort free, and its major flaw is that the more popular it becomes, the easier it will be for spammers to break it.

Conceptually, a challenge-response email system is just that: When someone sends you an email message, your email server responds with a challenge that the prospective mailer must respond to. If the mailer responds correctly to the challenge, you receive their message. Otherwise, the message is trashed as spam. To keep from annoying your regular correspondents, you create and maintain a whitelist of all email addresses or Internet domains that you will *always* accept mail from. A sender who is on your whitelist will never be challenged. A sender who passes the system's challenge may be added to your whitelist if you so choose.

C-R email systems depend on the fact that spammers do not have the time or manpower to respond individually to challenges. Keeping this crucial fact true is the primary technological difficulty in creating a challenge-response email system.

Captchas: Riddle Me This to Email Me!

The challenge offered to a prospective mailer shouldn't be something that can be easily defeated by a computer program. Most challenge-response email systems use something called a *captcha*, which is a simple puzzle that the prospective mailer has to solve in order for email to be allowed through. The simplest and earliest captchas were simply a word or phrase expressed in a graphical bitmap, a *picture* of a word. The word is sometimes "fuzzed out" or distorted in some way to make it harder for a computer program to recognize (see Figure 10.1). Although a human being can glance at a picture of the word *nozzle* and recognize it easily, a computer must use an optical character recognition (OCR) program and spend quite a bit of compute time on it.

Figure 10.1
A simple graphical captcha.

To my knowledge, spammers have not yet begun using OCR software to crack captchas, but that's only because C-R email systems are still relatively rare. If C-R mail systems become widespread enough, the "OCR attack" will be used. For this reason, modern captchas are more likely to ask questions that are like those intelligence-test puzzles you suffered through in third grade. For example, a captcha might consist of six small photos of cuddly animals. Five are photos of puppies and one is a photo of a kitten. The prospective mailer is asked which picture doesn't fit in with all the others. Most people will understand that the photo of the kitten is the odd one and will cite that one. The software behind the captcha must also be smart enough to know that "cat," "kitten," "kitty" and "calico" are all "good" answers.

Whitelists Are Everything

A challenge-response email system is basically a militantly enforced whitelist: If you're on the list, your mail gets through. If you're not, you have to solve the puzzle or your mail will be bounced back to you. This means that adding people to and maintaining your whitelist is the full burden of a C-R system, and it has some nonobvious aspects.

The most significant is that much email comes from robots. If you buy things online, you will get a fair number of very important messages from server-side programs that do not have the ability to respond to C-R system challenges. Your challenge messages to them will bounce, you will not receive the shipment notice or other account information, and the futile email traffic that results just clutters up a global Internet already groaning under the spam burden. Email newsletters come from server robots, as do notices from online message boards like phpBB. All these robots have to be added to your whitelist or you will not receive messages that you have been used to receiving.

Adding an e-commerce site to your whitelist is not necessarily easy. When you complete a purchase transaction online, you may receive messages from companies or Web sites completely unrelated to the ones from which you buy the goods. Furthermore, you generally have no way to know this ahead of time. I routinely receive messages from third-party payment processors that handle credit card payments for online stores. Until the first message arrives, you have no idea what the third party's email address is and thus cannot whitelist it—and until you whitelist the third party, you won't receive any mail from them. It's an ugly catch-22.

Other Problems With C-R Email Systems

My problems with C-R email systems are many, and at this point I might as well just run down the list:

√ C-R systems add significantly to the global Internet's burden. Each time delivery of a spam message is attempted, a challenge message is sent back to the supposed spammer. No spammer I know can cost-justify manually solving a captcha, so the challenge messages are simply ignored. Each attempted spam wastes twice as much bandwidth as spam that is conventionally delivered and then eaten by client-side filters.

√ A challenge returned to a spammer verifies that your email address is real. You might well ask, So what? If C-R systems block spam 100 percent (as they all claim), why is this a problem? Read on.

√ Some spammers have reportedly begun to forge the addresses or domains of commonly whitelisted entities to get spam through C-R barriers. Think about it: Almost everybody buys from Amazon, so if you whitelist all mail from amazon.com, a spammer simply has to forge the From field to **ship-confirm@amazon.com** (or anything from amazon.com) and their spam will sail right through. A sufficiently clever spammer might use this ploy only if their automated spamming software received a challenge from your C-R system and recorded that fact as a flag in your record in their database. Spammers are getting desperate, and I predict that this great gaping flaw in C-R systems will be widely exploited if C-R systems become common-place. Because C-R systems depend utterly on whitelists, there's no good way (and maybe no way at all) to close this loophole.

√ C-R systems annoy the hell out of a lot of people, and many simply won't bother to solve the captcha and won't try to contact you again. If you're a Public Professional and your line of work depends on being reachable by the general public, C-R email systems are *poison*.

C-R email systems are not 100 percent invulnerable to spam, and the more popular they become, the more spammers will be motivated to defeat them. They make it difficult to receive email newsletters or shop online, and they annoy people you might want to hear from. Use a Bayesian filter like POPFile instead—99.6% accuracy isn't bad at all!

Why Spamming Should Not Be Illegal

Of all possible antispam techniques, the worst is making spamming against the law. I'm against antispam legislation and here's why:

√ We've tried it; legislation doesn't work. The much ballyhooed CAN-SPAM Act, which went into effect January 1, 2004, had no effect that can be measured. Most people I have spoken to are now receiving significantly more spam than they did before the law went into effect.

√ Legislation is only as effective as our willingness to enforce it, and with terrorism by far the #1 concern of American law enforcement, little is being done to enforce state and federal laws against spam.

√ Well-funded direct marketing lobbies have worked hard to defeat and water down any law intended to restrict spam. In fact, the CAN-SPAM Act preempts all state laws against spam and explicitly allows spammers to send you one initial message and then require you to request that you be taken off the mailing list. This is a spammer's dream law: It provides spammers legal immunity from state laws and forces you to give spammers your email address to be removed from *one* mailing list (spammers may have any number of them) without any restriction on selling your (now verified) address to legions of other spammers.

√ Because the From field of an email message is so easily forged, people or companies can be framed by their enemies or competitors and forced out of business defending against false accusations of spamming. Ambitious prosecutors trying to build a reputation don't care whether an accused spammer is innocent; they only want to win.

√ Badly drafted laws could prevent innovative antispam technologies from being developed and deployed. The direct marketing industry, having been mostly forced out of telephone telemarketing, would love to spam instead. You can be sure that their lobby will do whatever they can (and they are very imaginative people!) to make sure that future antispam laws sound great while actually preventing effective antispam technology from reaching the market, not to mention protecting spammers from legal action.

No matter how much you hate spam, any antispam law is worse than no law at all.

Keep a Cool Head and Win the War

The war on spam is a lot like the war on thistles or the war on mosquitoes. Total victory (as we achieved in the war on smallpox) is impossible, but we have gotten better and better at keeping the enemy from having a major impact on our lives. Getting where we are was work, and staying ahead of the game is work, but most of us have decided that the results are worth the effort.

New technologies on the horizon will help even more. Various systems have been proposed to verify that the From field of a message contains the actual address of the sender. The great gaping hole in the Internet email protocols is simply that: There is no mechanism at all providing *authentication* of the sender. If an authentication technology is developed and deployed broadly, forging of email sender addresses will become impossible and a lot of spam will be nuked at the server without fear of false positives.

This will happen, but it may be a few years off yet. In the meantime, we're left to confront the spam problem and decide what to do. Having tried almost everything, my overall conclusion is that for the moment, nothing beats client-side Bayesian spam filtering. POPFile (as described in detail in Chapter 9) works better than anything else you can buy or download, and best of all, it's free.

Summing Up

The technologies I've described in this chapter are, for the most part, acts of desperation. They lean toward the *eradication* of spam, even if it means that legitimate messages are lost or that innocent parties must suffer collateral damage. Most are excessively complex and depend to some extent on someone else making decisions about what is spam and what isn't. In my view, that decision should always be yours, or (as with POPFile) it should be the decision of a utility that you understand and control. After all, it's not really about spam; it's about taking back control of your inbox and ensuring that real email gets through. A cool head will win the spam wars, even if you have to manually nuke a message here or there. Anger is harder on you than on spammers.

We're now ready to (finally!) say goodbye to the spam wars and turn some attention to the other, far scarier war: the war against malware. Spam is an irritation, but malware can bring down your computer, wipe out your data, make you an unknowing spammer, or put you at the mercy of increasingly clever identity thieves. Put on your degunking helmet. It's going to get scarier before it gets better.

Protect Yourself Against Viruses, Trojans, and Worms

Degunking Checklist:

√ Learn what malware is and why it plagues even the most experienced computer users.

√ Find out how serious the malware problem really is, and how malware is different from spam.

√ Discern the differences between viruses, worms, Trojan horses, back doors, adware, spyware, and phishing.

√ See how social engineering plays a part in the malware wars.

√ Uncover the truth about who hackers and crackers are, what they do, and why they do it.

√ Learn about software flaws and why they exist.

√ Build your own malware defense strategy.

Here's a cautionary tale for you: I've been in the personal computer industry since before there was a personal computer industry. (I built my first from loose parts with a wire-wrap gun in 1976.) I haven't been without a computer since 1976, and I've been familiar with viruses since the first virus made news in 1986. I've had Norton AntiVirus since it was first released in 1990. I'm careful about these things…and yet, in 2001, a virus got me. Me, a programmer and multicredentialed geek.

How could this happen? Easy: I had to turn Norton AntiVirus off while debugging a program I was writing. Debuggers and antivirus utilities often don't play nice together. While I was working, I even remembered to disconnect my machine from the network. Alas, when I was finished and reconnected the network, I simply forgot to run Norton again. A day or two later, I was reading email and bang! BadTrans.B started running.

I saw the flash of a dialog that vanished as soon as it appeared, and things like that make my antennas twitch. I shut down Outlook Express immediately, before BadTrans could get more than two or three copies of itself mailed to other people in my address book. Nothing worse than that happened, and Norton AntiVirus cleaned out the scoundrel for me after I rebooted.

BadTrans was one of the cleverer viruses of its era, and one of the first to exploit the many flaws in Microsoft Internet Explorer. I didn't have to open an attachment to get BadTrans. Because of the flaw in IE, when Outlook Express brought the virus down to my machine, IE blithely loaded it and ran it.

There are several morals to this story:

1. Virus writers are diabolically clever.
2. Even geeks get viruses.
3. If you get complacent, you'll get nailed.

In this chapter you'll learn that fighting the malware wars is a serious business, and that you *must* pay attention and put certain measures in place against malware—or you will pay the price. But don't panic like Dorothy and her friends, who ran through the haunted forest in Oz chanting, "Lions, and tigers, and bears, oh my!" until they got themselves completely unhinged and into much deeper trouble. Pay attention, take appropriate action, keep a cool head, and put into practice the virus degunking techniques that you'll be learning starting with this chapter.

Develop a Malware Master Plan

This chapter will provide you with the background information you need so that you can start to develop a master plan for dealing with the complex malware issue. Understanding malware is much more difficult than understanding spam, and the stakes are a lot higher. The first step in the degunking process involves getting familiar with the various categories of malware. This will help you get past the inevitable confusion that comes from overlapping categories and poor use of terms by nontechnical journalists. In the next several chapters, you'll learn how to put a set of malware degunking techniques to work, along with the security techniques that you must use to protect yourself.

√ Chapter 12 will present virus degunking techniques and virus protection options.

√ Chapter 13 will explain how to degunk adware and spyware, as well as "drive-by installs" permitted by your Web browser. You'll learn want these nasties do and how to remove them.

√ Chapter 14 will show you how to degunk Internet worms, how they work, and how to protect yourself against them with both software and hardware firewalls.

√ Chapter 15 is about Internet hoaxes, "phishing" scams, and the infamous "419" Nigerian scams. All of these fall under the category of "social engineering," which is a sort of malware that runs in your mind rather than on your PC.

As with spam and a lot of other things, the malware wars involve a fair amount of psychology, forethought, and simple caution. Knowledge is your best weapon. Let's get underway.

Understand the PC Malware Bestiary

Much of the problem in dealing with malware lies in simply understanding the jargon. What I'll do first is define the major terms I'll be using in this and the next several chapters. The rest of this chapter discusses what your risks are and what steps you can take to protect yourself.

Malware

Malware is a relatively recent coinage that applies to *all* software that does "bad stuff" on an innocent user's computer, no matter what that bad stuff is or how the malware gets in and accomplishes it. Viruses, worms, Trojan horse programs, adware, spyware, and "back doors"—are all malware. Malware as a category generally does not apply to specialized tools used by network intruders, virus authors, and spammers because those tools run on their machines, not yours.

Viruses

This is the most ancient genera of malware. Viruses were first discovered "in the wild" in 1981 on the Apple II computer, and the conceptual research that predicted computer viruses goes back as far as 1949 when "self-replicating software" was first discussed in academic research papers. Viruses and worms are both self-replicating software, but in current jargon, a virus is self-replicating software *that requires the action of a user* to get control of a PC.

There are two general categories of virus: Executable viruses and embedded script viruses. Executable viruses are true computer programs, created with the same programming tools used to create word processing programs and email clients. Embedded script viruses are scripts written in the scripting languages built into word processors and spreadsheets. These scripts are hidden in ordinary text documents and spreadsheets, and when a user opens the document or spreadsheet, the virus runs.

Currently, almost all viruses are either downloaded from Web sites or Usenet newsgroups or else transmitted via email. Both scenarios require that the user run a program by installing a downloaded application or by opening an email attachment. (Unfortunately, in the Windows world, "open" means "execute," rather than "inspect" or "look at," a Microsoft idiocy without which viruses would be far more rare than they are.) Every now and then a virus appears that exploits some newly discovered "security hole" in an email program or a Web browser and manages to execute even without being opened by a hapless user. (This is what happened to me in 2001.)

Worms

A *worm* is a species of malware that uses flaws in network software to move directly from machine to machine over a network, typically the Internet. Above all, you need to know this: *A worm doesn't always need you to do anything to run it.* Unless you block it somehow, it simply walks in, sits down, and takes over. (Worms can also be sent to you in email attachments, and such "blended threat" worms blur the line between worms and viruses. BadTrans, which nailed me in 2001, is a little of both.)

Worms typically take advantage of flaws discovered by the bad guys (whom I typically call "black hats," more on which later) in popular software, which these days is almost always Microsoft software. As I've explained earlier in this book, it's not that Microsoft software has more flaws than other software, but rather that Microsoft software is everywhere. A worm needs to able to jump from one machine to another over a direct connection, which means that both sides of the connection need to be running the flawed software. If a piece of software is to be found on only one out of 20 PCs in the world, the likelihood that a worm can jump from one machine to another is poor. On the other hand, when Internet Explorer is installed on 9 out of 10 PCs in the world, a worm can safely assume that almost any machine it can reach will be open and infectable.

Worms are stopped by firewalls. There are several kinds of firewalls, and I'll discuss them in detail in Chapter 14. My advice on worms is simple and urgent: *Do not connect to the Internet without a firewall.*

Trojan Horses

We all know the story of the Trojan horse, which was hollow and full of Greeks with a grudge against Troy. The ancient Trojans weren't sufficiently suspicious of gifts from strangers—and I think the gods punished them by making their name synonymous with…software that has bad stuff inside it. The term is misused by many, but the gist is this: A Trojan horse program looks like a legitimate piece of software, but it's written as a device to get access to a user's PC. Trojan horses often look for passwords or credit card information and then "phone home" with the stolen data. Others distract the user with a piece of animation or a simple game while the program turns off the speaker in the user's dialup modem and then dials one of those "900" style phone numbers in some other country, racking up charges while the clueless user plays the silly game. Screen savers are famous for being Trojan horses, and I advise against installing them unless you bought them on CD in a shrink-wrapped box at a computer store. Windows comes with its own built-in screen saver. Use it.

A Trojan horse program does *not* attempt to reproduce itself, nor does it mail itself to other users or (like a worm) jump directly to new machines across the Internet. Of course, if one of your friends mails you a "cool screen saver" and you run it, it's still a Trojan horse, even if it arrives by email.

The term *Trojan horse* is the most misused of all terms in the malware wars. If you read Web pages, you'll often see *Trojan horse* and *virus* used interchangeably. Real Trojan horse software is relatively rare compared to worms and viruses. The best way to avoid Trojans is to *know what's in the software that you install.* Don't just download something from a Web page and install it. Research the item you're drooling over, and once you download it, scan the downloaded file or files with your virus checker *before* installing it.

Back Doors

Believe it or not, there is machinery built into Windows to allow a Windows-based computer to be remotely controlled from anywhere in the world over a network connection like a cable modem, DSL, or dialup. Once such a remote control connection is established, the person on the other end of the line can run programs, monitor keystrokes, and create, edit, and delete files; basically they can do almost anything that you yourself can do while sitting at the keyboard.

This sounds scary—and it is—but remote control connections have legitimate uses, and they are not considered malware unless they are installed without the user's knowledge or permission. Good remote control software should make its presence clearly known and should not "hide" once installed. Once a remote control program gets sneaky, well, it becomes malware.

Back door is an informal term for a remote control program that hides, and allows someone else to control your PC without your permission. How back doors get installed varies. Some are installed by viruses. Some are installed by Trojan horse software. Some are installed by worms.

The most famous back door program is called Back Orifice. Back Orifice has been around for several years now, and it shone a bright light on just how wide open Windows 9.*x* networking is to meddling by outsiders. Whatever the intentions of its creators may have been, it's possible to be infected by Back Orifice, and you need to guard against it.

The best way to defend against all back doors (apart from being *very* careful about what you install on your PC!) is to use a two-way firewall like ZoneAlarm Pro. ZoneAlarm watches for programs that attempt to connect to the Internet from *inside* your PC, as a back door would, and will not allow the connection unless you grant permission. Of course, once ZoneAlarm detects a back door on your PC, you will need to remove it somehow, and that requires specialized software. More on this in Chapter 14, concerning firewalls.

Adware

There are two kinds of "free" in the software business: There is really and truly free software, much of which goes by the modifier *open source.* This is software that you pay nothing for, in either money or attention. The other kind of software is *ad-supported,* meaning that although you don't have to pay money for it, you must pay in attention by looking at ads that the software displays in one corner or in a separate window.

The border between spyware (see the next section) and adware is very fuzzy and getting fuzzier all the time. Adware must keep bringing in new ads from an ad server somewhere, so it must connect to the Internet to request and download the ads. The temptation to report whether or not you clicked on an ad displayed by a piece of adware is strong, and when adware does that, or when it keeps a log of what you click on when you surf the Web (whether it claims to do so anonymously or not), it becomes spyware.

Even when adware simply displays ads and does not "phone home" to report on your Internet habits, it takes a certain amount of your PC's processor power to do its work, not to mention the bandwidth it uses to bring down new ad graphics to display. Worst of all, this ad downloading machinery is not always uninstalled when you uninstall an adware application. It sits there running with nothing to do, slowing your PC down.

Adware comes with a price: reduced PC performance and the sort of gunk that I covered in detail, with co-author Joli Ballew, in our book *Degunking Windows*. You need to ask yourself whether a given application is worth that price, but keep in mind that much adware is also spyware.

My recommendation: Use open-source software, or buy commercial packages that do not "phone home" for ads to display or anything else.

Spyware

Some adware is especially aggressive, and in addition to downloading ads that dance in the corner of an adware application, it may keep statistics on what Web sites you go to when you surf the Web, or even what applications you run on your PC. It then reports these statistics back to a central server, where they are used to gauge how well the ads are working and build statistical profiles of software users that will enable adware people to design more effective and targeted ads.

At this point, adware becomes spyware. It doesn't matter that such statistics are claimed by adware firms to be gathered "anonymously." Given that adware must report your IP address when it connects to its ad server, I contend that there is no such thing as "anonymous" adware.

Spyware, like adware, consumes your PC's processor power and bandwidth. If you download and install a lot of spyware or adware, you can have a dozen or more little ad robots running in the background, messing up your Registry and slowing your PC to a crawl.

Some spyware is a form of Trojan horse, in that the application that installs the spyware has no ads or any other obvious connection to what's really going on. A popular trick is to offer people "free smileys" to sprinkle into their email messages. After the package is installed, the smileys are indeed there for you to use, but they're simply a cover for a system that monitors your Web surfing habits for a marketing company and reports back every site that you visit. This may be reported in 2-point type in the middle of a deliberately inflated 3,000-word end user license agreement, but who reads those?

To avoid spyware and adware, be very careful with the word *free*. Before installing a "free" application, go up on Google and do a search like this:

smileys spyware

Beware when the vendor of a "free" package (software, smileys, toolbars, animations, whatever) claims, "There is no spyware in our products!" Can you see them crossing their fingers, over there on the other side of the planet? No? Didn't think so. Get a second opinion. The Web is rich with reports of what "free" products bogged down user PCs with spyware and adware gunk. A very cogent analysis of the "free smileys" spyware scam can be found here:

www.eagle-wing.net/ClickPicks/Internet/Spam-07.shtml

Spyware and adware are very prevalent in gray-area fields of interest like file sharing and porn. If you must partake, be aware that you will be in the crosshairs of marketers whose ethics are unknown and questionable.

Spyware and adware can be removed safely with products like Ad-Aware and Spybot Search & Destroy. I'll have more to say on how to use these very useful products in Chapter 13.

Social Engineering

Computer security experts have a highfalutin term for what bad guys do when they trick clueless PC users without using technology at all: *social engineering*. This is the art of getting people to do things that are not in their best interest, by persuasion, lying, or other psychological trickery.

Much social engineering succeeds because most people are basically honest and want to be helpful. An ancient example of social engineering involved a scammer who called people on the phone and claimed to be a telephone company technician up on a telephone pole fixing something (sometimes with recorded background sound effects like wind blowing and birds chirping) and needed a little help from the person called. The "tech" asked the person to push a few buttons on the phone (like 9, 0, #), which allowed the scammer to make long-distance calls on the duped person's account.

In the current day in the PC world, most social engineering is a very specialized species of scam called *phishing* (see the next section). Social engineering can be a problem any time you possess trusted information (your own passwords or those of co-workers) or a privileged position in terms of, for example, network permissions. A fast-talking scammer once called AOL tech support to ask for help and, after talking with the tech support person, casually mentioned that he was selling his car quickly to generate some cash. Sensing a good deal, the AOL tech asked for more details, and the scammer emailed the AOL tech a document with a photo of the car and specs…but the document was in fact a Trojan horse that installed a back door (see earlier in this chapter) *inside* the AOL firewall. The scammer then mined the AOL internal network for usernames and passwords.

It goes against the good nature of many people, but be suspicious when people ask you for help. Always ask yourself, how could this person be scamming me? Be especially vigilant when helping involves passwords or other insider information. Scammers are everywhere.

Phishing

Phishing is basically social engineering with a technological assist. In virtually all cases, an email is sent to millions of people, claiming to come from eBay, PayPal, or a major national bank and asking for personal information. The email demands that you "verify your account," "reauthorize your password," or any of a multitude of other things, all of which ask you to enter account names, passwords, personal identification numbers (PINs), and so on. The messages often threaten to close your account ("with a loss of any unpaid balance in the account") if you refuse. There is an official-looking Web link that you must click to open a session and comply.

Of course, it's a scam, and the Web link will take you to a bad guy's server somewhere in Central Slobovia, where your passwords and PINs will be recorded so that the bad guys can clean out your account, or open new accounts via identity theft.

The scam email (always in HTML format) contains logo graphics that look authentic, and they *are*—because they were stolen from the bank or other organization from whom the message claims to come. (You can save graphics to disk from anybody's Web site, Citibank's as easily as Clueless Joe's Blog.) The

Web link can show one destination (PayPal.com) and still take you to another, typically a nameless "raw" IP address.

Protecting yourself against phishing is simple: *Never go to a bank or other firm with which you have an account by clicking a link in an email.* Always open a browser and type in the bank's URL.

Hackers and Crackers and the Colors of Hats

In one sense, using terms from biology like *virus* and *worm* when speaking of malware is a mistake. I've met people who think of viruses and worms as forces of nature or something that arose spontaneously from flawed software, as flies were once thought to arise spontaneously from decaying garbage. Not so—malware is computer software, written by human beings, just as video games, databases, email clients, and other software is.

So who are these guys? (Yes, they're overwhelmingly male.) Bright, focused, quick studies, often very young, socially challenged in many ways—just like "good" computer programmers. Years ago, we called these passionate program-mers *hackers,* borrowing a term used for over a century to denote expert horse-men, who could make a horse do anything they wanted and do it with style and grace. Computer hackers were those people who didn't take no for an answer when solving a programming problem. They were in it for the chal-lenge and the knowledge, and they went *deep*—probing the limits of both software and hardware, making both do what lesser lights considered impos-sible. I used to call myself a hacker, and still think of myself as one, but these days, I don't dare say so out loud. The word *hacker* now means "bad guy who breaks into computers and does nasty things." More recently, people have be-gun speaking of "black hats" instead of hackers, and most of us like that a lot better. In the old cowboy movies, the bad guys wore black hats and the good guys white hats.

Good hackers and bad hackers mostly have the same attributes and skill sets. The difference lies in their ethics. Bad hackers break into networks, write worms and viruses, and steal data. Good hackers devise defenses to keep the bad ones out. It's a constant arms race, good versus bad, black hat versus white hat. We've come to call those who work at protecting computers and networks from malware and black hat exploits "white hats."

Like most issues divided crisply into two sides, it's not always that simple. There is a group called the Cult of the Dead Cow, who created a popular remote control utility called Back Orifice. Although its members have been secretive about their own identities, the group has been very open about the software itself and have actually released its source code to the public. Back Orifice has some legitimate uses, and the Dead Cow guys have stated that one of their goals was to rub Microsoft's nose in how utterly insecure Windows is. In that they've been *massively* successful.

This doesn't excuse the damage that people have done with Back Orifice, but it also suggests that there is a lot of muddy water between the two streams. I've started calling certain parties "gray hats" because they create software that can cause damage but may also have some beneficial effects, such as exposing software flaws and prodding balky software vendors into fixing them.

What you need to understand to keep it all in perspective is that none of these guys is coming after you personally. Malware is impersonal, written sometimes as a stunt to show off one's black hat skills and sometimes with a criminal agenda (such as stealing passwords) but very rarely as a personal attack. There are black hat gangs who go after one another, but like the Mafia, they're not generally interested in ordinary people on the street. This is good, because if a black hat wants to get into your network or PC, he can probably do it. Malware, however, is just software, and software is not as clever as a human being. It can only do what it was written to do. If you take the proper precautions, you can stop malware cold.

Basically, be careful, put your security utilities in place and keep them updated, and don't let the myth of the black hats scare you.

Security Holes in Software

A security hole is a software flaw. A hole is a program bug that a black hat can exploit by writing a piece of malware that takes advantage of the bug or one of the bug's side effects. Modern software is *spectacularly* complex. A major application can represent millions of lines of program code, and there will always be bugs lurking somewhere in that immense tangle of computer instructions. Black hats have become experts at probing for weaknesses in modern software by using debuggers and other programmer tools.

The vast majority of security holes in modern software falls into a single, regrettable category called *buffer overflow* flaws. A buffer overflow flaw cooks down to this: Computer programs contain regions set aside for data manipulation. These regions are called *buffers,* and they are generally of a fixed size. Buffers are often adjacent to executable program code, and sometimes they are adjacent to (or even contained in) an extremely critical portion of a program called the *stack.* The stack contains many things, but its most important use is storing return addresses from program functions. These addresses, if changed, can literally alter the course of program flow.

When a buffer is on or near the stack in a vulnerable application, a black hat can write a program that forces too much data into the buffer. The buffer fills and then overflows to overwrite adjacent program code or return addresses. Although this may appear to be simple random vandalism, it isn't random at all. The black hat has very carefully chosen the data crammed into the buffer. The buffer is actually filled with executable program code, and the overflow portion overwrites addresses on the stack with new addresses chosen by the black hat, addresses that now direct the PC to execute the malware code with which the black hat has filled the buffer. Bang! The application has been modified and the malware now controls the show.

Don't worry if your head spins when you try to understand what I've just described. All you need to know, really, is that a buffer overflow allows a piece of malware to fill a buffer with new code and run it. This new code can execute other malware programs from disk and literally take over the entire PC.

How do security holes happen? In their unending quest for greater program speed, programmers have trimmed every "unnecessary" bit of code from their programs, including some code that we now understand to be *very* necessary, like code that checks to be sure that buffers never overflow. These speed optimizations might have been understandable 10 or 15 years ago, when there was no Internet, few black hats, and PCs weren't nearly as fast as they are today. Modern PCs have speed to spare, especially for things as essential as buffer overflow protection. There is no longer any excuse for writing code containing buffer overflow flaws.

That leaves the hundreds of millions of lines of code written years ago and now installed on our computers. Buffer overflow flaws are fixed by software vendors as quickly as they are found, but there are a lot of them, and some of them are *very* difficult to spot. Over time, new programs will be written with protected buffers and other measures to keep malware from taking control of an application and then the entire PC. Until then, security holes will be an issue and we will have to put other measures in place to guard against malware that takes advantage of older, flawed software.

What measures? If you keep viruses and worms from running on your PC, they can't fill any buffers and take over. With an up-to-date antivirus utility and a good firewall, the chances of malware taking advantage of software security holes are *much* less—and as much as I dislike saying it, the less Microsoft software you use, the better your chances are of avoiding security holes because (by their very ubiquity) Microsoft software attracts most of the attention of the black hats. Definitely download and install any security updates that Microsoft offers, but don't fool yourself into thinking that the black hats will ever run out of security holes to exploit!

If you're moderately to mostly technical, a terrific article on buffer overflow flaws can be found here:

www.linuxjournal.com/article.php?sid=6701

A superb page of links to articles on the buffer overflow problem is here:

**https://engineering.purdue.edu/ResearchGroups/SmashGuard/
The%20SmashGuard%20Page.htm**

Where the Risks Are

Having read all that, you might properly ask, What are my risks? How likely am I to encounter these things? To put the risks in perspective, let me take this short section to list some of the circumstances that put you at risk from malware.

√ An Internet connection is how worms get in. The connection can be broadband or dialup; slow connections are no safer than fast. If you don't need an Internet connection, you're not at risk from Internet worms, and if you can unplug your Internet connection when you're not using it, you're not at risk while it's unplugged. Anytime you're connected to the Internet, you are a target.

√ Email attachments are how most viruses (and some types of worm) get in.

√ Microsoft software (Internet Explorer, Outlook, Outlook Express, and to a lesser extent Office) puts you at greater risk of malware attacks than any other vendor's software. This is simply because it's everywhere, not because it's somehow worse than other software.

√ File sharing software seems rife with spyware, and the spyware that comes with it seems unusually virulent. Also, if you install software coming from who knows where over a peer-to-peer file sharing network, you are at high risk of installing Trojan horse software, back doors, and viruses.

√ Downloading software from Usenet newsgroups is a risk for Trojan horses, back doors, and viruses. You have no idea where that stuff comes from.

√ Trivial installable freebies like smiley collections, toolbars, screen savers, and animations have a terrible reputation for being spyware. Research such items before you install them, but better still…resist.

√ Porn sites (paid or free) seem to be very rich sources of spyware, scripting viruses, and Trojan horse nasties.

√ Pop-up ads can be used by black hats to trick you into allowing "drive-by installs" of Trojan horse software, keystroke loggers, and spyware. If you suppress pop-ups somehow, you will not be at risk.

Malware Defense: From a Height

In the next few chapters, I'll take up malware defense in detail, citing specific products and giving step-by-step instructions. For the moment, there are several general principles to follow to keep yourself safe in our increasingly anarchic and heavily networked world:

√ NAT firewall. *Before* you connect to the Internet, put a firewall in place. If you have broadband, an inexpensive router/switch with a built-in Network Address Translation (NAT) firewall is strong protection and easy to install and use.

√ Software updates. Apply all Windows updates. However, don't try to download and install them until you've installed a firewall.

√ Software firewall. In addition to (or if you're a dialup user, instead of) a NAT firewall, install a two-way software firewall like ZoneAlarm Pro, which can detect viruses, worms, and back doors trying to "phone home."

√ Don't allow install on demand. Disable "install on demand" in your Web browser. This will be primarily for Internet Explorer, but other Web browsers may offer this "feature" as well. Turn it off!

√ Antivirus program. Install a reputable and regularly updated antivirus program, and keep your update subscription current. If the antivirus program supports automatic, on-demand updates, enable them.

√ Email attachments. Don't open email attachments before scanning them with an antivirus program. Most antivirus programs can easily scan individual files.

√ Virus scan. Run a full-system virus scan at least monthly, and preferably weekly.

√ Don't open links in spam. Never click a Web link that comes to you in a spam message, or in any message that looks suspicious, even if it claims to come from someone you know.

√ Research all software before you install it. Use Google to determine whether a given "free" product is truly free or contains adware or spyware or, worse, a Trojan horse. *Antivirus programs and firewalls will not stop these!*

√ Choose software carefully. The more popular a piece of software is, the more likely it is to be targeted by malware. If at all possible, avoid using Internet Explorer, Outlook, or Outlook Express.

√ Read the news. Stay ahead of malware by paying attention to industry news on the subject.

That's the view from a height. If you keep these items in mind while using your computer, you have a very good chance of not being crippled by an unwanted electronic visitor.

At this point, it's time to get down and build some defenses. Viruses first: They're our oldest threat, but in many respects, they're the easiest to understand and stop. As with most degunking skills, a little psychology and a little technology could make your record of resisting virus infections as good as or better than mine!

12

Defeat Those Viruses

Degunking Checklist:

√ Don't leave removable media in drives when you shut a PC down.

√ Make sure Windows is configured to display file extensions for all file types.

√ Disable macros in all Microsoft Office applications unless you desperately need them.

√ Shop carefully for an antivirus utility, making sure that it's suitable for your PC.

√ Hold email file attachments in *great* suspicion.

√ Scan all downloaded files for viruses before you open them.

√ Consider using two different antivirus products to scan for viruses on your PC.

√ Once you have an antivirus utility installed, configure it to do a full-system scan once a week.

√ Supervise the use of your PC by others, and do not allow people to install software on it without your permission.

I've always been a little leery of using biological metaphors for computer concepts. Computer viruses are *not* living things, and otherwise intelligent people (albeit nontechnical people) have worried unnecessarily about whether two computers sitting side by side can pass computer viruses between them without some sort of connection. (Ubiquitous Wi-Fi wireless networking, of course, confuses the issue even more.)

Well, they can't. Computer viruses have only certain high-level resemblances to biological viruses, and it's important not to carry the metaphor too far. Terms like *transmission vector, infection,* and so on take on a certain ominous, mythic aura when applied to computer viruses, and it can make you crazy (or paranoid) if you let it.

Better by far is to understand what computer viruses are, how they get into your PC, and how to protect against them. That's what this chapter is about.

Understand What Viruses Are and What They Do

Computer viruses is one of the two major categories of self-replicating software. (The other category is worms; see Chapter 14.) To be "self-replicating" means that a virus makes other copies of itself. This self-replication involves attempts to spread the additional copies to other PCs though emailing itself to other PCs or by attaching itself to a legitimate piece of software. When a virus is running on a PC, that PC is said to be "infected."

To be a virus, a piece of software simply has to be able to reproduce and spread. Apart from that, it doesn't have to "do" anything, like format your hard drive or corrupt files. There are occasional "proof-of-concept" viruses released by virus writers that do nothing but spread, usually by some new and novel method. They do not necessarily damage files or have any other effect.

Most viruses, however, have a mission of some sort. They carry code that does something on the PCs that they infect. This code is called the virus's *payload*. Proof-of-concept viruses do not have a payload. Sometimes, a novice virus programmer will tinker up a payload-free virus for fun, just to see if he can get it into the news. Most viruses, however, have a payload of some sort. When they run on a PC, they do something.

In years past, virus payloads were usually destructive. They damaged files, reconfigured Web browser home pages, or put up mocking message boxes. Such viruses still exist, and more will appear over time. There is a trend, however, for current viruses to have payloads that do something a little more subtle. The most notorious of this new breed are viruses that plant spam relay stations as their payload. These relay stations are actually special-purpose email servers. They are used to relay spam from the spam's originator so that the originator cannot be traced. A PC infected with this kind of virus becomes a *spam zombie*. As much as 40 percent of spam currently comes to us through spam zombies, which make the spam wars a lot more difficult to fight.

Spam zombies are more like parasites than predators. They need to keep the infected PC running, and running well. Furthermore, they need to hide as completely as possible so that the owner of the infected PC doesn't find out what's going on and then attempt to remove the virus payload.

This trend is likely to continue, and we're going to see more virus payloads that create some sort of parasitical function on infected PCs. Spam relays are a current reality; other possible parasitical payloads might include file sharing relay nodes to confuse investigators trying to enforce copyright laws. Some viruses have been seen to search for passwords or email addresses and harvest this data for transmission to an Internet site owned by black hats and spammers. The latest I've seen in the news are viruses that look for webcams connected to PCs and relay images back to their authors of what people are doing within sight of the webcams.

What this means is that viruses will not always damage your PC and will not always immediately make their presence known. You may be infected, perhaps for months or even years, and never even know it. This is important because viruses may be making your PC do illegal things, like relay spam or transmit child pornography. Even if your PC seems to be working as well as it always did, it may be harboring nasty stuff. You owe it to yourself to scan for viruses regularly and take all due efforts to keep them from infecting your PC.

My emphasis in this chapter (and in this book generally) is on prevention. Antivirus software can only do so much. If you install an antivirus utility and continue doing stupid things, you will still be at risk for picking up viruses. (More on this later.)

How You Contract PC Viruses

Even if all software were perfect and there were no "security holes" in Microsoft's software or anybody else's, there would still be viruses and people would still contract them. Unlike worms (which generally do depend on security holes to function), viruses depend on *you* to execute them and allow them to propagate.

There are five general ways to contract a computer virus:

√ By booting from an infected diskette, Zip disk, or flash drive

√ By having macros enabled in your office suite and opening an infected document or spreadsheet

√ By allowing "install on demand" through your Web browser and browsing a virus-infected Web site

√ By executing an infected program that you downloaded from somewhere or got from a friend

√ In the majority of cases these days, by opening an infected email attachment

Not all of these scenarios are equally likely. Years ago, booting from infected floppy diskettes used to be the #1 virus transmission route, but today these boot sector viruses are increasingly rare. Most older PCs cannot boot from Zip drives, and few PCs, even new ones, can boot from USB-based flash drives. (USB flash drives need driver software that is usually only available *after* the PC boots up.) And who boots from floppies anymore? Still, if you do, scan them before you boot from them!

You can easily disable macros in Microsoft Office applications, and once they are disabled, that transmission route is closed. I'll show you how a little later. Ditto Web browser "install on demand," which is mostly an issue in Microsoft Internet Explorer. Turn off "install on demand" in IE or whatever other browser you may be using (some don't have it, and most call it by a different name) and you're in the clear. (I explain how to turn off "install on demand" in Chapter 13.)

The fourth and fifth methods for contracting viruses are the big ones. Nearly all the time, you will get viruses in one of those two ways: by running an infected program or by opening an infected email attachment. The two ways are actually the same because "opening" an executable file under Windows runs it. The difference is that email attachments, an attempt is usually made to try to trick you into thinking that they're some other kind of (non-executable) file and thus safe to open.

Watch Out for "Dangerous" Files and Their Extensions

So which file types are safe, and which are dangerous? The question turns on whether a file type contains executable code. No executable code, no viruses— it's (almost) that simple. Pure data files are typically safe, and this includes image files, sound and video files, and certain specialized document files like Adobe's Portable Document Format files (with a .pdf extension). I've assembled a table of file types known not to support viruses in Table 12.1.

Table 12.1 File Types That Do Not Support Viruses.

Extension	What It Is
.avi	Video file
.gif	Image file
.jpg, .jpeg	Image file
.mp3, .mp2	Sound file
.mpg, .mpeg	Video file
.pcx	Image file
.pdf	Adobe document file
.png	Image file
.tif	Image file
.txt	Simple text file

File types that consist entirely or partly of executable code are the ones to be careful with. I've assembled the most common executable file types in Table 12.2. Before opening any file of a type listed in Table 12.2, scan it first for viruses. Most good antivirus products install a context menu item in Windows Explorer so that when you right-click on a file in Windows Explorer, you can kick off a virus scan by selecting the "Scan selected item for viruses" context menu item.

Table 12.2 File Types That May Contain Viruses.

Extension	What It Is	Type of Virus It May Contain
.bas	BASIC program file	Executable
.bat	Batch file	Executable or script
.class	Java programs	Executable
.cmd	Windows command script	Script
.com	Executable program file	Executable
.doc	Microsoft Word document	Macro
.dot	Microsoft Word template	Macro
.exe	Executable program file	Executable
.htm, .html	HTML document	Script
.ocx	ActiveX module	Executable
.pif	Program information file (PIF)	Executable
.ppt	Microsoft PowerPoint presentation	Macro
.scr	Screen saver	Executable
.vbs	VBScript program file	Script
.vsd	Microsoft Visio drawing file	Macro
.vss	Microsoft Visio template file	Macro
.xls	Microsoft Excel spreadsheet	Macro
.xlt	Microsoft Excel template	Macro

TIP: Note well that Table 12.2 is far from exhaustive. There may be other, less-common file types capable of containing viruses. It's good discipline to scan any file with an unknown or unfamiliar extension for viruses. It only takes a couple of seconds, and the time is very well spent.

Microsoft Office Files and File Extensions

Some people, when looking at Table 12.1, might object that I omitted RTF files (they have the extension .rtf, which stands for rich text format). These rich text files cannot themselves contain viruses, and a genuine RTF file is always safe to open. However, there is a truly scurvy trick that virus writers play with Microsoft Word macro viruses and rich text files. Here's how it works:

1. The virus writer creates a Word macro virus and embeds it in a Word document file.

2. The virus writer then changes the file extension of the document file from .doc to .rtf and distributes the virus via email, just as with any email virus.

3. A PC user receives the RTF file through email. Thinking that RTF files are safe, he or she opens the file with Microsoft Word.

4. Word ignores the .rtf file extension and inspects the last few hundred bytes of the file to see what file format it actually is. Recognizing its own file type, it then loads the bogus RTF file as a DOC file. The embedded macro virus runs, and the PC becomes infected.

The lesson here is simple: When dealing with Microsoft Office applications, *you cannot trust any file extension.* Office applications ignore the file extension and look inside the file at the data itself to determine what file type the file is. You can see the format specifier yourself by dragging and dropping a Word file onto Notepad. Notepad doesn't understand Word files (and it can't run macros, so you're safe trying this) but instead attempts to display the Word file verbatim. You'll see a lot of garbage characters, but right at the end of the file you'll see "Microsoft Word Document" and sometimes a version number. (Word 2000 will say "Word.Document.8" because Word 2000 is actually version 8 of Word.)

Because file extensions can be changed so easily, the *only* safe way to open *any* file in Microsoft Office is to turn off macros in Office first, before you open anything. Macros can be very dangerous and if you're using them you're playing with fire. I'll show you how to disable Office macros later in this chapter.

Havoc from Hiding Windows File Extensions

Windows is, in many respects, a virus writer's dream. When you install a fresh copy of Windows, or bring home a new PC on which Windows was preinstalled, file extensions are by default hidden for known file types. In other words, if you have a file named whatchamacallit.jpg, Windows Explorer will by default display it as simply whatchamacallit. You won't see the .jpg and thus won't know what type of file it is.

In the Windows philosophy, that's OK. The idea is this: Just double-click it and Windows will take appropriate action. Double-click an image file and it will open Internet Explorer to display the image. Double-click a Word document file and it will open Word to display the document for editing.

Double-click an executable file and Windows will execute it. Errkk.

Windows's habit of hiding file extensions has gotten many people in the habit of double-clicking a file just to see what sort of file it is. If the file happens to contain a virus, that turns the virus loose.

TIP: Never double-click a file you're not familiar with, especially if you can't see its extension and don't know what kind of file it is. Scan it first with your antivirus utility to be sure it's "clean."

Windows also allows more than one period character to be present in a file name. This may seem innocuous at first, but take a look at this perfectly legal Windows file name:

whatchamacallit.jpg.exe

This looks like it has two file extensions, but in truth, only the last three characters (and the period character) are truly a file extension. Confusing? Indeed. Now, look at the very same file name when Windows is set to hide file extensions:

whatchamacallit.jpg

That's an image file, right? Safe to double-click, right? *Wrong.* It's an executable file, and it could well be a virus.

I think you get the idea.

If your copy of Windows hides file extensions, unhide them right away. I explained how to do this in Chapter 6, under the heading "Clean Your Attachments Folder."

How Viruses "Space-Shift Right" to Hide File Extensions

Even if file extensions are displayed under Windows, the black hats still have a trick they can play on you. Windows file names allow spaces. Now, suppose you saw a file with the following file name:

whatchamacallit.jpg.exe

This is completely legal, but looks weird indeed and should set your antennas twitching immediately. On the other hand, Figure 12.1 shows you what Windows Explorer would display for that file name given a typical arrangement of columns in the Windows Explorer view pane.

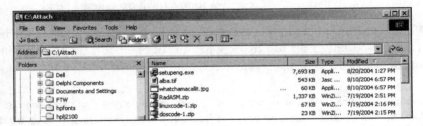

Figure 12.1

Hiding file extensions by inserting spaces.

Here, the *real* file extension (.exe) is hidden under the Size column, and all Windows gives you as a reminder is three little dots, which many people (in the heat of trying to get as much work done per unit of time as possible) might well miss.

A lot of recent email viruses use this trick. A file attachment will download, and when you use Windows Explorer to browse it, you may easily forget that the real file extension is hidden. The trick is used for viruses that come down in ZIP compressed archive files as well. We say it so often it's become a mantra, but it's worth saying again: *Never open any file attachment until you've scanned it for viruses.*

TIP: *Modern commercial antivirus utilities have automatic update features that download up-to-date virus signature files on a weekly or even daily basis. Still, you may have the bad karma to be hit by a brand-new virus in its first wave, before the antivirus people have had a chance to distill out and distribute an update. In that case, you may become infected by a virus if you open an infected attachment, **even if the antivirus utility says the attachment is clean.** (The poor antivirus utility can recognize only the* *viruses it has signatures for!) If you get email attachments that you want to open but want to be **really** safe in doing so, let them sit undisturbed on disk for at least a week. By that time your antivirus utility will almost certainly have distributed the signature (check to be sure an update came down!) and when you scan the attachment, the jig will be up and the virus will be spotted.*

GunkBuster's Notebook: Safe Viewing of Suspicious Files

A guy I know got a consulting gig from the widow of a computer geek, who had left several machines with tens of thousands of files on them. His widow wanted to know what was on the machines, but she was a technophobe and had heard enough about malware to be leery of fooling with the PCs and the files stored there. My friend was smart and could see immediately that the deceased geek was a file sharing fanatic, and that set off a number of alarms. So he proceeded carefully, beginning with a virus scan and then cataloging what was on the PCs.

One of the tools he used was Quick View Plus, which is a *file viewer*. Its sole job is to take a data file and display it as cleanly as possible. It does so in a way, furthermore, that will *not* trigger scripting or macro viruses. It supports 225 different data formats, many of them from programs that have long vanished over the horizon, like DOS WordPerfect. Displaying a file in Quick View is safe, even if the file contains a virus. Unlike Microsoft, Quick View seems to understand that "open" means "look at," *not* "run"!

Quick View was originally sold by Jasc and is now distributed by Avantstar, for $35. (Go to **www.avantstar.com**.) It's not as easy to find as when Jasc was the distributor, but if you hunt you can find it, and used copies can often be had on Amazon.com and eBay, sometimes for as little as $10. If you must deal with obsolete file formats, or Microsoft Office data files from multiple, untrusted sources, it's a must-have.

Disable Microsoft Office Macros

Microsoft Office documents and spreadsheets can contain executable program code, written in a macro programming language called Visual Basic for Applications (VBA). When you open an Office document containing such executable code, the code runs. VBA viruses are still an issue, especially within large organizations that have Office installed on hundreds or even thousands of PCs connected to a common network.

Putting executable code in what most people think of as text documents is bad, especially since fewer than 1 percent of Office users ever write or even use VBA macros. Macros are a little more sensible in spreadsheets, but either way, unless you know that you need VBA macro ability, you should disable Office macros on all your Office applications. Alas, you must disable them separately within each application.

Disabling macros is done by setting macro security to High. When macro security is set to High, only macros from a list of trusted sources will be allowed to run. All other macros will be disabled. Here's how to do it:

1. Bring up the Office application in question (any but Access; see later.).
2. Select Tools | Macro | Security.
3. Click the radio button marked "High" (see Figure 12.2).
4. Click OK.
5. Shut down and restart the application.

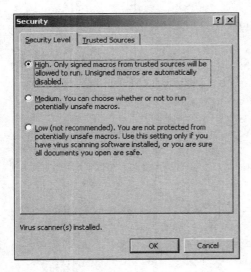

Figure 12.2

Setting Microsoft Office macro security to High.

This sequence will work identically for Word, Excel, PowerPoint, and Outlook. It will *not* work for Access. Access uses a different system for its macros, and macros do not run automatically when a database file is opened. If you receive a database file for Access (the extension is .mdb), you can inspect its macros by selecting Tools | Macros | Visual Basic Editor. When the VBA editor screen appears, select Tools | Macros. A box will appear listing all macros present in the database file. If any are unfamiliar to you, don't run them!

Macro Viruses in Office Add-Ins and Templates

Even when you've set the macro security level to High, that's simply for document or spreadsheet files. Templates and add-ins are another matter. By default, Office applications trust *all* templates and installed add-ins. Such blanket permissions are trouble in this virus-rotted world. In truth, *you* should be the one deciding *individually* what Office templates and add-ins to trust. Third party add-ins can carry viruses, and trusting them all without exception is simply stupid. You're better off having Office ask your permission for each add-in or template rather than trusting them all indiscriminately.

For Word, Excel, or PowerPoint, do this:

1. Select Tools | Macro | Security.
2. Click the Trusted Sources tab.
3. Uncheck the check box at the bottom, labeled "Trust all installed add-ins and templates" (see Figure 12.3).
4. Click OK.
5. Shut down and restart the application.

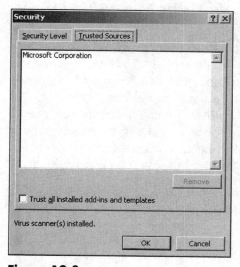

Figure 12.3

Removing blanket permission for templates and add-ins.

Each time you attempt to use a template or add-in, the application will ask you for permission by displaying the dialog shown in Figure 12.4. With macro security set to High, you must trust the source rather than simply the macro. Trusting Microsoft's macros, templates, or add-ins is fine. When you see the dialog shown in Figure 12.4, indicating an attempt (from a source you trust, like Microsoft) to run macros or an

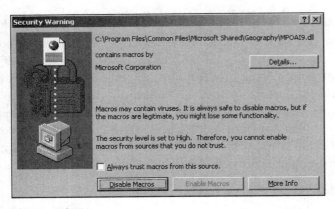

Figure 12.4

Granting macros permission to a trusted source.

add–in or open a template, click the check box labeled "Always trust macros from this source." When you do, the button labeled "Enable Macros" will become live. Click it and the macros in question will be allowed to run.

GunkBuster's Notebook: Office Macros and Legal Liability

Why am I so hard on Microsoft Office macros? Simple: *An office macro virus is a virus with your name on it.* When you send out a Word document or an Excel spreadsheet to a client, customer, or some other organization, you can be held legally responsible for damage done by macro viruses in those documents or spreadsheets. Corporations typically don't send computer programs to one another, but documents and spreadsheets are passed from company to company by the hundreds of billions every year.

Suppose a Word document carrying your company's letterhead is sent electronically to a customer and a virus inside the document gets loose and infects every document on the customer's file server. Whether there is damage or not, it may take days of high-priced techie time to put things right and get it all cleaned up. You will probably lose the customer, your reputation will be damaged, and you may find yourself talking to the customer's legal department. I'm not a lawyer, but I've been in the document business for a while, and if you don't believe me, ask your own legal counsel.

Macros are not worth the risk. There is little or nothing to be done with them that can't be done in other ways. The only sane IT policy is to turn macros off on all your copies of Microsoft Office and forbid their use by staff without exception.

Choose an Antivirus Utility

The most frequent question I'm asked about viruses is actually the least useful: What antivirus product should I buy? The answer is actually tricky and comes in two parts:

√   If you're careful about what you do on your PC, almost any current antivirus product will protect you virtually 100 percent of the time.

√   If you're careless about what you do on your PC (and especially online), it doesn't matter what antivirus utility you use. You're gonna get stung.

The point here is that antivirus products can only do so much. All of them require your cooperation, and none of them is absolute proof against really stupid activity. (It is amazing, though, how much they *will* catch.) In terms of cooperation:

√   You must install them.

√   You must use them to do regular system scans and scans of incoming files.

√   You must keep them up-to-date. (When does that update subscription run out?)

In terms of stupid activity, here are the biggies:

√   Mindlessly double-clicking on email attachments "just to see what they are." Heh. You'll find out!

√   Downloading massive numbers of files from Usenet newsgroups or peer-to-peer file sharing networks and then opening those files without scanning them.

√   Installing software from an untrusted source, especially using something other than a manufacturer's original silkscreen-labeled CD.

Against such stupidity, the gods themselves (even those named Norton or McAfee) contend in vain.

GunkBuster's Notebook: "Cool-Down" Time for Hot Files

Brand-new viruses are often introduced "into the wild" by begin uploaded them (or files infected with them uploading) to Usenet newsgroups or peer-to-peer file sharing networks. If you do a lot of file trading or downloading from such sources, you run a fair risk of contracting a virus so new that your antivirus utility won't have a signature for it in its virus signature database. Almost every person I've spoken with who has gotten viruses with a reputable antivirus utility in place and up-to-date was a heavy file trader or Usenet downloader

It's certainly true: The more files that pass through your hands, the more likely you are to see a virus; that's simple math. Where you get files does matter. If you get them from friends and they've been lying around on someone's hard drive for months, your antivirus utility will almost certainly be able to clear them. On the other hand, if there's a possibility of receiving files directly from virus writers or other black hat types, your antivirus utility may not be current enough to be foolproof. If you must traffic in files from untrusted sources, here's a suggestion: Download all such files to a directory that you create for the purpose...and let them sit for at least a week, to let the antivirus vendors catch up with newly released viruses. After downloaded files spend a week in the cooler, make sure your antivirus utility has been updated within a day or two and then scan the downloaded files.

This may be a tough discipline to enforce on yourself, but it's actually cheap insurance. Caution is the most effective antivirus utility there is!

Using Software Reviews for Purchasing Decisions

Never buy a software product without looking at reviews first—and not just at one site, but at several. In the case of antivirus utilities, it's not just the money at stake; it's the long-term proper functioning of your PC and the protection of your data.

When reading reviews, don't forget that every person's PC and software situation is different, and this usually accounts for the presence of both glowing and blistering reviews on the same product in the same place. Antivirus software is touchier than most, and it has a tendency to conflict unpredictably with other software. It's also more sensitive to the speed of the processor and the amount of memory installed. It's more important to look at the general picture, weighing the number of positive reviews against the negative.

It's also important to look at the site on which the reviews are published. As a former magazine editor with 15 years' tenure, I can tell you that advertising-supported magazines and Web sites will be much more reluctant than store sites like Amazon to publish a negative review. Also, user-written reviews will probably be more honest (if not necessarily more informative) than reviews coming from professional writers and columnists. Take notes as you read reviews, on paper or in a Notepad file, indicating how many positive or negative reviews you have read and where you found them.

Here are some good places to look for reviews:

√ Amazon is by far the best because it is not primarily advertiser supported and it sells almost everything. You'll find more user-written reviews here than almost anywhere else on the Web.

√ ZDnet.com publishes well-written and researched reviews of a great many computer products. Keep in mind that it is an ad-supported site.

√ About.com publishes both reviews and factual technical articles, which on the whole are well written and targeted at intermediate PC users.

√ Avoid TopTenReviews.com. Like most sites that focus on features grids, its reviews appear to count features much more than actually test them!

When reading reviews that mention prices, remember to check prices at the computer store or online. Prices change regularly and without notice.

What All Good Antivirus Utilities Should Have

Testing antivirus software is difficult because so much of its performance must be measured over a long period of time. As with the war on spam, it's a statistical game. Nearly all antivirus utilities will tag any virus that's been in the wild for two weeks or more. What's tougher to test is how quickly the vendor responds to new threats, and there's really no good way to do that.

Still, there are some things you should look for as you are shopping for antivirus utilities:

√ Automatic updates for virus signature data. Automatic updates for program code are good, but not essential.

√ The ability to scan individual directories or (especially) individual files, by way of a context menu (right-click) item in Windows Explorer.

√ The ability to scan memory for already running viruses.

√ The ability to schedule automatic scans of your entire PC on a periodic basis.

√ The ability to "clean" or "disinfect" infected files when they're found.

√ The ability to watch email attachments for files.

Things to Watch Out For

While reading reviews and asking friends at user group meetings, there are some potential "black marks" to look out for in antivirus products. Here's a quick list:

√ Some antivirus products rely heavily on Microsoft's Internet Explorer for their update mechanism. This is generally done to avoid conflicts with firewalls, but it's not a good idea to rely on IE for *anything* security related these days, and you're better off not using it at all.

√ In an effort to be all things to all people, some antivirus products have added features for catching worms, Trojan horses, spyware, adware, Windows Messenger service pop-up spam, and spam relays. This would be fine, except that such products are really targeted at modern, very fast, and memory-rich PCs. If you bought your PC in 2000 or before, such products will slow your machine down unacceptably. These products are also complex and difficult to install and configure.

√ Pertinent to the last point, some of these more recent, all-encompassing malware detectors will conflict with other software and (because some malware tries to disable antivirus software) are often very difficult to completely uninstall. Troubleshooting can be a nightmare. If they work well, you're golden. If they don't, you're in serious trouble!

√ Many modern antivirus products block Windows scripts by default. If you're using software that relies on Windows scripts (and you won't necessarily know if that's the case), that software will cease to work. Script blocking is fine unless you need the scripts. This issue goes well beyond Microsoft Office, and script blocking will interfere with Visual Studio, ASP content, MicroLogic's InfoSelect, and a lot of vertical market products that integrate with Office applications or IE. Make sure that in any antivirus product you're considering, script blocking can be easily and selectively turned off.

√ Some antivirus products come bundled with software firewalls. In my view none of these bundled firewalls is as good as standalone products like Zone Alarm Pro. Don't install them if you can avoid it because multiple firewalls installed on one system are usually trouble, especially for nontechnical users. (I'll come back to the firewalls issue in Chapter 14.)

√ To beef up their showing on magazine and Web site feature comparison charts, some antivirus products toss in spam filters, Registry cleaners, file and directory cleaners, and so on. I always hold such "incidental software" in great suspicion. If it's simply an add-in for product bragging rights, it may not be the best in its class and was probably what the vendor could license for cheap or throw together in a hurry. Antivirus software should stick to the knitting. It's about viruses. Don't bother with the other stuff.

Do You Need Multiple Antivirus Utilities?

If you prowl the Web reading discussions of the war on viruses, you'll occasionally hear people debating whether it's best to have more than one antivirus utility installed. For reasonably careful people it's overkill. On the other hand, if you're equipping a PC with antivirus software in a case where the PC has been used for a while without any virus protection at all, it may be useful to *manually* scan the "dirty" system with at least two major antivirus products.

That having been said, be aware that only one antivirus package can typically be active in memory at a time. You can install more than one on your PC, but you can only *run* one at a time. Furthermore, if you have one active in memory doing real-time scanning, shut it down before doing a manual scan with another package. Don't try to have two or more antivirus products in memory at once, scanning for viruses. They *will* conflict, and weird things will happen.

What I Recommend

Many authors of guides like this always punt when it comes to actual product recommendations, perhaps trying to avoid endorsing a particular product. I always find that attitude irritating: Hey, I paid for a book full of advice, now what's your advice?

So here's what I have to say about the majors. I have not tested all antivirus utilities by any means, but I've tested all the majors, and more than that, I've *used* them for a period of time, on my own personal machines—sometimes a lot of time. (I've used one version of Norton AntiVirus or another over the years since 1992.)

√   Norton AntiVirus 2001 is simple, effective, and easy to use—and it will not stress PCs from back to 1997 or so. (Figure a Pentium 266 as a minimum machine.) Unfortunately, Symantec has begun refusing to renew LiveUpdate subscriptions for Norton 2001, so the product may now be worthless. (It only renews subscriptions for its antivirus products for three years.) **www.symantec.com**

√   Norton AntiVirus 2002 is much like Norton 2001, but some features were added and it may require a Pentium 450 and more memory to use it well. Keep in mind the time limit on LiveUpdate subscription renewals. **www.symantec.com**

√   Norton AntiVirus 2004 is a terrible mess. (If you don't believe me, read the reviews on Amazon!) It requires a very fast machine (I would almost say 1.8 GHz or faster) and a lot of memory. Its main problem is the mountain of new features that Symantec has tried to cram into what was once a fairly simple, even elegant package. I had a lot of trouble installing it and found the performance of the PC after I got it working (which took some time and close attention) unacceptable. Uninstalling it was difficult. Fortunately, it was on a lab machine, and I just nuked the entire Windows partition as I do on lab machines every few months. You probably won't have that option. Alas, the venerable Norton AntiVirus product line seems to be at the end of the road. Don't buy it. **www.symantec.com**

√ McAfee VirusScan 2004 (version 8) is effective and reasonably easy to use, but it relies on Internet Explorer and ActiveX controls to do its virus signature updates. Setting it up is tricky (especially if IE is not your primary browser), but I am also very leery of the security risks that lie in using IE as an integral part of a security-related product. There are many security holes in IE, and there will be more because it's the favorite target of black hats everywhere. **www.mcafee.com**

√ Panda Software's Titanium Antivirus is quite simple, effective, and very fast, even on relatively old (and slow) PCs. It's very easy to install and does not rely on Internet Explorer. Among the Big Three, it's the one I now recommend, especially for nontechnical people. (When my now-unrenewable Norton 2001 subscription expires, Panda's Titanium will replace it.) Panda Titanium is one of an increasingly small minority of antivirus products that will work under Windows 95. One caution: If you connect to the Internet via dialup, don't try to buy it online. The downloadable file is *very* large and will take many hours to come down. Order the boxed product instead. **www.pandasoftware.com**

Beyond Norton, McAfee, and Panda, there are 15 or 20 more products worthy of consideration. PC-Cillin 2004 is fast and works well, but like many other modern products, it tries to do too much and its firewall is terrible. Kaspersky Labs Anti-Virus Personal 5 shows a lot of promise, but it's subtle and may confuse nontechnical users.

Beyond that, current antivirus products become *quite* obscure.

And that said, I recommend against using obscure antivirus products. Unlike a lot of software, antivirus utilities are useless without intensive, *fast,* ongoing support, especially in terms of creating signatures for new viruses and delivering them via auto-update as quickly as possible. You need a vendor with staying power. If the vendor of the antivirus product you're using goes under and stops updating the product, it's worse than useless because you may still think you're protected against viruses when you're not. Remember that you're buying a company as much as (or more) than buying a product!

Using Trial Products

Nearly all antivirus vendors provide free trial versions of their software, which typically operate for 30 days before expiring. Most such products are easy to uninstall (the recent Norton AntiVirus versions are an exception), so you can try a product for a few days and see if you "get" it and nuke it and try something else if you don't.

If you're really nontechnical, it might be useful to find someone with some tech experience to help you install, evaluate, and then uninstall antivirus trial products. It's extremely tricky to troubleshoot some antivirus software, especially when it conflicts with other software you have installed and use regularly.

GunkBuster's Notebook: Free vs. Commercial Antivirus Utilities

I like free software as much as anyone, but antivirus utilities represent one category of software where I feel that free isn't as good as paid. The reason is simple: What you need in a virus utility isn't simply a program that scans files for viruses. You need an ongoing update of virus signatures that is accurate and (this is crucial!) timely. The antivirus program software itself is almost incidental. The virus signature update files are the heart of your virus protection. If they're spotty (meaning that they don't contain signatures of all viruses doing the rounds, perhaps omitting "low-risk" viruses) or if they're old (meaning that they can spot any virus up through…2003), they're worthless. If a virus signature for a given virus isn't in your signature files, *your antivirus utility won't see it.*

Although free antivirus utilities exist, I question whether an organization without a continuous and predictable revenue stream can be both accurate and timely with virus signature updates. This becomes more and more critical as time goes on and more viruses and subtler viruses are released. Getting new viruses into signature files *fast* costs money, and maintaining a server farm to allow you to download those signature updates every day costs money.

There's also the issue of long-term survival. If the maintainer of a free virus protection system gives up and quietly closes shop one night, those automatic updates stop coming and the clock's ticking toward the moment that a virus will try to execute and the free utility won't be able to stop it.

Basically, it's not the initial cost, but the ongoing maintenance. Most commercial antivirus utilities have update subscription fees of $20 to $30 per year. That's about $2 a month. It won't break you, and it's probably the most important single service-related cost associated with your entire computer. Just do it.

Installing a Typical Antivirus Product

Installing an antivirus product isn't any more difficult than installing any other major application. If you've installed any significant software at all, the process will be familiar to you. In this section I'll briefly explain how Panda's Titanium Antivirus product installs. Virtually all other antivirus products install pretty much the same way.

You can buy a boxed product version of Titanium Antivirus, or you can download a 20 MB file over the Internet. The downloaded file is a Windows installer; the CD is autorun and will kick off the installer shortly after Windows detects it in the CD drive.

After asking you to select an installation language (English, Spanish, German, and so on), Titanium Antivirus looks for other installed antivirus utilities, and if it finds one, it pops up a dialog that recommends that you uninstall it. This isn't strictly necessary, if you're careful not to have two antivirus products running at the same time. On the other hand, if you don't intend to have two antivirus products installed, definitely uninstall the earlier one before continuing the install.

Titanium Antivirus will next ask if you if you wish to scan memory and hard drive for viruses during the install. If you're installing your first antivirus utility on a PC that's seen some use for a period of months or more and you haven't ever scanned it for viruses, I recommend scanning both memory and files during installation. This will be sure that you're starting "clean," and will prevent any virus skullduggery that might try to interfere with Titanium Antivirus's installer.

On the other hand, if you're changing antivirus utilities and have scanned the PC in question on a regular basis, it's enough to scan memory during installation. Still, to be completely safe, I recommend selecting both by checking the two check boxes (see Figure 12.5).

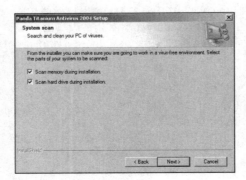

Figure 12.5

Selecting scans during Titanium Antivirus installation.

As fast as Titanium Antivirus is, on a slow machine with a lot of files, the scan may take as much as half an hour or more because it includes *all* files, not simply executable files. It will display a dialog with a progress bar to let you know how far along the process is (see Figure 12.6).

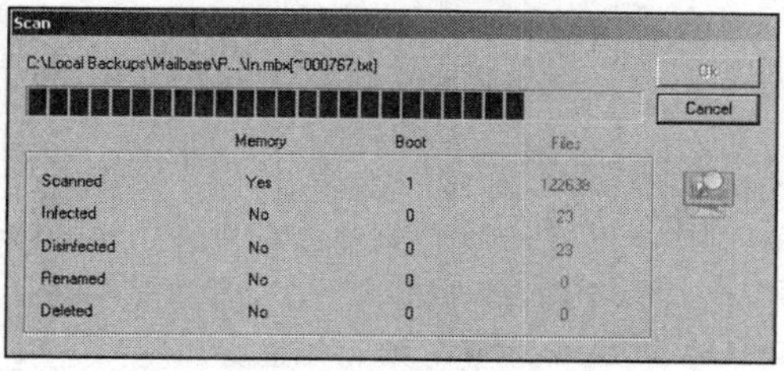

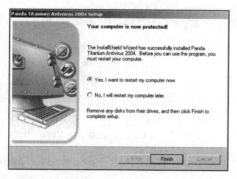

Figure 12.6

A virus scan progress bar.

After the scan is finished, Titanium Antivirus will verify its install directory with you and then perform the actual install. This will take only seconds on a reasonably quick PC. After the install, you'll have to reboot the PC (see Figure 12.7).

Figure 12.7

Choosing to reboot after a completed installation.

Once you've rebooted, Panda Titanium is running—and you're protected. However, depending on how recent the downloaded or boxed installer was, you will probably need to update the virus signature files, even after a new install. Titanium Antivirus will pop up a window over the taskbar tray to remind you to do this. You can also double-click the taskbar tray icon to bring up the Titanium Antivirus status window and request an update by clicking the "Update antivirus" link in the window (see Figure 12.8). Panda's automatic update machinery will take it from there.

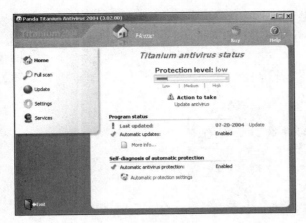

Figure 12.8
Updating the Titanium Antivirus signature files.

Most other antivirus installations follow this same general sequence. All will require that you reboot to complete the installation, and most will suggest (or even require) that you give permission to download updated virus signature files.

Using a One-Off Virus Removal Utility

If you don't have virus protection of any kind of your PC, sooner or later you will get stung. In extremely rare cases, you may receive (typically through a spam message) an email virus so new that your antivirus utility doesn't yet have a signature for it and won't spot it. If you're dumb and open email attachments that you're not expecting (and not simply from people that you don't know!), that brand-new virus can slip past your antivirus utility and infect your system.

If you know what virus it is, you can often download a free one-off removal utility from a reputable antivirus software vendor. I've removed viruses and worms from client PCs on a number of occasions using such utilities. Symantec (the vendor of Norton AntiVirus) makes such utilities freely available almost as soon as a virus is first spotted "in the wild." Go to the Symantec Web site, at this URL:

http://securityresponse.symantec.com/avcenter/tools.list.html

You'll find a list of many viruses, with downloadable tools for removing them from your PC. Note that such tools do *not* repair damage to files or directories caused by a virus infection! If your system is still functional, it will detect and remove the virus in question. Repairing the damage to the system once the virus is gone is up to you.

In most cases, you may not be entirely sure what virus is running on your system, and there's no foolproof way to tell, especially if you're nontechnical. If you think you have a virus and don't know what it is, buy and install a good antivirus utility and do a complete system scan. Running such a scan automatically once a week is a good idea. Don't let it go months between scans!

Summing Up—Use Good Virus Hygiene Daily

Good virus protection is necessary, but an installed antivirus utility is not a license to run any program you want and open any attachment that comes in the door. I've mentioned the problem of brand-new viruses and worms several times in this chapter; that's one risk. If your antivirus utility isn't regularly updated, it won't help you, and the older it gets, the more nearly worthless it is.

Keeping the viruses out of your system requires your cooperation. In closing this chapter, let me summarize a few points of good day-to-day virus hygiene:

√ Install a well-supported antivirus utility as soon as you get a new PC, or as soon as you reformat and reinstall the operating system on an existing PC.

√ Don't let the virus signature update subscription run out! The utility will tell you when you need to renew it. Do it. It's a small price to pay for keeping your PC alive and clean.

√ Schedule a weekly full-system virus scan. All good antivirus utilities allow you to do this. A full-system scan may take some time, but schedule it to run at 8 P.M. on a Friday night while you're out on a date and you'll never even know it's happening.

√ Never open an email attachment that you're not expecting, even if it seems to come from someone you know. If an unexpected attachment comes in from a friend or co-worker, email that person and ask if they did in fact send it to you.

√ Even when an attachment is sent from a known party, scan it with your antivirus utility before doing anything with it.

√ If someone sends you a zip archive with files in it, don't scan the archive. Instead, extract all the files to a directory *without* running them and then scan the extracted files. Some of the better antivirus utilities can scan files while they're still inside a zip archive, but not all of them do.

√ If you download software from Web sites or (especially) from Usenet newsgroups or peer-to-peer file sharing networks, scan the downloaded files with your antivirus utility before you attempt to install them. Better still: Let them sit in a directory for a week to allow your antivirus software to "catch up" with brand-new viruses.

√   Disable macros in Microsoft Office applications unless you desperately need them.

√   Do not leave removable media in disk drives when you turn a PC off. If you accidentally boot the PC with an infected diskette, Zip drive, or (more rarely) CD in a drive, a boot sector virus could take hold in your system.

√   Don't allow other people to open files or install software on your PC. This is especially important if you have teenagers at home and crucial if you know that they frequent newsgroups or file sharing networks.

If you can stick with all of that, you're very unlikely to become infected by a virus. Remember, it's happened to me only *once* in all the time I've had computers (almost 30 years now!) and that was because I took my antivirus utility down for technical reasons related to low-level programming and forgot to put it up again. If you work good virus hygiene into your daily computing habits, you're about as safe as you're ever going to be.

From viruses, at least.

Dealing with spyware, adware, and worms is another matter, with a whole different set of ways to be careful. Let's move on to adware and spyware.

Avoid Adware, Spyware, and Browser Bugaboos

Degunking Checklist:

√ Research a game or utility *thoroughly* before you install it to see whether it installs adware or spyware as a ride-along.

√ Install both Ad-Aware and Spybot Search & Destroy and run them regularly.

√ Avoid using Internet Explorer unless you can't possibly avoid it. *Huge* numbers of black hat exploits target security holes in IE.

√ Disable "install on demand" in whatever browser you're using to avoid "drive-by" installs of malware.

√ Use the Mozilla Firefox browser to suppress pop-up ads.

√ Don't go to porn or warez sites, which are notorious for planting browser exploits on unwary surfers' Web browers.

√ If you must surf to unsafe sites, create and use a limited privileges Windows user account when doing so.

S everal years ago, I downloaded a new game after seeing a review on the Web. The game was actually good enough that I eventually paid for it. However, the "free" version came with something a little extra: A talking purple ape named Bonzai Buddy. Created using Microsoft's Agent software (which also gave us Mr. Paper Clip and that animated puppy helper), Bonzai Buddy appropriated a significant chunk of my desktop screen, squirming around and speaking through my sound card in an annoying voice, cracking bad jokes, and trying to sell me things.

Bonzai Buddy left a fair amount of gunk on my PC, and getting rid of him completely was surprisingly tricky. The experience left me with a profound caution of what we now call spyware and adware. It also reminded me that there are two kinds of "free," as I've mentioned before and will again shortly.

In this chapter I'll take up what I call "minor malware," which includes adware, spyware, and various black hat exploits that are attracted to Internet Explorer like flies to...shortcake. As with almost all degunking solutions, the answer is about 60 percent psychology and 40 percent technology. Basically, the more dumb things that you do, the harder the cleaning up will be. Work smart and clean less—it's just as true of your PC as it is of your desk or your garage.

Adware vs. Spyware

Many people speak of adware and spyware as though they were interchangeable and heap their excretions on both equally. Although the boundary between them can get fuzzy sometimes, we need to be fair here:

√   Adware is software (like a game or utility) that displays ads or sales pitches of some kind without attempting to send information on your activities back to HQ.

√   Spyware may also display ads, but it "phones home" with information about what Web sites you visit.

Technically, even spyware doesn't log your keystrokes or search your hard drive for passwords. Malware that does things like that breaks the law and is more properly considered a Trojan horse. The idea behind spyware is to gather data about what users are interested in so that ads may be targeted more precisely to them and, as a secondary benefit (as a service to the advertisers), to see how many people are actually looking at the ads. This is currently legal, even if most of us consider it a gross invasion of privacy.

Apart from the privacy violation issue, adware and spyware are bad news for two main reasons:

√ They take system resources, sometimes a lot of them. Adware runs all the time you have the supported package open and running. Worse, some adware or (especially) spyware packages install themselves as Windows services, which means that they run in the background, all the time, even when you're not using the supported package. One adware item installed and running may not slow your system down very much. But if you've installed five or six adware-supported software packages, your system may slow down to a crawl or crash, especially if it's old, slow, and memory starved.

√ Adware and spyware have a habit of playing fast and loose with Windows resources and may conflict with unrelated software and cause system crashes. In response to adware removers like Ad-Aware, some adware developers have begun fighting back, making their products more difficult to remove from your PC. One particularly obnoxious spyware package actually uninstalls Ad-Aware on systems where it finds Ad-Aware already installed. Adware and spyware are thus a major source of gunk on your Windows system.

The Two Kinds of Free

This is a good place to recap my warning about the two very different kinds of "free" in the software world:

√ There is really and truly free, no catches. Much of the best software you can use these days is free and open source, meaning that the original program source code used to create the program is included. Not all freeware comes with source code, but freeware that is truly free asks nothing from you as a condition of running it. (Some freeware authors request donations, and it's honorable to send the author something if you like the program.)

√ Then there is "free"—with a catch. The most common catch is that you have to allow the software to download ads and display them in one corner of the software's main window. You may also have to allow the software to report back to its HQ what ads you clicked on, or even what Web sites you navigated to in your Web browser, quite apart from the ads themselves. Adware and spyware are this kind of "free," which really isn't, especially when you consider the havoc it can wreak on your PC.

Know What You're Installing!

The cornerstone of my advice regarding malware gunk will always be this: Be aware of what you're doing, and don't do stupid things. All the technology in the world won't prevent you from falling prey to malware if you just keep on keeping on as you always have.

Avoiding spyware and adware is pretty simple, though the impatient will doubtless squirm: *Research the "free" product you're thinking about downloading and using.* Research it *thoroughly.* Half an hour checking it out may well save you several lost days trying to undo the damage that some "free" product causes.

Google these (where *product* is the name of the product you're researching):

Is *product* **adware?**

Is *product* **spyware?**

Don't just read one or two items, and pay attention to when a given item was posted. Old reviews may not apply to new releases of the same package.

TIP: Sometimes a product may or may not be spyware or adware, depending on its version. The immense amount of bad publicity in the last year or so has made some vendors drop the adware/spyware feature (and sometimes go to a paid business model) rather than have warnings that "SlobShare is spyware!" posted all over the Web. The BearShare peer-to-peer file sharing utility was adware for a long time, but in mid-2004 it moved to an adware-free model. I predict that this will be a trend, so keep your eyes open!

One way to tell if a product is open source (and hence truly free) is to look on a Web site called SourceForge (**http://sourceforge.net**), which caters to the open-source community. You'll find a search feature on the main page. If a product you're interested in is hosted on SourceForge, it's open source and thus truly free, without any adware or spyware. You can download the product there as well.

GunkBuster's Notebook: Look for Where the Category Experts Hang Out

The very best way to find out where adware and spyware hide is to ask what I call "category experts." These are people who are fanatical about a given software category because it's their hobby, line of work, or general passion. There are enthusiast forums catering to almost every software category, and this is where the category experts hang out, answering questions and tendering opinions. For example, if you're interested in file sharing utilities (which are notorious hotbeds of adware and spyware), you *must* read the forums at **www.zeropaid.com** and **www.slyck.com**, both of which are portals to the file sharing community. Category experts will know the ugly details on almost any piece of software in their category, and if you can find an enthusiast forum for your category, you're ahead of the game.

Finding forums in a given category can be surprisingly difficult. One trick is to use Google to search for the name of the category and one of the popular forum software products. Here are the best-known ones:

√ phpBB

√ vBulletin

√ Snitz

√ DCForum

The reason this works is that almost all of these forums have a small-print statement such as "Powered by phpBB" or "Powered by vBulletin" at the bottom of every forum page. Take advantage of these "Powered by..." tags and create a Google search like this:

"OCR software" "Powered by phpBB"

What Google will return are pages in online forums where the text *OCR software* appears. Many may be off topic, but scan a few and you're likely to find a forum devoted to the software category that you're researching. Most forums have rules and "Intros for Newbies" and you should read them carefully to avoid coming off as an idiot the first time you post something—like a question that's been asked 20 times in the past week.

Good Adware/Spyware Research Sites

There is a great deal of interest in spyware and adware, and there are a lot of excellent sites for people researching these topics. Some of the sites are security-expert oriented and are quite technical, but many have material (such as lists of known adware/spyware products) suitable for nontechnical people as well. Here the two best that I know of:

√ Counterexploitation (**http://cexx.org/**). Probably the best of breed, with excellent spyware/adware lists, advice on removal, and a discussion forum for questions.

√ DoxDesk (**http://doxdesk.com/parasite/**). Provides a nice list of spyware and adware, with a script that can determine if your copy of Internet Explorer (V5 or above) is infected with known malware.

Note that some of the largest spyware/adware companies have been very aggressive in filing lawsuits against small Web sites who list them as spyware or even adware. One such litigator involves a product called Gator, created by

Claria. Claria's definition of spyware is not the same one the rest of us use, and that's been a source of considerable confusion. Fortunately, whatever it actually is, most of the spyware/adware removal tools will remove Gator from your PC.

Use Anti-Spyware Software

The spyware/adware plague has spawned a growth industry in removal tools. Much like antivirus utilities, these products will scan your PC for spyware and adware, present you with a list, and then remove the items you specify.

Why not remove all of them? Who'd want that stuff? Note well that removing adware from your PC may make the application that installed it unusable. In one sense this is OK—part of the "deal" is that they gave you the software for free...*if* you agreed to look at their damned ads. The fact that this agreement is buried at the end of 24 pages of dense legalese in the end-user license agreement (EULA) makes that logic questionable in my view, but it's still the way things work and you need to be aware of it.

Most of these tools are commercial and cost from $20 to $70. However, two of the very best are free, though donations are requested: Lavasoft's Ad-Aware and Patrick Kolla's Spybot Search & Destroy. Which do I recommend? Both! I've found that each has abilities the other lacks, but together they can get all but the very worst spyware and adware off of your system. (However, if you only choose one, choose Spybot.)

Installing and Using Spybot Search & Destroy

Spybot S&D downloads as a conventional Windows installer. Install it as you would any Windows application, by running the installer. (It doesn't come with any spyware or adware!) Download it from the author's site:

www.safer-networking.org/en/index.html

The first time Spybot runs, it will ask if you want it to back up the Windows Registry. This is a good idea, though it takes some time, especially on older and slower PCs. It will also check to see if any updates have been made available since the release of the version that you downloaded. Downloading and installing these updates is important. As with antivirus utilities, Spybot cannot remove adware or spyware it doesn't know about. New spyware species appear all the time, and the Spybot team does a wonderful job keeping up with it, but you must download and install the updates from Spybot's HQ to take advantage of this feature.

When you run Spybot, it will come up with the window shown in Figure 13.1. To kick off a scan of your PC for spyware gunk, click the Check for Problems button.

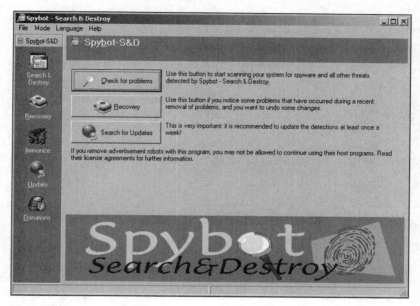

Figure 13.1

Spybot Search & Destroy's user interface.

Spybot will begin scanning for known adware and spyware. There are a lot of adware/spyware signatures in Spybot's database, and if you have a lot of files on your system (or a slow PC), this step may take awhile. I've seen it take half an hour on a full hard disk in a slow machine, and that may not be worst case. As it scans, it will display a growing list of adware/spyware items that it has identified and tagged for removal.

Spybot will present the full list of items for you to look at when the scan is done. The list is hierarchical. The main list is by the name of the spyware or adware technology (for example, Avenue A). Each technology item can be expanded by clicking on the + symbol in the left margin. In the expanded list, individual files belonging to the parent technology will be shown. See Figure 13.2 for an example.

Each item will be shown with a check in the check box to the left of the item name. This check mark means that Spybot will delete the item on its "Fix Selected Problems" scan. You can uncheck any specific item by clicking the check box. Any item without a check mark will be left on your system after the scan.

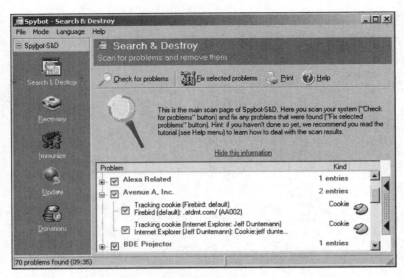

Figure 13.2
Spybot's display of identified spyware and adware.

To remove the items that Spybot has identified, click the Fix Selected Problems button. Spybot will initiate a scan of the identified spyware and adware components, removing them from your hard drive. Only the items that you deliberately unchecked will be passed over.

If you're like most people, the first time you run Spybot (or Ad-Aware), a *lot* of spyware and adware gunk will turn up. However, once you've cleaned the gunk from your PC, running the utility once every two weeks—or once a month, if you don't do a great deal of Web surfing or software installation—will keep spyware and adware gunk to a bare minimum.

Why Keep Adware?

Keeping certain adware (or even spyware) on your PC may be necessary if there is an ad-supported product that you want to continue using. More and more, ad-supported software checks to see if its associated adware has been removed, and if it is, the product may refuse to run.

How will you know? There's no general way to know until you attempt to run a product and it fails. In that case, reinstall the software (including its adware) and run Spybot again. If you had it remove everything it found during its previous run, the only adware you should see after the second run will be the adware supporting the product you want to retain. Take note of it—you will have to uncheck its components before the next run or the product will refuse to run and you'll have to install it yet again.

This is a lot of fooling around. Almost all software has competitors. Look around for something that does the same job, only without adware or spyware. You may have to pay for it—maybe as much as $20! If you're lucky you'll find a truly free application. Either way, it's better than having some "free" program clog your PC with gunk!

GunkBuster's Notebook: Don't Panic over Cookies!

Unless you're really careless about what you install on your PC, most of what utilities like Ad-Aware and Spybot will find will be cookies. Cookies cause a lot of confusion and it's worth clearing up some misconceptions here.

A cookie is a small file that is created on your hard drive by the Web browser when directed by a Web site. It's a way for a Web server to "recognize" who you are when you navigate to a Web site. That way, the site can say, "Welcome back, Peter Novilio!" without your having to enter a username and a password. A cookie is not only unique to you, it's unique to you working from a particular Windows account. (More on Windows accounts a little later.) The Web site of the *New York Times* placed a cookie on my PC to identify me, as did the Netstumbler Forum server and several e-commerce sites that I use regularly, all of which was done with my blessing. Cookies save me time and keystrokes, especially on sites I use many times a day for research (like the *NYT*) that would otherwise require me to log in each time I went there to look something up.

Cookies are not programs and do not consume computer processor power or memory. They're quite small and take only a little hard disk space. Although they can be planted by adware or spyware, cookies *themselves* are not adware or spyware. Cookies are bad only when they are the tools of nosy adware or spyware, and in those cases, they should be removed by Ad-Aware or Spybot. Nuking all your cookies will force you to manually log in to any sites that had relied on cookies to identify you. It's possible to forbid a browser to place a cookie on your PC at all, and while some (slightly paranoid) people do that, it's really overkill. Some e-commerce sites will not do business with you unless you allow the use of cookies.

My advice: Let an anti-adware/spyware utility choose cookies for deletion based on their association with known adware or spyware systems.

Installing and Using Ad-Aware

Although Spybot Search & Destroy is my personal favorite, I also use Lavasoft's Ad-Aware. I've found, over the last year or two, that each program finds things that the other doesn't. Spybot is simpler and a little more conservative. Ad-Aware is more complex and finds a few more adware items than Spybot typically does. It also floods you with information that I consider irrelevant, like Most Recently Used (MRU) item entries in the Windows Registry. These have no relation to either spyware or adware, and I've often wondered why Ad-Aware takes up time looking for MRU entries.

That said, however, Ad-Aware is worth having, if you're willing to give it some study and read the online help. You can download it from Lavasoft's Web site:

www.lavasoftusa.com

What you're looking for is the free version of the product, Ad-Aware SE Personal Edition. Lavasoft sells a number of more advanced versions of the product, but its paid product line is targeted at large companies and universities and doesn't have much that typical home users need beyond what the free product offers.

Ad-Aware looks and works a lot like Spybot. Its main display is shown in Figure 13.3. You click its Start button and it scans files on your PC against a database of tens of thousands of known spyware and adware components, and a handful of other things.

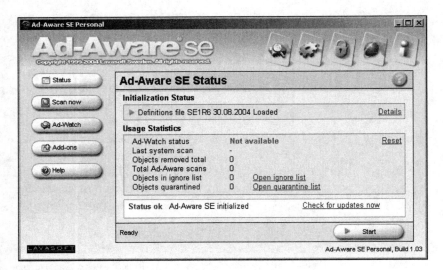

Figure 13.3

Ad-Aware's main window.

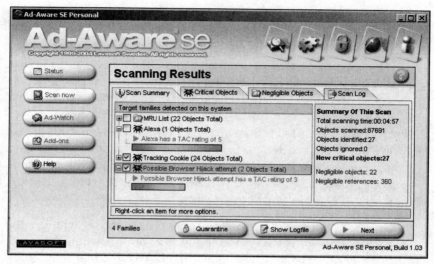

Figure 13.4

Ad-Aware's display of identified adware/spyware components.

When its scan is finished, it displays a list like that shown in Figure 13.4. If you click on the + box to the left of a listed item, you will see a Threat Assessment Chart (TAC) value to give you some sense for how serious a threat an identified item is. I feel that anything with a value of 5 or less is not an especially serious threat.

Ad-Aware uses some loaded verbiage that I think might be confusing or needlessly alarming, especially to nontechnical people. For example, as you can see in Figure 13.4, an item called a "browser hijack attempt" is provided and has a TAC rating of only 3…and in fact the item is a Web shortcut leading to AOL's ever-present "Try me free" pitch. Irritating as AOL's marketing may be, that's not what I would call "hijacking"!

Unlike Spybot, Ad-Aware does *not* default to marking every item found for elimination. You must place a check in the empty check box to the left of an item to mark it for deletion, otherwise Ad-Aware will leave the item in place. Once you have check-marked everything you wish to remove, click the Next button to kick off the cleanup process. Ad-Aware will eliminate all items that you marked for deletion.

GunkBuster's Notebook: Is Adware/Spyware Inoculation a Good Idea?

Both Spybot Search & Destroy and Ad-Aware were originally designed to remove spyware and adware *after* it has been installed on your PC. Both products now offer a feature that amounts to "inoculation" against the installation of spyware and adware. Spybot calls this the Immunize feature; Ad-Aware calls it Ad Watch. In both cases, the product installs an engine that watches for files with certain names as they are written to disk and prevents those files from being written, and it also prevents adware/spyware executables from running.

So what's not to love here? My concerns are mostly with system performance. If you have too many software guardians installed on your PC watching too many things at the same time, your system will slow down. Older, slower machines may slow down to a point where you won't find their performance acceptable. Another concern is that the newer antivirus products also watch for the installation of adware and spyware, so you may have multiple utilities doing the same thing, all consuming PC resources while they're doing it—and possibly conflicting with one another in the process.

Virus protection software and a good firewall are essential, so if you don't have a muscular enough PC to handle all three, adware/spyware inoculation is the least necessary. Besides, with some simple steps (covered earlier) and a little common sense and caution, you can avoid nearly all adware and spyware.

Watch Out for Phony Spyware or Adware Removers

As if spyware and adware weren't bad enough, we now have software that claims to remove spyware—but is in fact spyware itself! This is a form of social engineering, and simple fraud. Some self-proclaimed spyware removers are world-class malware. One supposed anti-spyware product apparently installs something called Favoriteman, an infamous spyware item that installs its own favorites in your IE favorites menu.

Many of the phony remover products are stolen and modified versions of Spybot Search & Destroy. A good example is SpyBan, which had no anti-spyware features at all but was a Trojan horse program that installed all kinds of malware before aborting. Quite a few of these phony products have been forced off the Net (SpyBan is one of them), but many others are still out there.

The solution? Thoroughly research *anything* before you install it, and when unsure, stick with brand-name products.

Implement an Adware/Spyware Strategy

1. Run Spybot first. If you uncover a lot of gunk, remove it using Spybot and then install Ad-Aware. If you uncover only a little gunk, Spybot may be all you need.

2. Install Ad-Aware and do a full scan.

3. Ignore any MRU items found. They have nothing to do with adware/ spyware.

4. Look at the Critical Objects list. Check anything with an Ad-Aware TAC rating of 6 or more. If anything sounds familiar to you or is something that you know you use (for example, the Alexa toolbar), leave it unchecked so that Ad-Aware will not remove it. Ad-Aware is a little more aggressive than Spybot. Research things on the Web that you're not sure about, to see what they are.

5. If after you run your scans and remove all identified adware or spyware you find that some of your installed applications will not run, reinstall the balky applications and do another scan with Ad-Aware. Make a note as to which adware/spyware elements have returned, and (assuming you want to continue using the ad-supported products in question) avoid removing those adware/spyware elements in future scans.

GunkBuster's Notebook: Is Alexa Spyware?

If you have Internet Explorer installed on your PC (and who doesn't?), you probably also have something called Alexa, and both Ad-Aware and Spybot will tag it during their adware/ spyware scans. There's been a lot of argument about what Alexa actually does and whether it qualifies as adware or spyware.

Here's the scoop. Alexa is owned by Amazon, and it's a service that finds Web links that are "related" to the one in your Internet Explorer window. There are two ways that Alexa finds its way onto your PC:

√ In its simplest form, it's installed with Internet Explorer, as the menu item Tools | Find Related Links.

√ You can install the full Alexa toolbar from **www.alexa.com**.

With the Alexa Web site, Amazon is trying to do for the Web what it does for books: give you popularity statistics and allow you to post reviews. The "related links" menu item is similar to the "People who bought *Moby Dick* also bought…" feature on Amazon.com. It's basically "People who clicked on Snopes.com also clicked on…" and this depends on Alexa gathering statistics on who's clicking what. If you use Alexa, it reports your Web surfing history. If you don't use it, it doesn't report anything. Alexa is an implementation of something called *collaborative filtering*, in which many people share their insights to produce a statistical database that helps sort out popularity or relatedness among a large number of items, like products or Web sites.

The fact that it adds your Web surfing history (anonymously) to its statistical model technically makes it a species of spyware, and if the concept bothers you, definitely let Ad-Aware or Spybot remove it from your PC. On the other hand, Alexa doesn't try to hide what it does, and many people swear by it as a research tool. (I'm lukewarm on it myself.) My point here is that there are some gray areas in the spyware wars, and you shouldn't panic when Ad-Aware puts a big red bug in a window beside the name of something it's found.

Be Mindful of Browser Bugaboos

Of all the various security holes and malware exploits that have been documented in PC software, a large proportion of them involve Web browsers. Part of the problem may be that Web browsers represent an "intimate" connection between your PC and a server somewhere else in the world, about which you know very little. Many different kinds of data can come over that connection: words, pictures, animations, sounds, music, movies. The Web, moreover, was designed to be a universal platform, able to deliver future forms of content that we haven't even imagined yet. Its designed-in versatility allows the PC-Web server connection to be misused very easily by black hats, who have become extremely adept at delivering gunk in the form of malware. Some of that gunk is "sticky" gunk that comes down silently, hides well, and is very difficult to remove.

I call the various exploits based on Web browsers "browser bugaboos." In the following sections we'll talk about what they are and how you can avoid them.

The Hazards of Internet Explorer

The vast majority of browser bugaboos are focused on Microsoft's Internet Explorer Web browser. This is due to a number of factors:

√ Microsoft's design philosophy was "trusting." It assumed that IE's machinery would not be misused and did not deliver it with adequate security enabled.

√ IE is simply everywhere; it has about 90 percent of the browser market. This makes it a prime target for black hats looking for software to subvert.

√ IE's fundamental browser extension technology, ActiveX, is a serious hazard.

The Internet Explorer security issue became so bad during the first half of 2004 that some of Microsoft's own people admitted in public forums that they consider IE too dangerous to use themselves. Having studied the problem at length, I've come to agree. Although Microsoft's most popular products (IE, Outlook, Outlook Express, and Office) all have serious security issues, if you must unload one of them, Internet Explorer is the one to dump.

As a replacement, I recommend Mozilla Firefox. I've used Firefox as my primary Web browser for almost a year and have had no trouble with it, except for an occasional Web site created with Microsoft-specific extensions to HTML. The browser itself is fast, stable, and much more resistant to the sort of gunk attributable to browser bugaboos.

Download Firefox from the Mozilla Web site:

www.mozilla.org/products/firefox/

It installs very easily (detailed instructions are on its Web site) and "just works."

At this point, we need to address some of those browser bugaboos in detail.

Drive-By Installs

A lot of adware and spyware seems to appear by a sort of black magic. I've helped numerous people who swear they've never installed anything dicey (which was true; some had barely installed *anything*) or opened any email attachments, and yet when their PCs bogged down, a scan I did with Spybot Search & Destroy revealed layers and layers of adware and spyware gunk.

My clients were left scratching their heads and wondering if it was evil spirits. Not so—it was something a lot less spooky (but no less gunk-y), which we've come to call *drive-by installs*.

It comes as a shock to a lot of people, but it's true: If you surf to a Web site with a misconfigured Web browser (especially Internet Explorer), *that Web site can silently and automatically install malware on your PC.* This stealthy dropping of malware on a PC through a Web browser is a drive-by install.

Drive-by installs are made possible by a Web browser feature called "install on demand." Several Web browsers support this, but Microsoft's Internet Explorer is the most prevalent. Internet Explorer allows the automatic download and installation of something called ActiveX components. These are small programs created specifically to be downloaded and installed inside a Web browser to enhance the browser's ability to display Web content. The idea was that if a Web surfer came to a site that wanted to show an animation or play music, the site would download an ActiveX *browser helper object* (often you'll hear people speak of these as "BHOs") to do the work. It's a good idea, but Microsoft naively assumed that the feature would not be misused—and alas, install on demand ActiveX components became the most-abused Web browser feature in Internet history. As useful as they can sometimes be, your best bet is to disable install on demand on any Web browser you might be using.

Disabling Install On Demand in Internet Explorer

Disabling install on demand in Internet Explorer is easy, and probably the single most important "tweak" to IE that you can ever make—apart, perhaps, from abandoning it entirely. Here's the step-by-step:

1. Select Tools | Internet Options.
2. Click the Advanced tab.
3. Look down the page of options until you see two adjacent options: Enable Install on Demand (Internet Explorer) and Install on Demand (Other). Both are checked by default. Uncheck both (see Figure 13.5).
4. Click OK.
5. Close and restart Internet Explorer.

Beefing Up Security in the Internet Zone

The Internet is a wilder and woollier place than it was when Internet Explorer was designed, and if you must use IE (which I no longer recommend), at least turn security to High in the Internet Zone. By default, security is set to Medium in the Internet Zone. Changing this value to High will probably keep most malware from coming down to you through known exploits.

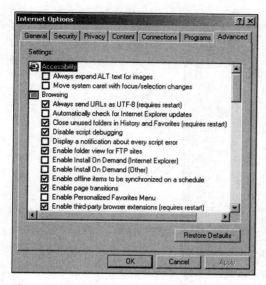

Figure 13.5

Disabling install on demand in Internet Explorer.

Note that I said "known." The real problem with Internet Explorer is its ubiquity, prompting the black hats to be constantly searching for new exploits. Even with IE security set to High in the Internet Zone, it's very possible (even likely) that new exploits will be discovered that operate irrespective of the security level in any zone.

Here's how to jack up the security level in Internet Explorer's Internet Zone:

1. Select Tools | Internet Options.

2. Click the Security tab.

3. Make sure the Internet Zone is selected in the icon bar at the top of the dialog.

4. Click the Default Level button at the bottom of the dialog.

5. Move the slider bar at the left of the dialog up to High (see Figure 13.6).

6. Click OK.

7. Close and restart Internet Explorer.

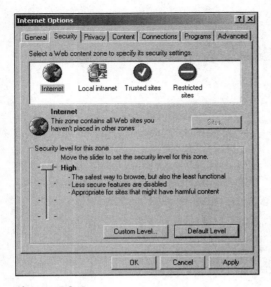

Figure 13.6
Setting Internet Explorer Internet Zone security to High.

Disabling Install on Demand in Mozilla Firefox

There is a feature in Mozilla Firefox analogous to install on demand, though it doesn't go by that precise name and isn't as "loose" as that of Internet Explorer. Firefox allows the downloading and installing of extensions, but it always prompts you before it installs them. Nonetheless, malware extensions exist, and unless you know you need to install a Firefox extension (and have researched it thoroughly to make sure it's legitimate), I think it's a good idea to disable the ability of a Web site to install an extension. That way there's no possibility that you will allow installation by mistake. (It's been done!) If you need to install an extension at a later time, you can always reenable extension installation.

Step-by-step:

1. Select Tools | Options.

2. Click the Advanced icon in the left margin.

3. Scroll down to the Software Update section.

4. Uncheck "Automatically download and install updates to extensions" and "Allow Web sites to install software" (see Figure 13.7).

5. Click OK.

6. Close and restart Firefox.

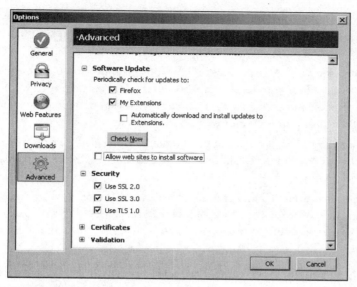

Figure 13.7
Disabling install on demand in Mozilla Firefox.

Block Pop-Ups!

Another very common browser bugaboo is the pop-up window. These are very common as advertising on the Web. Sometimes they "pop under" and are created *beneath* your current browser window, and you don't see them until you close your browser window. Then you have to close the pop-under window or windows. You may also have had the experience of navigating to an extinct Web site that has been bought by "pornsquatters" who buy the domain and mount a porn site pitch on the domain. Trying to "back-up" or close the window triggers one obnoxious pop-up after another, and you're left trying to kill them individually, like some madcap online version of the old "whack a mole" carnival game, only with dirty pictures instead of moles.

While annoying in the extreme, such pop-ups do not damage your PC. Pop-ups can be more sinister, in conjunction with spam-based phishing scams. (I'll have more to say about phishing and Internet scams in general in Chapter 15.) You get a spam that warns you that your eBay (or PayPal, or bank) account will be closed unless you verify your account information. A link in the email takes you to an authentic-looking Web site and a pop-up window appears, with fields to fill in with your account login and password, and possibly credit card numbers as well. If you fill in those fields and click OK, your information is whisked off to some black hat hideaway on another continent, who then pick the account clean and perhaps even establish new accounts under your name and credit rating.

Pop-ups are occasionally useful, but the bad guys have rendered them too dangerous to use. I powerfully recommend that you block pop-ups completely. This can be done in any of several ways:

√ Switch Web browsers. Mozilla Firefox has a powerful pop-up blocker that is enabled by default. If you frequent a Web site that has useful pop-ups (these do exist), Firefox allows you to build an exception list containing sites that will be allowed to pop up windows over the browser.

√ Install a software firewall with a pop-up blocker. ZoneAlarm Pro is the best of these, hands down. I'll explain firewalls in general and discuss ZoneAlarm in Chapter 14.

√ Install a separate pop-up blocker utility. There are many of these available, but if you use a browser with a pop-up blocker or a firewall with a pop-up blocker, a separate utility is unnecessary and will be one more thing using cycles on your PC!

My favorite pop-up blocker for Internet Explorer (which I now use only on sites that require it) is not a pop-up blocker at all but the Google Toolbar. You can download it free from the Google Toolbar site:

http://toolbar.google.com/

There's a nice page for testing the effectiveness of a pop-up blocker technology at Emerald Technology, Inc. They have mounted a page that will attempt to pop up windows using several pop-up mechanisms. If you navigate to this page and don't see any pop-ups, you're protected!

www.emeraldpopstop.com/testpop.aspx

Finally, the very recent and controversial Windows XP Service Pack 2 modifies Internet Explorer so that it now blocks pop-up windows. I do not at this time recommend installing Service Pack 2 (it breaks a number of existing applications, especially older ones) and provides nothing that you can't obtain by installing a good firewall and moving to a browser other than Internet Explorer.

GunkBuster's Notebook: Disabling Internet Messenger Pop-Ups

There is a species of pop-up window that has nothing to do with the Web or with Web browsers at all. These are much less common than Web pop-ups, but apart from being annoying, they have their own technical dangers and should be blocked as well.

These so-called *messenger service pop-ups* are caused by misuse of a network service that's built into every copies of Windows: Windows Messenger Service. It's used to send messages across local area networks. It can also be used to send messages over the Internet, which was never the intent of its inventors.

Of course, if you're at home and don't have a network (or if your network consists of your PC and your spouse's PC, or maybe one for the kids) the Windows Messenger Service is of very little use. It's best to disable the service, which will end messenger pop-ups completely. Here's how:

1. Select Start | Settings | Control Panel.
2. Double-click the Administrative Tools applet to run it.
3. Double-click the Services item.
4. Look down the list of services for the Messenger service. Double-click Messenger.
5. In the dialog that appears, pull down the Startup Type list and select Disabled.
6. Click the Stop button. It will take Windows a few seconds to stop Windows Messenger Service. Once it's done, you'll see "Service Status: stopped" in the dialog (see Figure 13.8).
7. Click OK.
8. Reboot your PC.

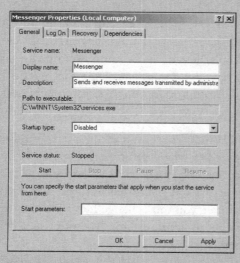

Figure 13.8
Disabling Windows Messenger Service.

Use Limited Windows Accounts for Web Surfing

One way to limit the damage that malware (of any species) can do to your system is to limit its privileges on the operating system. You have this power if you're running either Windows 2000 or Windows XP. (For Windows 95, 98, or ME you're out of luck.) The easiest way to limit malware's privileges is to limit *your* privileges, and that involves creating a limited user account.

First of all, what are "privileges"? In Windows, certain actions are controlled by the operating system's innermost machinery. These actions include reading, writing, and deleting files; installing software; and changing important Windows parameters. Windows jargon refers to these controlled actions as *privileges,* and Windows regulates which Windows account has permission to perform which actions.

When you boot Windows, you "get in" to Windows through an *account.* The default account on Windows 2000 and XP is administrator, which in geek talk is "root" or "superuser." An administrator account has *all* powers over Windows, its software, and its files. You may never have noticed that Windows has accounts because by default, you don't "log in" to an account. Windows simply boots up and there you are—in the superuser account called administrator.

When you're logged into Windows as administrator, you can do anything that Windows can do: install software, read/write/delete files, fiddle with all Windows settings. And when you're logged in as administrator, any malware that gets in and begins running has all the same privileges that *you* do, because it's running under that same administrator account. You can totally trash Windows as administrator, and so can malware.

If you create a more limited Windows account and log into Windows through that account, malware is limited to whatever privileges you gave to the limited account. If you forbid the account to install software, malware can't install anything (like a spam zombie server) and can't mess with the Windows Registry. When logged in as a limited user, you can't change files created by anyone (like yourself) who logged in earlier as administrator. Malware can't change those files either, so they're protected.

The downside, of course, is that while you're logged in to a limited user account, you can't install software, change Windows settings, or read/write/delete files created under other user accounts, even if the person who created those files was you, working within those other accounts. This makes working under Windows less convenient, and thus few people ever actually do this. However, what sometimes makes sense is to create a limited user account and use that account only when you're doing risky things. Most of the time, you log into Windows as administrator, with all those godlike powers. When you need to live dangerously, log out as administrator, and log back in as a limited user. Then you can't do certain things—but neither can any malware that busts in while you're working.

What sorts of things are considered "living dangerously"? That depends on who you talk to, but the two biggies (for ordinary Windows users) are these:

√   Reading email

√   Surfing the Web

Most of the malware that ordinary users encounter comes in at one of those two times: Viruses generally happen to people while they're downloading their email, and most Web browser bugaboos occur while surfing the Web. If you perform these two functions from a limited user account, your chances of suffering a malware attack are *much* less. Worms can enter your system anytime you're connected to the Internet, so a limited user account protects you against worms only if you limit your Internet connection to those times you're logged in as a limited user. This is not easy to arrange, so most people don't do it. Rely on firewalls to prevent worms from getting in; I'll discuss this in detail in Chapter 14. (A limited user account, of course, will greatly limit the damage that a worm can do if it does get in somehow.)

Creating a Limited User Account in Windows

Windows's privilege and permissions machinery is very complex, and understanding it completely takes a lot of study. Fortunately, you don't have to understand it completely (or even understand it very much at all) to created a limited user account. Microsoft has anticipated the need for this sort of account and has built a sort of template for limited accounts into Windows. When you create a limited user account, you use this template.

Here's how you create a limited Windows XP user account:

1.   Click Start | Settings | Control Panel.

2.   Double-click on the Users Accounts applet to run it. What you'll see looks like Figure 13.9.

3.   Take note: If you haven't already created an administrator-class user, you can't create a restricted user. I'm not sure of the logic here, but that's how Windows works. What I recommend is creating an administrator-class user with your own name first and to use that account when you do your "normal" work in Windows.

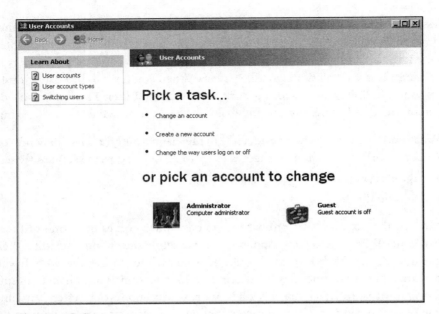

Figure 13.9

The Users and Passwords applet.

So either way, click Create a New Account. The new window will look like Figure 13.10. Enter a name for the new account and click Next.

4. The window you'll see at this point is where you select the type of user account to create. If you haven't first created an administrator account, the Limited user type will be grayed out and inaccessible. In that event, clicking Create Account will create an administrator account. Once you have created an administrator account, you can select the Limited type and create a limited user account under the name entered in Step 3.

That's all you need to do for Windows XP. The process for Windows 2000 is similar, but a little simpler. Step by step:

1. Click Start | Settings | Control Panel.

2. Double-click on the Users and Passwords applet to run it.

3. Make sure that the check box labeled "Users must enter a user name and password to use this computer" is checked. Otherwise, it's impossible to log in as different users at different times.

4. Click Add.

5. In the next window, enter a name and a description for the user. Click Next.

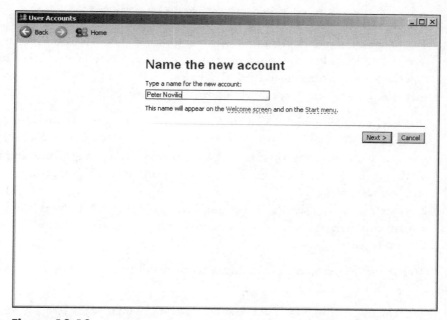

Figure 13.10

Entering a name for a new Windows account.

6. Here's the key step: Click Restricted User in the window that gives you the choice of user types. Then click Finish. (See Figure 13.11.) That's all you need to do!

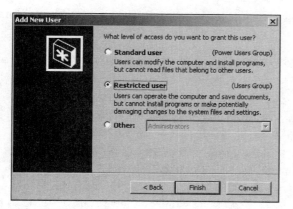

Figure 13.11

Selecting a user type under Windows 2000.

Fast User Switching in Windows XP

To change users under Windows 2000 requires logging out from the current user account and logging into a new one. This takes a certain amount of time, especially on an older or slower PC. Windows XP added a very handy feature that makes switching users almost effortless: *fast user switching.*

Fast user switching allows you to "freeze" an account and move quickly to another one. The frozen account remains in memory, with all its settings in place, and any programs that you left running remain running. For example, if you're working on a document in Microsoft Word in an administrator account and you want to do some Web research, you can fast-switch to the limited user account that you created and surf the Web. The copy of Microsoft Word will remain running (and your document will remain open) while you're over in the limited user account.

To use fast user switching to change accounts, do this:

1. Click Start | Log off *username.*
2. The Log Off Windows window appears in the center of the screen with two buttons, Log Off and Switch Users. Click Switch Users.
3. The user selection window appears, displaying all existing user accounts. Choose the account you want to switch to and click on its icon. Windows then switches to that account.

It's really pretty quick (much quicker than logging out completely as one user and logging back in as another) and allows you to leave work "in progress" in an administrator account while you duck out to surf the Web in a limited user account.

If you're not used to having multiple accounts under Windows, there are some things to keep in mind:

√ Each account has its own desktop and desktop settings. You will have to create some desktop icons and arrange them to your preference and select the background color or wallpaper for each new account.

√ Some older software (released prior to Windows 2000) may not work correctly under a limited user account. If a piece of software that you've been using successfully under the administrator account malfunctions under a limited user account, that's probably why, and there's really nothing to be done but use newer software.

√ You may not be able to change—or even see—files that you yourself created while logged into another account.

√ It's a good idea to switch to an open account and shut down any running applications before shutting down the PC as a whole.

TIP: *If you're fond of navigating to porn sites or warez sites on the Web, it's a very good idea to create and use a limited user account when you do. Those are the types of sites most likely to attempt to plant browser-based malware on your PC. Such malware can be difficult to remove, especially once it can install software on disk. Do your "dark side of the Force" surfing under a limited user account and the malware will have a much harder time taking hold on your PC.*

Summing Up—Peddlers Not Invited

Everybody, it seems, wants a piece of your PC as a way of getting a chunk of your wallet. Adware and spyware assault you with ads, and Web sites pepper you with pop-ups. It can make you crazy, but such "minor malware" is fairly easy to prevent, and free software is available to allow you to remove it. Summing up the advice in this chapter:

√ Research "free" software thoroughly before you install it. It might be really and truly free, or it might install adware or spyware.

√ Turn off "install on demand" in your Web browser.

√ If possible, move to a Web browser other than Internet Explorer, which is the prime target of the world's black hats. Mozilla Firefox is the best, and it's free.

√ Install and use a well-known adware/spyware remover like Ad-Aware or Spybot Search & Destroy. (Don't install a "no-name" product. Some are phony and install malware!)

√ Make sure you have a pop-up blocker in place. This might be a specially equipped browser like Firefox, a good software firewall like ZoneAlarm, or a utility designed to block pop-ups, like the Google Toolbar.

√ If you must surf to dicey Web sites (which are more likely to plant malware), create a limited privileges Windows user account and log into Windows through that account.

Avoiding all this kind of gunk can be done, and isn't even that difficult. Having taken the steps outlined in this chapter, I get virtually no adware or spyware on my PC and haven't seen a pop-up window in over a year.

We're closing in on the last and scariest type of malware there is: Internet worms. In the next chapter I'll explain how these little fire-breathing monsters operate and how you can block them with firewalls and a little common sense.

Use Firewalls to Stop Those Worms

Degunking Checklist:

√ Many worms target security holes in Microsoft Internet Explorer. Use a different Web browser (like Mozilla Firefox) if you possibly can.

√ Before you connect a PC to the Internet for the first time, even through a dialup connection, install a firewall.

√ Do not use the Windows XP Internet Connection Firewall. It is not "two-way" and conflicts with routers.

√ When a "two-way" firewall (like ZoneAlarm) spots an unknown program attempting to contact the Internet, deny the request and run a virus check immediately.

√ If you have a broadband connection to the Net, buy and use a router appliance containing a NAT firewall, even if you don't have a local area network.

√ Install a good antivirus utility and keep it current. Antivirus utilities can protect against "blended threat" worms that (like viruses) ride in on email attachments.

Afriend of mine in California went to stay with his father for a few days to help the man recover from surgery. He took his PC with him to enable him to work while he was there and bought an analog modem to connect to the Internet through a dialup ISP. At home he had broadband and worked through a router appliance and never had any trouble. However, within *thirty seconds* of connecting to his dialup ISP, his PC went crazy. It crashed and would not boot up. He hadn't gone to the Web. He didn't open any email attachments. He didn't have time, in fact, to do much of anything.

A worm got him.

He never discovered which worm precisely, for in disgust he reformatted his hard drive and reinstalled Windows completely. He also went down to CompUSA and bought a software firewall product, which he installed on his PC before attempting to dial up to the Internet again.

My friend discovered the essential difference between a virus and worm: The worm doesn't require that you "do" anything. All a worm needs is a network connection between the PC where it's running and your PC. Then all it needs to do is jump.

If you're not scared yet, you should be. But the good news is that I'm going to show you in this chapter how you can protect yourself against nasty worms.

Understand That Worms Are Viruses with Legs

Word is out in the black hat underground: Viruses are so, well, *yesterday*. Worms are where it's at. Viruses depend on people or computer mechanisms outside themselves to move from PC to PC. A worm, by contrast, contains its own transportation. To move from PC to PC, worms use flaws in software used to access the Internet (most often Internet Explorer) and flaws in local area networks connected to the Internet. A worm basically starts running on one PC and begins scanning the Internet for another vulnerable system. Once it finds a vulnerable system, a copy of the worm jumps to that system. As soon as that jump is completed, both worms begin scanning for more vulnerable PCs. In a matter of minutes, a single copy of a worm can spread to hundreds or even thousands of Internet-connected PCs.

Apart from how they get around, worms and viruses have a lot in common. They are both malware, and both have the potential to destroy data, disrupt your PC's settings, or even make your PC unbootable. Like viruses, they sometimes have a mission of some sort (called a *payload*), and sometimes they are simply designed to spread as far and wide as possible before being contained and eventually wiped out.

The Nature of Worm Gunk

Like viruses, worms are big-time gunk generators. The ways that worms gunk up your PC are similar in some respects to the ways viruses, adware, and spyware do:

√ Worms require memory and processor cycles to run. On older PCs, they may require so much memory that they crash your PC as soon as they begin running. In bad cases, your PC may thus be rendered unbootable.

√ Worms write themselves and their payloads to disk, creating file gunk.

√ Worms can change the names of files on your PC as means of hiding. Worms sometimes rename parts of themselves to one of several privileged files under Windows, so that you cannot shut down their processes through the Windows Task Manager. This interferes with Windows operation and makes the worm harder to remove. It may also crash your PC and render it unbootable.

√ Worms add keys to the Windows Registry and muck around with various system settings, making your PC slow or unstable.

√ Worms that plant spam relays add to the general amount of spam gunk that besets the world, clogging the Net and everybody's inboxes.

As with any kind of gunk, prevention is *way* better than cure. A bad worm can be so hard on your PC that you may be required to do what my friend did: reformat your hard drive and reinstall Windows from scratch.

Worms with a Mission

One reason worms are becoming more popular is that we've become quite adept at slowing the spread of viruses. But the other reason worms have become popular with black hats is that they spread so quickly. If the idea is to install a payload on 10,000 PCs in a big hurry, a fast-spreading worm is now the way to do it.

As with viruses, a lot of worms plant spam relay servers as payloads that turn an infected PC into a "spam zombie." The other major payload for worms are *distributed denial of service (DDoS)* clients. These are very simple programs that do one thing: At the command of their remote black hat masters, they zero in on a particular Internet server somewhere (often a Web server belonging to a large company) and flood it with thousands of simultaneous requests for connections. The flooded server can't handle all those connection requests and in most cases must simply shut down until the DDoS storm ceases.

The Life Cycle of a Worm

Understanding how to stop worms begins with understanding how worms operate. Worms have a well-defined "life cycle" that consists of several distinct stages. Disrupt any of these stages and worm propagation ceases and the worm can't spread:

1. *Breaking in.* A worm establishes a conventional Internet connection to an uninfected PC. It uses a security hole in some piece of software running on that PC to break in and copy to PC memory a portion of itself from a previously infected system. The worm, having gotten into memory, begins running on the new PC.

2. *Moving over.* Having established an illicit connection to the new PC, the worm then copies its "body" to the new PC and writes itself to disk.

3. *Digging in.* With itself both running in memory and written to disk, the worm changes the PC's configuration so that it is launched every time the PC reboots. The worm may also hide itself in several ways and make itself more difficult to find and remove.

4. *Planting the payload.* If this particular worm carries a payload (a spam relay or DDoS client or password cracker program), the payload is now installed on the infected PC.

5. *Scanning for new victims.* The worm has now done everything it needs to do to fully infect the PC. It then begins scanning a range of IP addresses, probing for still more PCs. This probing operation looks for systems that have the security hole or other vulnerability that the worm uses to break in. The worm may scan hundreds or thousands of new systems until it finds a vulnerable one. (This may take all of 30 seconds!) Once a vulnerable PC is found somewhere, the worm initiates the "break-in" code and the cycle begins again.

Some worms change the order slightly (some, for example, propagate to new systems before planting the payload, in order to infect more systems more quickly) but most worms follow this sequence of events pretty closely. A few worms are called *blended threat worms* because they use multiple means of propagation. The commonest blended threat is a worm that spreads by both direct PC-to-PC connection and email attachment, as though the worm were a virus. Worm authors like email attachments because a worm can get past an outward-looking firewall (like the NAT firewall in a router, which is covered in more detail later in this chapter) by riding in on an email attachment.

Interfering with the Worm Life Cycle

The worm needs to be able to complete its life cycle to plant the payload and propagate to new, uninfected systems. If you interfere with any stage in the worm life cycle, you can stop the worm in its tracks. Here are some methods that people use to inhibit worm operation:

√ *Avoid vulnerable software.* Like virus writers, worm writers need a "critical mass" of vulnerable, infectable systems. To be infectable, a system must carry a security hole of some kind that a worm can use to break in. The overwhelming majority of these security holes are found in Microsoft software, simply because Microsoft software is everywhere. Systems that do not use certain Microsoft products (especially Internet Explorer) are less vulnerable to worms.

√ *Prevent illicit file transfers.* The worm is a computer program, and like all computer programs, it is stored in one or more executable files. These files have to be transferred from an infected PC to an uninfected PC using some kind of file transfer protocol, like File Transfer Protocol (FTP), Trivial File Transfer Protocol (TFTP), or Hypertext Transfer Protocol (HTTP). If a firewall prevents these protocols from being initiated from outside the PC, the virus can't "move over" to the PC.

√ *Prevent software installation and system reconfiguration.* If a PC is running a restricted user account under Windows, the operating system will not allow the worm software to install itself, nor will it allow the worm to change the Windows Registry to launch itself at bootup.

√ *Spot the worm or payload files as they're being written to disk.* Worms are sometimes spread through email attachments as well as direct PC-to-PC connections. Most good antivirus products can therefore recognize worm files and will prevent the worm from writing itself to disk. Unfortunately, many worms "come out of nowhere" and can infect tens or hundreds of thousands of systems before the antivirus companies can distribute worm signatures. Antivirus products will thus only stop "old" worms (where "old" may be as little as a week) and are not considered primary worm protection. They are a good backup, though, as a firewall will not necessarily stop a worm from entering your system via an email attachment.

√ *Prevent the worm from scanning or connecting to new systems from the PC.* A good firewall is "two way"; that is, it blocks both connections coming into the PC from outside and connections originating inside the PC that attempt to connect to new systems elsewhere on the Internet. A firewall knows what software is allowed to connect to the outside world (like your Web browser) and stops all other software from making connections to the Internet.

Realistically, this gives you the following options for protecting yourself against worm attacks:

√ *Be careful about using certain Microsoft software.* You may be stuck with Windows (Mac users aren't targeted for worms because there are so few Macs out there), but you can move to non-Microsoft Web browsers and email clients.

√ *Install a two-way software firewall.* This is your very best protection against worms, and if you do nothing else, do this, no matter what kind of Internet connection you have, broadband or dialup.

√ *Install a router with a Network Address Translation (NAT) firewall.* This is an option only if you have a broadband Internet connection, but if you do, it's cheap and easy protection that works well in conjunction with a software firewall.

Your Worm Defense Strategy

Defending against worms is different from defending against viruses. Most of the time you won't get hit by a worm by doing stupid things. (Again, worms sometimes spread via email attachments, as though they were viruses.) Your defense is mostly technology. The strategy I advise is this:

1. Install a software firewall on your PC *before you ever connect it to the Internet.* There are many firewall products out there, but the one I use and endorse is ZoneAlarm from Zone Labs. I'll explain how to install and use it later in this chapter.

2. Have an antivirus product installed, running, and up-to-date, and follow all the good virus hygiene practices I outlined in Chapter 12. Antivirus products can provide some backup defense against older worms, especially those blended threat worms known to spread via email attachments.

3. If you have a broadband connection to the Internet, install an inexpensive router appliance that contains a Network Address Translation (NAT) firewall. These router appliances are intended to connect several PCs into a local area network, but even if you have only one PC, the NAT firewall is good backup protection for your software firewall.

The Prime Directive in Worm Defense

The strategy outlined in the preceding section is really all you need to follow. However, there is one point involving worm defense that I cannot emphasize too strongly, and in fact I call it the Prime Directive in Worm Defense. The point is this:

Do not connect a PC to the Internet without installing a firewall first!

You should follow this directive whether your Internet connection is a broadband connection or a dialup connection. The reason for the Prime Directive is this: There are worms bouncing around the Internet constantly. Every so often a worm is turned loose by some careless person who opens an infected email attachment that can do considerable damage.

Learn the Essentials about Firewalls

Firewalls are not optional or "nice to have." They are the single most important security technology you can use. A firewall is a sort of digital doorman, standing guard at the network port of your PC. The network port is how you connect your PC to the Internet, and everything that comes to you from the Internet comes in through that network port. A firewall controls what sorts of connections are allowed to be made to your PC from outside and also what software is allowed to initiate a connection from inside your PC to the outside world. A good firewall thus looks both outward and inward, closely managing the data that moves in both directions between your PC and the Internet.

The two general kinds of firewalls that are used to protect PCs installed in homes and small offices are as follows:

√ *Software firewalls* are programs that install on your PC, just as antivirus utilities or any other software packages are installed.

√ *Network Address Translation (NAT) firewalls* are built into router appliances that are used to create local area networks in homes and offices. These router appliances are small inexpensive boxes that are connected between your PC and your broadband modem. They also allow you to connect your PC to other PCs or laptops with cables or even wireless connections, for fast file transfers between PCs. Alas, although routers usable with dialup connections exist, they are rare and quite expensive, often $150 or more.

A NAT firewall in a router is a nice-to-have, but a software firewall is absolutely essential, and I'll cover those first.

Using Software Firewalls

Software firewalls come in a number of forms. In this book I'll be talking only about a category called *personal firewalls* that are designed to be installed in a single PC and protect only that PC. Most other types of software firewalls are designed to run on servers and protect whole networks of PCs.

Personal firewalls install on your PC, and they monitor data connections originating from outside your PC and from inside it as well. This two-way nature is extremely important:

√ Controlling connections from outside your PC (typically, from somewhere on the Internet) is important because worms, scripts, and various other black hat exploits attempt to connect to unprotected PCs from outside. Worms are simply computer programs, and against a software firewall they have little or no chance.

√ Controlling connections from inside your PC prevents a worm or virus from "phoning home" or spewing spam messages by the thousands after it's infected you. Sometimes, the only way you can tell that you've been infected by a "stealth" worm is when your firewall informs you that something a little bit odd is trying to connect to the outside world from inside your PC.

Personal firewalls are only concerned with connections to the Internet. The sense here is that if you control the sorts of connections that can be created to or from your PC, the types of data moving through those connections doesn't really matter.

Software firewalls definitely stop illicit connections to your PC, but they go further and stop port scans and pings from outside. A *port scan* is a sweep of network port numbers on your PC. An "open" network port can be sensed with certain network software, and if a port is found to be present and open to the outside world, a black hat or a piece of black hat software somewhere can then attempt to break in through that port. A *ping* is a signal sent to your PC using a common network protocol, asking your PC to respond. A system pinging your PC is basically asking, "Are you there?" and the reply from your PC (sometimes called a *pong*) says, "Yes, I'm here."

Software firewalls also prevent black hats from communicating with Trojan horse programs or other "back doors" installed on your PC by viruses or worms. A virus may install a spam relay on your PC, but if the spammer can't contact it through the spam relay's back door, the relay can't start sending spam.

Using NAT Firewalls

Many computer security experts object to calling NAT firewalls "firewalls." It's certainly true that in terms of its technology, a NAT firewall (more properly called a NAT server) works entirely differently from a true software firewall. On the other hand, one of the side effects of what NAT does is a sort of protection that is very firewall-like. That's why practical minded computer geeks call them firewalls anyway.

NAT firewalls are not as easy to explain as software firewalls, and it's not critically necessary that you understand in detail how they work. So if the following discussion makes your eyes glaze over, feel free to skip to the next section!

NAT means *Network Address Translation.* Every PC on a network (whether a small local area network or the global Internet) has an Internet Protocol (IP) address. An IP address looks like this: 263.24.0.71. It's a group of four numbers separated by periods. When you connect to the Internet through your ISP, your ISP's servers provide your PC with its very own and completely unique IP address. This address is required anytime a connection is made between your PC and a server or computer on the Internet. Your IP address is used every time you connect to an email server to read your email or to a Web server to surf the Web. Your IP address is also used by worms that try to infect your PC. If a worm can't determine your PC's IP address, it can't break in and infect your PC.

Put as simply as possible, a NAT firewall is a way to hide your PC's IP address from the outside world.

NAT works by acting as a translator between the public IP address that your ISP gives you and a private IP address that is not visible from the Internet. This private address is known *only* to the NAT server inside the router. See the diagram in Figure 14.1.

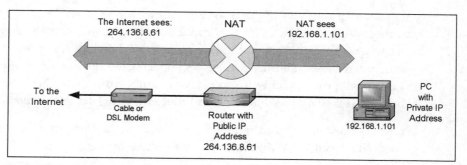

Figure 14.1

How a NAT firewall works.

The NAT server inside the router responds to the public IP address given to you by your ISP. The NAT server, in turn, gives your PC a private IP address that only it knows. The private IP address is private in another sense: It belongs to a block of IP addresses set aside as "local." These "local" addresses cannot be directly accessed from the Internet, but only from devices that are directly wired to the "inside" of the router and thus local to the PC using the address.

The NAT server makes incoming connections to your PC very difficult to arrange without its (the NAT server's) full cooperation. When your PC initiates a connection to an email or Web server, the NAT server takes note of that and allows the email or Web server to respond back to your PC. But a connection coming in "out of the blue" is simply ignored. If a worm attempts to scan your public IP address for vulnerabilities, the NAT server simply tells it to go pound sand. This is why the NAT server can be called a firewall. It stops unsolicited inbound scans and connections (like those from a worm scan) cold.

Unfortunately, if the worm gets into your PC some other way (by riding in on an email attachment, for example), the NAT firewall can do nothing to stop it. The NAT firewall is strictly "outward looking" and assumes that any connection initiated *from* your PC—even by a worm—is OK. This is why a NAT firewall is not, all by itself, complete protection against worms. However, it is *very* strong protection against automated exploits by scripts, worms, and other malware attempting to get at your PC from outside.

Later in this chapter, I'll explain how to install and use my favorite router product, the Linksys BEFSR41.

Install and Use ZoneAlarm

There are a fair number of good software firewalls out there. The one I have used the most is Zone Labs's ZoneAlarm. ZoneAlarm comes in both a free and a paid version; the paid version is called ZoneAlarm Pro. I like the paid version because it has a few additional features and updates, but the free version is very good and will protect you well, especially in conjunction with a NAT firewall in a router. (I'll cover NAT firewalls and routers a little later in this chapter.)

There is a firewall bundled with Windows XP called Internet Connection Firewall (ICF), but I don't recommend it, for these reasons:

√ It is strictly "outward looking" and will not prevent viruses or worms from "phoning home" to their dark masters.

√ It is inflexible and difficult to configure.

√ It conflicts unpredictably with NAT firewalls in routers.

√ If you have a local area network of several machines in your home, ICF will interfere with file and printer sharing among the PCs on your network.

ZoneAlarm addresses all these problems, and I have used it for almost two years now without any difficulties.

Getting ZoneAlarm

There's a kind of chicken-and-egg problem with obtaining a software firewall while adhering to the Prime Directive in Worm Defense: You shouldn't connect to the Internet without a firewall in place, and yet the easiest way to get ZoneAlarm is from the Internet.

Here are some suggestions:

√ Ask another person (who already has a firewall) to go up to Zone Labs's site and download ZoneAlarm for you. The URL is **www.zonelabs.com**.

√ Put a NAT firewall in place first and then connect to the Internet to download ZoneAlarm. (I explain how to install a router with a NAT firewall in the section "Install and Use the Linksys BEFSR41 Router" later in this chapter.)

√ Buy the paid version of ZoneAlarm in a box at a computer store like CompUSA.

In the following sections, I'll explain how to install and use the free version of ZoneAlarm. The paid version is installed and configured in almost precisely the same ways.

Installing ZoneAlarm

Here are the steps to follow to install ZoneAlarm:

1. Run the ZoneAlarm installer by double-clicking it.

2. You'll see a window asking for your name and email address. My experience has been that Zone Labs does not abuse the email address, so you can enter it without qualms. This is important because you won't know when updates are available unless you allow them to email you.

3. The next window asks for your approval of the product EULA. Check the "I accept" box and click the Install button. The product will write all of its files to disk.

4. During the install you'll see the dialog shown in Figure 14.2. Your choices here are the free version (ZoneAlarm) and the paid version (ZoneAlarm Pro). If you choose the paid version, you get a 15-day free trial, after which you can buy the paid version or your install will revert to the free version. The free version lacks features like the pop-up blocker and email virus/worm detection.

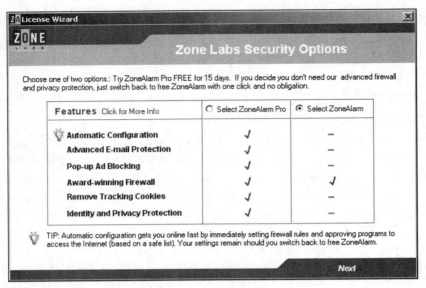

Figure 14.2
Choosing a ZoneAlarm version.

5. Continue working through the install wizard (it's a very talkative wizard, with a lot of screens that neither say nor do anything useful) until you come to the Configure Web Surfing Access dialog, shown in Figure 14.3. Here you

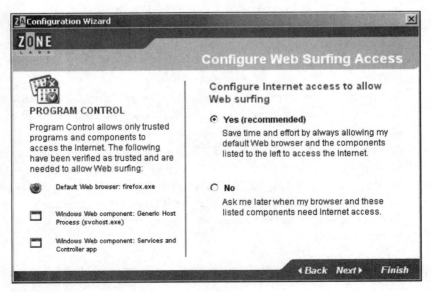

Figure 14.3
Preconfiguring Web browser permissions in ZoneAlarm.

are being asked to grant permission to access the Web to your default Web browser and the associated Microsoft services. By preconfiguring itself to allow these three items to access the Internet, ZoneAlarm is saving you a little bother later on, when you have to begin "teaching" ZoneAlarm what software is allowed to connect to the Internet from inside your PC. Make sure that Yes is selected and click Next.

On the last wizard dialog you have the option of running through a short tutorial on using ZoneAlarm. Taking the tutorial is a good idea. Finally, you have to reboot your PC.

Understanding ZoneAlarm Zones

ZoneAlarm depends on the concept of *zones* for any networks or external servers to which it connects. There zones are supported:

√ *Trusted.* Programs and networks you trust (your own, for the most part) belong in this zone.

√ *Internet.* This zone contains computers that you're not sure about—which includes virtually everything on the Internet.

√ *Blocked.* This zone contains computers or networks you want nothing to do with. Most of the time you won't be using this zone. Important: *You don't have to manually put networks or IP addresses of computers in the Blocked zone to prevent them from breaking into your PC!*

Configuring ZoneAlarm is easy because it doesn't require you to type in the names of any software products that are allowed to access the Internet. Instead, it asks you about networks and software packages as it encounters them, and you have the option of granting permission or denying it as you choose.

The first thing ZoneAlarm will ask you about is your network. A dialog titled New Network will pop up almost immediately after you reboot on installing ZoneAlarm. This dialog is asking whether the network connected to the PC should be placed in the Trusted, Internet, or Blocked zone (see Figure 14.4).

There are two possibilities here:

√ You are connected to the Internet directly, without a router between you and the Internet. If that's the case, make sure Internet zone is selected in the Zone drop-down list. Internet zone is the default, but make sure. The Internet does *not* belong in the Trusted zone!

√ You have a router between you and the Internet. (An IP network address beginning with 192.168 indicates a router.) If your router connects to other PCs, you'll need to place the network in the Trusted zone. If your router has

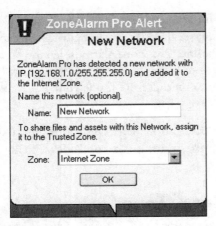

Figure 14.4

Choosing a zone for the connected network.

no other PCs on it, you can leave it in the Internet zone if you prefer, but I recommend putting the router in the Trusted zone so you can connect other PCs to it later on without complications.

Naming the network really isn't necessary. As with all ZoneAlarm permissions, you can change the network's selected zone later on if you change your mind about it or install a router for a home network.

Software Package Permissions

On the software side, ZoneAlarm begins by denying access to *all* programs and asking you which ones to permit as they attempt to get on the Net. Each time you run a program that needs Internet access, ZoneAlarm pops up a dialog over the taskbar tray (see Figure 14.5) asking you two things:

√   Whether to give the program access at all.

√   Whether to give the program access just this one time, or always, without asking permission each time. It does this by "remembering" you permission response.

In the figure, note the name of the executable that is trying to access the Internet. The program file is thunderbird.exe, which is the Mozilla Thunderbird email client. That's a "good" program (not malware). That means you need to both grant thunderbird.exe permission to access the Net and also have ZoneAlarm remember that permission so the alert won't pop up every time you try to check your email. That being the case, check "Remember this setting" and click Allow.

Figure 14.5.
ZoneAlarm's "New Program" alert dialog.

The first day you have ZoneAlarm installed, you'll be seeing pop-up alerts for numerous programs as those programs attempt to access the network for the first time since ZoneAlarm began watching the door. After a week or so, you'll see a New Program alert only rarely, such as when you install a new Internet application or use a program that you use only once in a long while.

GunkBuster's Notebook: Beware of Unexpected "Changed Program" Alerts

Ordinarily, once you give a program permission to access the Internet (and tell ZoneAlarm to remember that permission), you won't see another alert on that program until you upgrade the program. ZoneAlarm looks at not only the name of a program asking permission to access the Internet, but also the size of the program and possibly certain other things. (Zone Labs is understandably cautious about describing in detail how its products do their jobs.) The idea is to allow ZoneAlarm to tell when a program has *changed*. Once a program is changed (for example, when you upgrade to a new version), ZoneAlarm will pop up a Changed Program alert and ask you for permission to allow the changed version to access the Internet.

You can expect a Changed Program pop-up alert the first time you use a program after you upgrade it. That's normal. However, if all of a sudden you get an alert on a program that you gave permission to long ago and did *not* upgrade or reinstall, be careful! Malware has been known to delete a well-known program file and install itself under that file's name. In other words, you may contract a virus that deletes the existing file **thunderbird.exe** and installs itself as **thunderbird.exe**, hoping you'll think it's your familiar email client. (The fact that your installed copy of Thunderbird will no longer run should also make you suspicious!)

If you get a suspicious Changed Program alert on a trusted program that you did not recently upgrade or reinstall, save out all your other work and do a full-system virus scan immediately. Something is rotten somewhere, and if your antivirus program is up-to-date, it will very likely spot the culprit and allow you to remove it. (You may also have some reinstalling to do after that. This is war, buddy!)

Deciding Whether to Grant or Deny

How can you tell what a program is when ZoneAlarm pops up its permission queries? Some are simple: **thunderbird.exe** or **firefox.exe** are easy to identify as an email client and a Web browser. But how about **services.exe** or **spoolsv.exe**? There are in fact a number of programs that are part of Windows and should be allowed permission to talk to the network. The two best known are probably **services.exe** and **spoolsv.exe**, but there are others.

When unfamiliar programs turn up and ZoneAlarm asks about them, your best bet is to do a quick search on the Web. Googling on the name of the file in the pop-up alert should nail it.

TIP: One excellent site to look at for program executable file names is LIUtilities's WinTasks Process Library. You can Google right to it with a simple query: "wintasks process," where process is the full file name that ZoneAlarm is reporting, like spoolsv.exe. You may get more than one hit, but in my checking, LIUtilities is always the #1 search hit on that sort of query.

If more than one Web site refers to an executable as malware, you have reason *not* to grant permission—and abundant reason to do an immediate check for viruses, worms, spyware, and adware.

Although ZoneAlarm has a lot more configurable options for stopping worms and other malware (especially the paid version), there's very little else you really have to know. Once it's learned about all the network-enabled programs you use on a daily basis, it retreats into the background, silently stopping attacks from outside and watching carefully to be sure the programs inside your PC are the ones you want to be there.

Install and Use the Linksys BEFSR41 Router

Because I have had several PCs in the house for a good many years, I bought a router appliance years ago, when broadband first became available in my area. The device I bought was the Linksys BEFSR41, and it worked without problem or incident for almost five years before a power surge during a thunderstorm fried something inside it. The BEFSR41 includes a NAT firewall and a four-port switch. The switch allows me to connect up to four PCs to it to create a local area network. (The only reason I didn't buy another BEFSR41 after the first one fried is that I now have six PCs in the house and needed a router with more ports!)

The BEFSR41 is shown in Figure 14.6. Even though it has four ports for as many as four PCs, it works perfectly well with only one PC connected to it, and you get the full benefit of the NAT firewall. You can buy the BEFSR41 at most computer stores or discount appliance stores like Best Buy. I've even seen them at Home Depot.

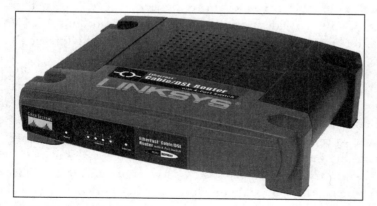

Figure 14.6
The Linksys BEFSR41 router. (Photo courtesy of Linksys.)

> **TIP:** *If possible, buy your router and have it there beside the PC and ready to go before the installer comes to hook up your cable or DSL broadband modem for you. There was a time, two or three years ago, when many of the cable companies distrusted routers and didn't want people to use them. Now, however, opinion has swung the other way and most cable systems do not object to routers on PCs. Emphasize to the cable installer that you're interested in the router for its NAT firewall and protection against worms and network intruders. These days, they understand the threat and will most likely connect the cable modem to the router for you. This avoids a possible problem with PC authentication to the cable system, which I'll cover after the installation section.*

Installing the BEFSR41

Before you attempt to install the BEFSR41 router, *power everything down*: PC, cable/DSL modem, and anything connected to them (monitor, scanner, whatever) that has its own power supply. All data connections are done with *Category 5* network jumper cables with RJ45 connectors on the ends. Category 5 jumper cables look like fat modular telephone cables with larger end connectors. Your cable or DSL modem probably came with one, and so does the BEFSR41, so you shouldn't need to buy any jumpers separately. However, if you do need one, they're inexpensive and available anywhere that computer accessories and supplies are sold.

Figure 14.7 shows how to connect the BEFSR41 router between your cable/DSL modem and your PC. On the back of your cable/DSL modem should be an RJ45 jack that accepts a jumper cable. It's usually marked "Ethernet" or "Network." I've never seen a cable/DSL modem with more than one RJ45 jack on the back, so you won't be puzzling over which hole to plug the cable into! Connect the cable/DSL modem to the jack marked "Internet" on the back of the BEFSR41. (Older versions of the BEFSR41 label this jack "WAN." This stands for "wide area network," and basically means "the Internet.")

On the back of the BEFSR41 are four RJ45 jacks numbered 1 to 4. A fifth jack is labeled "Uplink." Connect a jumper to any of the four numbered ports. Do not, however, use the Uplink port. This port is intended to "daisy chain" additional Ethernet switches to the BEFSR41, and if you don't know what that means, don't worry about it. (Just don't use the Uplink port!) Connect the other end of the jumper to the network port jack (generally marked "Network") on your PC or laptop. Very few PCs have more than one such jack, so it's a pretty sure bet that any jack into which your Category 5 jumper will fit is the right one.

Once the cables have been connected, power everything back up in the following order:

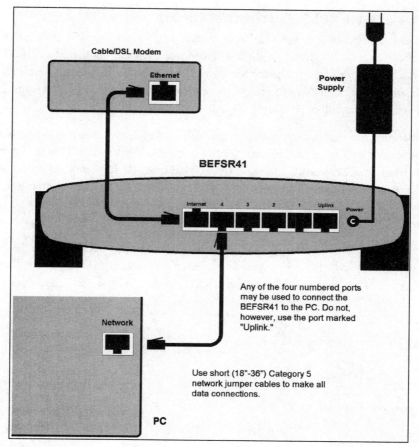

Figure 14.7
Connecting the BEFSR41 router.

1. The cable/DSL modem. Wait two or three minutes for the modem to perform its self-test sequence.
2. The BEFSR41. Again, wait two or three minutes for the device to perform its self-test sequence.
3. The PC or laptop.

Unless you did something wrong (or unless the cable company uses MAC address authentication to allow PCs to connect to its network; more on this in a moment), the system should be ready to use without any further configuration. To test it, bring up a Web browser and see if you can open any Web page. If you can, the router is in there working, protecting you against unwanted inbound connections to your PC from the Internet.

MAC Address Authentication

There's one possible snag involved in adding a router to your PC configuration. It happens mostly when people install a router *after* they have had a cable/DSL broadband connection in place for awhile. If you install the router between the PC and the cable/DSL modem when you first get broadband service and have the modem installed, you typically avoid the problem.

Although this will sound a little technical, it's important, so follow me as best you can. Your PC's network adapter has a unique ID number. This ID number is called the *Media Access Control* (MAC) address. (It has nothing to do with Macintosh computers!) A network adapter's MAC address never changes, and some cable companies use it to authenticate computers that connect to their broadband networks.

It works like this: (Follow along on Figure 14.8.) When you have cable Internet service installed, the cable system (through the cable modem) basically asks your PC what its network adapter's MAC address is. The PC identifies itself

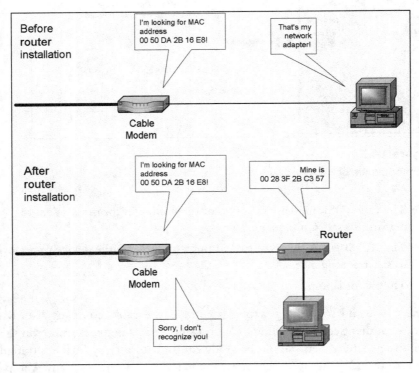

Figure 14.8

How MAC address authentication works.

with its network adapter's MAC address and the cable system records that MAC address on its servers. From then on, anytime your PC tries to connect to the cable Internet system, the system asks your PC for its MAC address. If the MAC address returned in answer to the cable system's query is *not* the same address logged during cable modem installation, the cable system does not let your PC connect to the Internet.

The cable companies do this so that people can't "tap in" to the cable with their own cable modems and get Internet access through the cable without paying for it. The PC network adapter's MAC address identifies the PC to the cable system as a legitimate paying customer.

Now, when you insert a router in between your cable modem and your PC, the cable system can no longer ask your PC what its MAC address is. When the authentication query comes down the cable, the router is the one that responds—and the router has its own, unique MAC address, which is not the same as the address in your PC's network adapter. The router's MAC address has not been recorded by the cable system, and so the cable system doesn't recognize it and it won't let your PC access the Internet.

There are a couple of different ways to deal with this problem:

√ Some cable systems will automatically reauthenticate a system after it's been disconnected from the cable for several hours. If you can stand to be without your Internet connection for 24 hours, disconnect the cable modem from the router, power down the cable modem, and don't attempt to reconnect the cable modem to the router for 24 hours. Then reconnect the cable and power up the cable modem. This may prompt the cable system to rerecord the MAC address that it "sees" (this time, the one belonging to your router) and make everything work together again.

√ If the first technique didn't work, call your cable company, explain that you've put a router in between the PC and the cable modem, and ask that they reauthenticate your system. They have to do this anyway every so often when people buy a new PC, which has a different MAC address than the one on the PC for which cable Internet service was originally installed. Because people generally change PCs more often than they change routers, having a router is actually to the cable company's advantage and will prevent tech support calls down the road when the PC at the account changes.

√ If the cable company refuses to reauthenticate your PC (and I haven't heard of this being done for a long time), you may have to "clone" the MAC address of your PC's network adapter and insert it into your router. This sounds scary, but it's not as difficult as all that—and the newer routers help you do it. Read on.

Cloning Your MAC Address

Unless you have the sort of authentication problems we've been discussing here, a router typically doesn't need any particular configuration. However, if configuration is needed, you can "log in" to your router using a Web browser and change its settings. The router comes from the factory with a preset local IP address. If you type this IP address into your Web browser, the browser will respond with a configuration page. This page does not come "from the Web" in the familiar sense, but comes from inside the router, which has its own little built-in Web server. You don't have to be connected to the Internet to bring up the router's configuration page. (This is a common misconception.)

For the BEFSR41, the default configuration page address is this:

http://192.168.1.1

Once you enter this, a username and password dialog will appear. If the BEFSR41 router is new out of the box, the username will be blank (don't enter anything in that field) and the password will be "admin." If you bought the router used, its previous owner may have changed the username and password. If that's the case, do a hardware reset on the router. (See the GunkBuster's Notebook titled "Resetting a Used Router" in this chapter.)

TIP: If your router is new, it's important that you change the user name and password from the defaults. There is a place in the configuration pages somewhere to allow you to do this. Read up on it in the router's documentation and change the username and password before use it for any length of time!

Once you enter the password and click OK, the router's main configuration page will appear. On newer versions of the BEFSR41, an option labeled "MAC Address Clone" will be present under the main Setup option. On older versions of the BEFSR41, click the orange Advanced button and then look for an option labeled "MAC Addr. Clone." The MAC address cloning screen for the newer routers is shown in Figure 14.9.

The great thing about the newer Linksys routers is that they do all the tricky work: They ask your PC's network adapter what its MAC address is and then "clone" that MAC address as their own. Basically, your PC's network adapter MAC address replaces the one built into the router. This makes the router "look like" your PC to the cable system, which will then allow your router and PC to access the Internet.

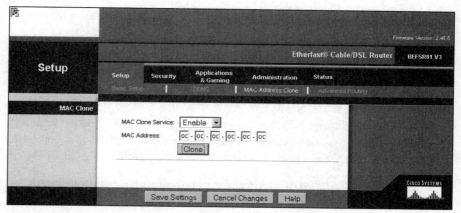

Figure 14.9
Router-assisted MAC address cloning.

To do the MAC clone:

1. Click the Enable radio button or select Enable from the pull-down list.

2. Click the button marked "Clone" or "Clone your PC's MAC." Your PC's MAC address will appear in the six numeric fields above the button. (This may take a second or two.)

3. Once the new MAC address appears, click the Save Settings button and you're done! Power everything down and then up again, and you should connect to the Internet again without further difficulty.

Tricky: MAC Cloning on an Older Router

Versions 1 and 2 of the BEFSR41 do not have a "Clone Your PC's MAC" button, alas. To clone your PC's MAC address on an older router, you have to find your PC's MAC address yourself and type it manually into the router.

For Windows 2000 and XP, you determine your PC's MAC address this way:

1. Select Start|Run.

2. Enter "cmd.exe" in the field and click OK.

3. A black "console window" will open. At the flashing cursor, type "ipconfig / all" and press Enter.

4. A great deal of textual information will appear. Scan down the list until you see "Physical Address" to the left of a group of six two-digit numbers separated by dashes, in the form 00-00-00-00-00-00. Copy those six numbers down exactly as shown. (Some of the numbers may contain letters from A to F. This is OK.)

For some reason, Microsoft chose not to call the MAC address by its real name and refers to it as "Physical address" instead.

For Windows 9.*x*, do this:

1. Select Start|Run.
2. Enter "winipcfg" in the field and click OK.
3. A small window will appear. Look for a field labeled "Adapter address" containing six two-digit numbers separated by dashes. Copy these numbers down exactly as shown. That's your network adapter's MAC address.

Once you have the MAC address written down, bring up the router's configuration screen. Here's the step by step to do the cloning operation:

1. Click the orange button labeled "Advanced" toward the upper-right corner of the display.
2. Click the gray button labeled "MAC Addr. Clone."
3. Type the six two-digit numbers you copied down into the six entry fields. Be sure you first backspace over the "00" digits or other numbers that may already be there. (See Figure 14.10.)

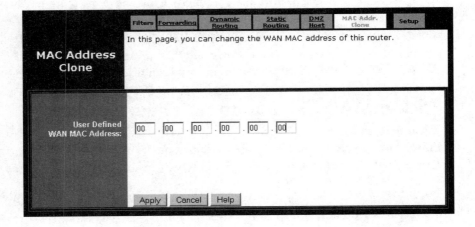

Figure 14.10

MAC address cloning on an older router.

4. Click Apply.
5. When the screen clears to white, reading "Settings are successful," click Continue.

After you've cloned the MAC address on either older or newer versions of the BEFSR41, power everything down (cable modem, router, and PC) and power them back up in order, as explained earlier in this section. Your router now has your PC's MAC address, and the cable system should now recognize the system as legitimate.

GunkBuster's Notebook: Resetting a Used Router

Routers like the Linksys BEFSR41 are extremely common on the used market right now for a simple reason: Millions of people have replaced a "wired" router like the BEFSR41 with a wireless router to create a Wi-Fi network in their homes. In fact, if you ask around, you may be able to score one for nothing at all.

There is a problem with used routers: Many have been configured by their previous owners for various reasons, and those configuration changes may not be what you need. Worse, they have probably changed the password and username and may not remember them.

Fortunately, nearly all router products (not simply the BEFSR41) have a "hardware reset" feature. This is in the form of a small button somewhere on the product, usually set back behind a tiny hole (perhaps 1/8 inch in diameter) and requiring a bent-out paper clip to press. When you press this button, the router will clear all of its settings to their default values, including the password and username. Assuming the router is not faulty in some way, it should then act precisely as it did when it was new.

It should be obvious, but note that the hardware reset button only works when the router is powered up!

Summing Up—Turning Worms Away

Worms are in many ways nastier than viruses in that they don't always depend on your doing dumb things to get a foothold in your PC. You can religiously avoid email attachments or software downloaded from newsgroups or dicey sites and still fall victim to a worm. On the other hand, keeping worms out of your PC is a little simpler than capturing viruses because worms must be able to establish a solid connection between an infected PC and your PC. Block that connection and you block the worm.

Here are the "big picture" things you should remember in regard to the worm wars:

√ *Never* connect a PC to the Internet without installing some sort of firewall first.

√ Always use a two-way software firewall to prevent viruses and other malware from "phoning home."

√ Even if you don't need a home network, install a router appliance with a built-in NAT firewall.

If you can remember and adhere to those three points, the worms may come a-callin' but your PC won't let 'em in!

Degunk Nigerian Rhapsodies, Hoaxes, and Other Smelly Phish

Degunking Checklist:

√ Don't believe everything you read in an email, even one that comes from family or friends. Healthy skepticism is…healthy.

√ Check possible hoaxes out at sites like snopes.com before you spread them any further.

√ Don't forward an email to everyone in your address book.

√ Watch out for easy money spam rip-offs: No one is going to give you a cut of a fortune to help smuggle it out of their country.

√ Don't fall victim to identity theft because of phishing.

√ Never attempt to access an important Web site, especially a financial or e-commerce Web site, by clicking on a hyperlink in an email message.

If you're like most people, you have a cousin/uncle/aunt/friend who sends you and many others a message every few days with a subject like "FW: Important warning! Look out for <xxx>," where you can fill in any of a multitude of different imagined or (very rarely) real threats, from rat urine on soda cans to exploding water cups in microwave ovens to genetically engineered "love bugs" with no natural predators that will eventually engulf the world.

The same people also send pleas for business cards to be sent to a sick child somewhere or astonished announcements that Microsoft will send you money (sometimes as much as $1,000) if you forward this message to someone else.

Such messages are hoaxes, often sent by well-meaning but credulous people who don't seem to be playing with a full deck. Some such hoaxes are jokes (often cruel jokes) and a few are "joe jobs," intended to damage someone's reputation.

We've all probably received a few pitches from aggrieved and persecuted persons in Nigeria (MANY OF WHOM HAVE STUCK CAPS LOCK KEYS) who are somehow sitting on millions of dollars, which they will share with you if you help them get the money (illegally) out of the country. And lately, I receive five or six messages every single day from eminent financial institutions such as Citibank demanding that I reconfirm my personal information or else they'll close my account. (Funny, I've never had an account there....)

What's going on here? Not all malware comes in the form of computer code. Some of it runs right inside our heads, hoping to feed off our good nature, or desire for gossip, our willingness to believe the worst about people, or our greed. We might call this "mental malware," and it includes many species of hoaxes and scams and a more recent invention of black hat identity thieves called phishing.

None of it is dangerous unless you let it sucker you in. This chapter will show you how to degunk mental malware and how to make sure you don't fall for it.

Degunk Those Viral Hoaxes

Way back in 1998, one of the staffers at my company forwarded an email message she had received to everyone who worked there. It was so completely gonzo that I saved it:

> People, listen up!
>
> Whenever you buy a can of coke or whatever, please make sure that you wash the top with running water and soap or if not available drink with a straw.
>
> A family friend's friend died after drinking a can of soda! Apparently, she didn't clean the top before drinking from the can. The top was encrusted with dried rat's urine which is toxic and obviously lethal!!!!! Canned drinks and other food stuff are stored in warehouses and containers that are usually infested with rodents and then get transported to the retail outlets without being properly cleaned.
>
> Send this to everybody you know!!!!!

Forty seconds of research on AltaVista (we didn't have Google back then) confirmed what I remembered from high school biology class: Urine from healthy animals is basically sterile, and the sorts of diseases carried by rats that can be fatal to humans are extremely uncommon in the United States.

Also, virtually all soda cans are boxed or shrink-wrap palletized as soon as they're manufactured and are never warehoused completely exposed. Soda manufacturers know precisely how most of us drink their products (bottoms up!) and they're not about to let themselves in for lawsuits by allowing exposed can tops to collect dust, dirt, or animal or human pathogens.

My poor co-worker had fallen for one of the hoariest Internet hoaxes out there. Being fundamentally good-hearted and a caring mother, she obediently forwarded the silly message not only to everyone in her personal address book, but also to everyone at the company. Doubtless there were others in the company who received it from her and sent it to everyone in *their* address books, from which it probably grew 15 legs and continued its digital gallop around the networked world, gunking up untold PCs as it went. I occasionally got variations on that same message for the next two or three years, and I hear that people are still passing it on.

Social Engineering Viruses

Things like this are a special form of virus, which some people call a mental virus or a social engineering virus because they rely on you to reproduce them by forwarding them to "everyone in your address book!!!!!"

Social engineering viruses exist in several different categories. Not all are hoaxes, but all are spam gunk and serious nuisances, and some can be downright dangerous if taken seriously:

√ Warnings about health threats (like rat urine, see earlier) or "silly science," like recent findings that the sun is going to explode in six years.

√ Political misinformation intended to sway elections or at least harass an opponent. ("John Kerry has a secret agreement with the Sierra Club to institute a $1,000 annual tax on all SUVs!!!!!")

√ Pleas for charitable assistance, usually in ways that require little of the recipient, like clicking on an ad or sending business cards to a sick child. (Almost none of them ask for money, how could you guess?)

√ Announcements of phony giveaways, which includes the infamous Bill Gates $1,000 hoax, phony coupons from various store and restaurant chains, and so on.

√ Prayer/inspiration chain letters, which threaten you with divine retribution (or at least bad luck) if you refuse to send the letter to at least 10 other people.

√ Jokes; usually cruel or tasteless.

√ Inspirational stories or messages.

√ Phony warnings about computer viruses or Trojan horse attacks, sometimes with "removal" instructions that do damage to your system by deleting essential Windows files. These are social engineering viruses with a vengeance: You are both the reproductive system *and* the payload!

Don't take such things seriously, don't act on them, and puh-*leez* don't add to the world's spam gunk by forwarding them to anyone else! The fact that they came from Aunt Mona (who spends her livelong day trafficking in Internet urban legends and prayer chain letters) should be reason enough to discount them, but if you want hard data, you need to take a spin through one of the various "hoaxbuster" sites out there, all of which exist to put these things six feet under.

The great-great-granddaddy of all hoaxbuster sites is Snopes (**www.snopes.com**), and the best way to get a quick check on a possible Internet hoax is to Google on the hoax topic like this:

snopes rat urine

Snopes is a wonderland of reality checks on an endless number of bizarre hoax topics (see Figure 15.1). Many of these are urban legends that go around without any help from computers, but a great many of them find their way into our

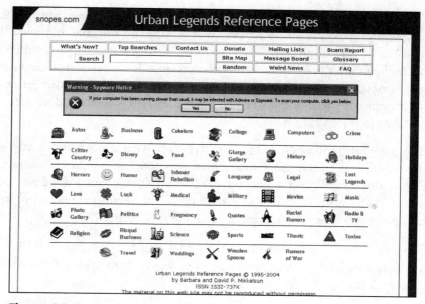

Figure 15.1

The Snopes.com main page.

inboxes on a very regular basis—with a lot of help from old Aunt Mona, who clearly needs a new hobby.

Other hoaxbuster sites I've used with success include these:

√ The DOE Computer Incident Advisory Center's Hoaxbusters (**http://hoaxbusters.ciac.org/**)

√ Nuketown Hoaxes (**www.nuketown.com/hoaxes/**)

√ Art Boese's Museum of Hoaxes (**www.museumofhoaxes.com/**)

So Why Are Harmless Social Engineering Viruses Wrong?

Two reasons, basically. The first is that *they are spam gunk.* If you forward them on, you are a spammer. They use valuable Internet bandwidth. Spam (including social engineering viruses) now accounts for perhaps 70 percent of all Internet traffic. When Internet machinery gets overloaded, packets get lost, messages are corrupted or dropped entirely, and legitimate traffic does not get through. If you're reading this book on spam and malware gunk, you're probably trying to be part of the solution—so don't be a part of the problem!

Second, and perhaps more important, "harmless" is a slippery concept. Some people, especially the lonely elderly and the superstitious, take things like "bad luck" or "God's displeasure" very seriously, and threatening such things can make their rather gray lives even more miserable. Jokes can hurt feelings. A lot of the jokes I get from the usual suspects are the sorts of things that go around the Internet because nobody would print them anywhere—and no, I am not going to give any examples.

You may not be the best judge of what's truly harmless. An apparently well-meant warning to remove a virus or turn on some sort of Windows security feature may sound good to you, but then again, if you're not a Windows techie, how do you know it's legit? You may think you're helping someone but in fact may be giving them a blueprint to disabling their entire PC.

The best rule to follow in dealing with social engineering viruses is this:

√ Delete *any* message that instructs you to forward it to anyone (or everyone) you know!

Avoid the Nigerian 419 Scams

By now, virtually everyone on Earth, plus the astronauts in the Space Station, has received at least one of a certain species of letter via email. The details vary, but the overall template is pretty much the same in every case. Rather than spending the next two pages describing these letters, I'll just toss in a pretty typical one, out of the countless examples that have turned up in my inbox over the past five or six years. In full:

FROM: BARRISTER AKIN ESQ.

      MOSES & CO

      ATTORNEYS/LEGAL PRACTITIONER

      NIGERIA

SUBJECT: WE NEED YOUR ASSISTANCE.

DEAR FRIEND,

COMPLIMENTS OF THE SEASON. GRACE AND PEACE AND LOVE FROM THIS PART OF THE ATLANTIC TO YOU. I HOPE MY LETTER DOES NOT CAUSE YOU TOO MUCH EMBARRASSMENT AS I WRITE TO YOU IN GOOD FAITH BASED ON THE CONTACT ADDRESS GIVEN TO ME BY A FRIEND WHO WORKS AT THE NIGERIAN EMBASSY IN YOUR COUNTRY. PLEASE EXCUSE MY INTRUSION INTO YOUR PRIVATE LIFE.

I AM BARRISTER AKIN MOSES ESQ. I REPRESENT MOHAMMED ABACHA, SON OF THE LATE GEN.SANI ABACHA, WHO WAS THE FORMER MILITARY HEAD OF STATE IN NIGERIA. HE DIED IN 1998. SINCE HIS DEATH, THE FAMILY HAS BEEN LOSING A LOT OF MONEY DUE TO VINDICTIVE GOVERNMENT OFFICIALS WHO ARE BENT ON DEALING WITH THE FAMILY. BASED ON THIS THEREFORE, THE FAMILY HAS ASKED ME TO SEEK FOR A

FOREIGN PARTNER WHO CAN WORK WITH US AS TO MOVE OUT THE TOTAL SUM OF US$75,000,000.00 (SEVENTY FIVE MILLION UNITED STATES DOLLARS), PRESENTLY IN THEIR POS-SESSION. THIS MONEY WAS OF COURSE ACQUIRED BY THE LATE PRESIDENT AND IS NOW KEPT SECRETLY BY THE FAMILY. THE SWISS GOVERNMENT HAS ALREADY FROZEN ALL THE ACCOUNTS OF THE FAMILY IN SWITZERLAND, AND SOME OTHER COUNTRIES WOULD SOON FOLLOW TO DO THE SAME. THIS BID BY SOME GOVERNMENT OFFICIALS TO DEAL WITH THIS FAMILY

HAS MADE IT NECESSARY THAT WE SEEK YOUR ASSISTANCE IN RECEIVING THIS MONEY AND IN INVESTING IT ON BEHALF OF THE FAMILY.

THIS MUST BE A JOINT VENTURE TRANSACTION AND WE MUST ALL WORK TOGETHER. SINCE THIS MONEY IS STILL CASH, EX-TRA SECURITY MEASURES HAVE BEEN TAKEN TO PROTECT IT FROM THEFT OR SEIZURE, PENDING WHEN AGREEMENT IS REACHED ON WHEN AND HOW TO MOVE IT INTO ANY OF YOUR NOMINATED BANK ACCOUNTS. I HAVE PERSONALLY

WORKED OUT ALL MODALITIES FOR THE PEACEFUL CONCLU-
SION OF THIS TRANSACTION. THE TRANSACTION DEFINITELY
WOULD BE HANDLED IN PHASES AND THE FIRST PHASE WILL
INVOLVE THE MOVING OF US$25,000,000.00(TWENTY FIVE
MILLION UNITED STATES DOLLARS).

MY CLIENTS ARE WILLING TO GIVE YOU A REASONABLE PER-
CENTAGE OF THIS MONEY AS SOON AS THE TRANSACTION
IS CONCLUDED. I WILL, HOWEVER, BASED ON THE GROUNDS
THAT YOU ARE WILLING TO WORK WITH US AND ALSO ALL
CONTENTIOUS ISSUES DISCUSSED BEFORE THE COMMENCE-
MENT OF THIS TRANSACTION. YOU MAY ALSO DISCUSS YOUR
PERCENTAGE BEFORE WE START TO WORK. AS SOON AS I
HEAR FROM YOU, I WILL GIVE YOU ALL NECESSARY DETAILS
AS TO HOW WE INTEND TO CARRY OUT THE WHOLE TRANS-
ACTION. PLEASE, DO NOT ENTERTAIN ANY FEARS, AS ALL
NECESSARY MODALITIES ARE IN PLACE, AND I ASSURE YOU
OF ALL SUCCESS AND SAFETY IN THIS TRANSACTION.

PLEASE, THIS TRANSACTION REQUIRES ABSOLUTE CONFIDEN-
TIALITY AND YOU WOULD BE EXPECTED TO TREAT IT AS SUCH
UNTIL THE FUNDS ARE MOVED OUT OF THIS COUNTRY.

PLEASE, YOU WILL ALSO IGNORE THIS LETTER AND RESPECT
OUR TRUST IN YOU BY NOT EXPOSING THIS TRANSACTION,
EVEN IF YOU ARE NOT INTERESTED. LOOK FORWARD TO
WORKING WITH YOU. THANK YOU.

TRULY YOURS,

BARRISTER AKIN MOSES ESQ.

The whole goal of these letters is to dupe *you* into beginning a conversation
with some shadowy Nigerian who claims to be "Mr. Akin Moses," and then
hand Mr. Moses and his friends the instructions for making an electronic funds
transfer into your bank account. Once the account information is in their hands,
instead of transferring that imaginary $75 million into your account, they will
siphon anything out of the account that might happen to be there and then
vanish. If you're smart enough to give them an empty account to work with,

they will begin asking for money for "documentation fees," or bribes, or something else that has the bare whiff of plausibility. The money moves one way, into Nigeria…or South Africa, or Sierra Leone, or Liberia, or some other troubled African nation. Nigeria was the first, and now all the other nearby countries are trying for a piece of the action. Alas, there appears to be more than enough grasping stupidity in the First World to go around.

Most people will look at this, roll their eyes, and ask, "What kind of knucklehead would fall for *that*?" I'm not sure, but so many knuckleheads *do* fall for it that literally hundreds of millions of dollars have flowed into Nigeria and other African countries on the back of this scam, most of it from the United States. It's a sort of international pigeon drop (go look it up) and the annual take is more than most of these nations post for a gross national product.

The scam is not new, nor did it begin with the Internet. In the early 1990s, I used to get one or two postal letters a year from Nigeria, addressed to "Business Owner" or "Business Executive" at our office address. The pitch was written on a typewriter and came in a hand-addressed envelope with very pretty Nigerian stamps on it. One was even perfumed. That they were able to do this by hand implies that they had a significant response rate, which doesn't say much for the intelligence (or moral fiber) of the average American.

There's nothing to be done about this from a law enforcement standpoint, either here or in Africa. Once your money is gone, it's gone. Nigeria is in a state of anarchy right now, and its own government officials have no real power to enforce Section 419 (hence the name of the scam) of the Nigerian penal code against the scammers. Westerners who have gone to Nigeria to either "buy their way in" or perhaps complain about not receiving their cut have been kidnapped, held for ransom, mutilated, or killed.

What you can do about it is keep an ear cocked for any signs that your more naïve relatives or friends are contemplating responding to one of these pitches. Do whatever you must to persuade them that it's a scam. Some people seem to have a mighty thin grip on reality, and those are the ones who become the prey of the Nigerian Money Mafia. Don't let it be you, or anyone you know.

Don't Be Victim to Identity Theft Because of Phishing Expeditions

Resisting viral inspirations and chain letters from Aunt Mona, and even those scam letters from Nigeria, is simply a matter of common sense and a little willpower. The messages they carry may not be truthful, but they're easy to recognize as gunk, and it only takes a second to nuke 'em till they glow. The final category of scams I'm going to treat in this chapter is another matter.

Here's the scenario: An email arrives in your inbox. In full:

Dear Citibank Member,

This email was sent by the Citibank server to verify your E-mail address. You must complete this process by clicking on the link below and entering in the small window your Citibank ATM/Debit Card number and PIN that you use on ATM.

This is done for your protection - because some of our members no longer have access to their email addresses and we must verify it.

To verify your E-mail address and access your bank account, click on the link below:

https://web.da-us.citibank.com/signin/citifi/scripts/email_verify.jsp

— — — — — — — — — — — — — — — — — —

Thank you for using Citibank

— — — — — — — — — — — — — — — — — —

Sounds a little odd, perhaps—especially if you don't have an account at Citibank. If you do have an account there, however, your first impulse might be to click on the link and just get it over with, grumbling about those damned computers and how nobody seems to be able to do anything right and keep things running anymore.

The Web link is always shown in full and appears to be at the citibank.com domain. If you do click on the link, you'll be taken to a Web site that looks authentic: Citibank logo graphics, professional design, Citibank links at the bottom, and so on. In the middle is a Web form for you to enter your Citibank credit card/ATM number, along with your PIN. What could be wrong here?

Answer: *Everything.*

The message didn't come from Citibank. The site to which the message took you wasn't at Citibank. When you type in your ATM card number and PIN, it won't go to Citibank. Instead, it will go to some shady guys in some difficult-to-determine part of the world, who will then empty out your Citibank account and (if the card is a credit card as well) shop the card out to its limit.

Zip! The hook is set, and you've been phished and you've been the next identity theft victim!

The New Scourge of the Internet

Scams like this are the new scourge of the Internet, shoving those pesky Nigerians aside as the currently hot way to bilk Americans out of their money. The Nigerians have to appeal to your greed, and not everybody is greedy—or stupid enough to believe those Nigerian tall tales. The people who impersonate Citibank, or eBay, or PayPal, or any of three dozen other major financial institutions around the country, only have to appeal to your desire to keep your bank account current and functional.

This species of scam is called *phishing.* (It has nothing whatsoever to do with the venerable rock band Phish, and one wonders what those poor guys think of it all.) Phishing is about impersonating a bank (or a pseudo-bank like PayPal or an auction site like eBay) and then "fishing" for ATM card and PINs, bank account numbers and passwords, and so on. Phishing spam messages are sent out by the tens of millions, so even if only one percent of the recipients have Citibank accounts, there is a strong possibility that one of those recipients will take the bait and bite.

Those who bite become victims of big-time identity theft, and it can take months of paperwork and creating new accounts to put things completely right again.

Impersonating a Web Site

If you're even a little bit skeptical, those Nigerian scam letters will smell phish, er, fishy to you as soon as you see them. Why would somebody in Nigeria single out someone in Dubuque (who works in a dentist's office and has never been to Africa) to help smuggle $75,000,000 out of the country? Anybody who would believe that has been watching *way* too much TV.

On the other hand, Citibank is a very big bank with a lot of customers. And "computer error" is a commonplace with truly mythic resonance in every American life. Who hasn't been told that "we can't do anything right now because the computers are down"? It sounds all too plausible. Computers are *always* messing up. Everybody knows that.

Furthermore, the Web site looks *exactly* like the Citibank Web site. You won't have seen that particular screen on the Citibank site before (because it doesn't exist!), but you've been to a number of the others, and all the logos and layouts look pretty much the same. If you click on the "Privacy Policy" link at the bottom, you'll go to Citibank's privacy policy screen. How could a bunch of crooks huddling in a yurt in Outer Slobovia have a site that looks so much like Citibank's site?

Here's how.

1.   Bring up your browser.
2.   In the URL field at the top, enter **www.citibank.com**.
3.   Select File | Save Page As (or File | Save As in Internet Explorer).
4.   Enter a file name somewhere on your hard drive.
5.   Click Save.

You've just "stolen" the front page of Citibank's Web site, including its graphics and all the HTML code that it took to display the page precisely as you saw it. It's absurdly easy to copy virtually any part of anybody's Web site and save it to disk. You don't have to be a shadowy black hat type with years of experience cracking networks.

With only a little work, you can go "beneath the surface" inside the saved HTML code and modify just a couple of Internet addresses. You then have a Web page that says Citibank all over it, but in the crucial places, contains the address of a temporary Web page hosted somewhere in Eastern Europe or Central Asia.

"Bait and Switch" Web Links

What about that authentic-looking Citibank URL in the scam email? (Look back to the phishing message on page 294.) *Phony.* The text displayed for a clickable Web link does not necessarily contain the destination URL for the link. Think for a second: How many Web links in Web pages display a URL?

Not many. Most say simple textual things like "Privacy Policy" or "About Us." In HTML, a clickable Web link has two parts:

1. The text that you see on a Web page, like "About Us."
2. The actual URL to which you'll go after clicking on the link.

Most of the time, #2 is invisible, and you only see #1. A crook can put *citibank.com* in the displayed text, and then put *crookedscammer.com* in the URL itself, which you won't see. This is in fact what is done in virtually all phishing scams. So it's a kind of bait and switch: You see citibank.com in the email message, but go to crookedscammer.com when you click the link.

How Not to Get Hooked

First of all, unless you're a die-hard techie, there's no point in trying to determine whether a given site is fraudulent by examining the Web page. Take a look at Figure 15.2. This is a screen capture of an HTML phishing scam message that I received recently. Looks authentic indeed—and it took me several minutes of close inspection of the underlying code to figure out where the damned thing was set to transmit the information it wanted from me.

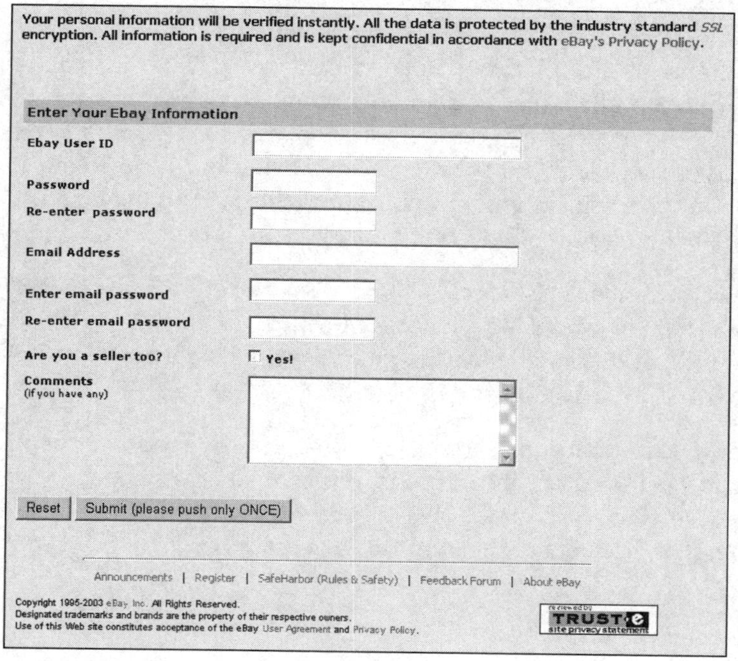

Figure 15.2
An eBay phishing scam.

The destination is in fact hidden in the code shown below. Can you find it?

```
<FORM action-3Dhttp://mc04.equinox.net/tools/netform.t method=3Dpost>
<INPUT= name=3Dtoaddress type=3Dhidden value=3Debay_sc@yahoo.com> <INPUT
name=3Dmailsubject= type=3Dhidden value=3D"MacConnect Information">
<INPUT name=3Dresponsepage= type=3Dhidden value=3Dhttp://www.ebay.com/
index.html>
```

I didn't think so—and I leave it as an exercise for the reader.

My point is that trying to determine if a message is genuinely from Citibank or not is futile. There's no good way to tell, especially if you're nontechnical. That being the case there's only one way to be absolutely sure you don't fall for a phishing scheme:

√   *Never go to an important Web site by clicking on a URL in an email message!*

If you need to check your online banking account, open up a Web browser and *type in the URL of the bank manually.* Always type it. Never click on anything to go there.

GunkBuster's Notebook: Using SpoofStick to Verify Web Sites

The heart of any phishing scam is convincing you that you're going to the eBay site (or some other important site with which you have a trusted relationship) when in fact you're going to an imposter site. Black hat scammers have numerous tricks to make their imposter sites appear to be the real thing. Even the address in the navigation toolbar can't be trusted completely.

How can you tell? It's difficult—which is why you're well advised never to go to a banking site (or something like eBay) by clicking on a URL in an email message or an instant message, even if it appear to be from someone you know.

A new tool from CoreStreet Software, called SpoofStick, can provide a little help. It's free and easy to install, and once you navigate to a Web site (however you do it), it will confirm the Internet domain of the site that you're actually on. In other words, if you think you're on ebay.com, look at SpoofStick's display bar. If it doesn't say, "You're on ebay.com," close the browser *immediately*.

Download SpoofStick from CoreStreet's Web site: **www.corestreet.com/spoofstick/**. There are two versions, one for Internet Explorer and one for Mozilla Firefox. The version for Internet Explorer is a 170 KB Windows installer that you download and run, as with any Windows installer.

The version for Firefox is a Mozilla XPI browser extension, and Firefox will install it for you, direct from CoreStreet's site. Here's how it's done:

1. Make sure that you have enabled Firefox Web installs. To check (or enable them if not), select Tools|Options and click the Advanced icon.

2. Under the Software Update header, see if the "Allow Web sites to install software" item is checked. If not, check it and click OK, and then close and restart Firefox.

3. Click on the link labeled "Download now" on the Mozilla version download page on the SpoofStick portion of the CoreStreet site. The dialog shown in Figure 15.3 will appear, asking permission to install the software. Click Install Now.

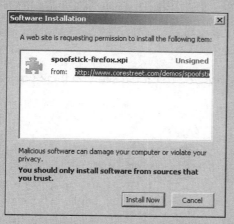

Figure 15.3

The Mozilla Firefox install permission dialog.

4. When the install is complete, close and restart Firefox.

SpoofStick does only one thing: It displays the current domain being viewed by the browser in a new toolbar beneath the other Firefox toolbars. (See Figure 15.4 for an example of SpoofStick doing its job and showing you an eBay page that isn't!) It can see past all known scammer tricks, and you can trust what it says. If you ever see what appears to be a discrepancy between where you think you are and what SpoofStick tells you, close the browser, open it, and type your destination URL again. Never enter personal or financial information into a Web site without

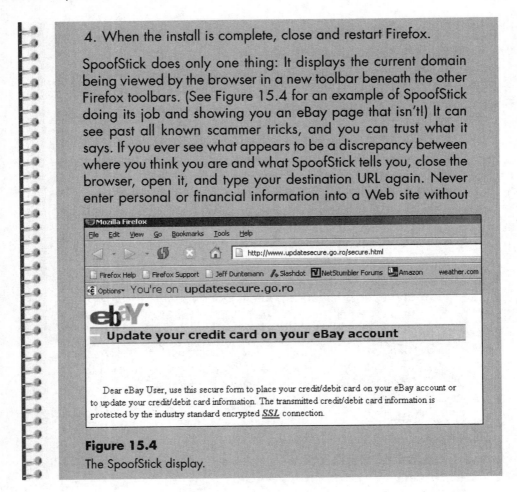

Figure 15.4
The SpoofStick display.

being *absolutely* sure that you're on the site you think you're on!

Summing Up

The best insurance against being taken in by hoaxes and scams isn't technological at all: It's simple skepticism, combined with a moral decision not to take part in any scheme that seems "shady" nor forward anything to "everyone you know" for any reason. Hoaxes can hurt when people believe them. Chain letters (even virtual ones) are illegal. Unlike viruses and worms, *hoaxes and scams can't work if you refuse to take the bait.* This is one case when "just say no" makes a lot of sense, especially if followed by "just hit Delete."

Degunking After a Malware Attack

Degunking Checklist:

√ Don't panic when your antivirus utility or firewall announces that it has stopped a malware threat. That's their job, and they're doing it.

√ If odd things begin to happen on your PC, stop your work, back up all your data, and run a full-system virus scan (followed by an adware/spyware scan) immediately.

√ Always let your antivirus or anti-spyware utilities do as much of the work of removing malware from your system as you can.

√ Before you assume that malware is responsible for a dead PC, make sure you're not the victim of a hardware failure.

√ If Windows won't boot and you still have data on the hard drive that hasn't been backed up, try booting into Safe Mode.

√ If Safe Mode won't work, obtain a Linux LiveCD and boot your PC into Linux.

√ If Windows won't boot, first attempt a nondestructive reinstall or repair of Windows.

I probably watch the Weather Channel too much. Every day, it seems, there's new footage of a flood plain somewhere with houses window-deep in water. In between the news footage are commercials from companies that repair water and smoke damage "like it never even happened." Talk about targeted marketing! Carol and I have an unbreakable dictum to which we've adhered throughout our 28 years of marriage: *Never live near water.* Lots of people like to live near water, and if you live near enough to water, sooner or later you end up calling one of those places that promises to fix your water damage "like it never even happened."

Odds are good that if you pay attention and take the psychological and technological steps I've outlined in the past several chapters, you'll never get hit by a bad malware attack. On the other hand, there is such a thing as bad luck. There are occasional floods in the Arizona desert—lived there; watched them on the evening news. (In Arizona, not only do you not live near water, you don't live near ditches, either!) If your luck is bad, you may run into a brand-new virus before the antivirus companies can distribute a signature for it. You may run into a worm that can get through a firewall by exploiting a security hole *in the firewall.* (This happened in the spring of 2004, to several of Internet Security Systems's products, including the popular Black Ice firewall. It wasn't pretty.)

So what do you do when your luck runs out and the bad guys lay waste to your PC? There's no gunk like the gunk that comes of a bad malware attack. At minimum it's renamed files or added (and pointedly *unwanted*) Registry entries. At worst it means lost data and an unbootable PC. In this final chapter I'm going to help you get your head around the challenge of recovering from a malware attack. This involves knowing what to do, and also knowing when you're in over your head. Yelling for help may sometimes be the sanest thing to do after an attack, but more than anything else, you need to simply keep your cool and not panic.

Understand the Five PC Defense Conditions

There's bad, and then there's *bad.* You can have a little water in the basement, or you can have water lapping at your front door and pouring in through the dryer vent. Not all malware affects your PC identically, and not all malware gunk is equally serious. To help sort things out, I've borrowed a card from the military and defined five "defense conditions" that may arise inside your PC. Only four of the following DefCons are due to malware, but the fifth can fool you. Read them carefully, and see which most closely matches your situation:

1. You discover a malware attack because your antivirus product spots a virus or your anti-spyware product spots some new spyware. Your PC appears to be working normally and nothing weird is happening. DefCon 1.

2. Your PC appears to be working normally; it's as fast as always, it boots OK, and all your files seem to be intact, but weird things have begun happening, things that never happened before and don't seem to be associated with Windows or any of your installed software. Pop-up windows come and go. One of your installed taskbar applications turns up missing. Your network port seems to be working overtime (judging by the taskbar tray indicator) whether you're doing anything network related or not. DefCon 2.

3. Your PC is running slow. It's crashing more than it usually does, and you're getting some weird signs: An application aborts without any indication of what's wrong, odd pop-ups appear, the desktop blanks and refreshes, and when it does, some of your taskbar tray icons vanish and the rest reappear in a different order. Some of your files may turn up missing or corrupt. It's become difficult to get any work done. DefCon 3.

4. Your PC goes through its startup sequence but Windows won't boot and it just hangs somewhere during the startup process until you shut off the power. DefCon 4.

5. Your PC is dead meat. Nothing lights up, the drives aren't spinning, or (worse) there's a smell of something burning somewhere. DefCon 5.

Each of these defense conditions requires a different strategy. I'll describe each strategy individually—but first, we have to ask a very important question.

Was It Really Malware?

In this chapter, we're going to be concerned primarily with DefCons 1 through 4. DefCon 5 is a special case: It's a hardware failure. Something in the PC's physical mechanism—its power supply or motherboard, most likely—has simply failed. This has nothing to do with malware. If your PC isn't working, the first thing you need to do is eliminate hardware failure as a cause so that you don't end up chasing black hats who aren't there!

Here are some guidelines for identifying hardware failure:

√ Make sure you have power to the outlet into which the PC is plugged!

√ If the PC is dead and you smell something burning, pull the plug—it's an electrical failure in the hardware, probably in the power supply.

√ Nearly all PCs have a power LED somewhere in front where you can see it. If you push the power switch and there's no light, it's probably a power supply failure.

√   All power supplies have a fan. After you turn the PC on (and you see the power LED light up), if you wet a finger and hold it near the fan's exhaust grill, you should feel air moving and (especially with modern PCs) hear the fan motor. If you don't detect a running fan, your power supply has failed.

√   If the power supply seems to be working but you see nothing on the display, make sure your monitor is plugged in, powered up, and connected to the graphics card in your PC. (Look for loose connectors!) On a CRT (non-flat) monitor, you should feel a tickle from static electricity if you hold the back of your hand to the glass front of the display. If the monitor is powered up and you feel no static electricity, your monitor may have failed.

√   If you power up the system and see nothing but a flashing cursor in the corner of the display, your motherboard has probably failed.

√   If the PC makes any of a number of sequences of beeping tones, there is a hardware failure of some kind in the system that could include the motherboard, the keyboard, or the mouse.

If you have more than one computer in the house, it can be useful to swap in another monitor to make sure your first monitor hasn't failed. This can be done with the keyboard or the mouse as well if you suspect those.

Debugging failed hardware further than this is outside the charter of this book. If you're nontechnical, you'll probably need help, from a technical friend or perhaps by taking the computer in for a look at a local computer dealer. One caution: If it's an old PC and the motherboard fails, you're unlikely to find a newer motherboard that will work in that system. Plan on getting a whole new PC. Old hard drives can be transplanted into new PCs, so you won't necessarily lose all of your data files, assuming that the hard drive is not the part that failed.

Is It Simply Plain Old Windows Gunk?

Sometimes, a DefCon 3 situation may have nothing to do with malware either. All Windows systems collect data gunk over time due to ordinary day-to-day work, installing and uninstalling applications, and writing and deleting files. This kind of gunk slows PCs down because of unnecessary, abandoned, or corrupt keys in the Windows Registry and also due to nearly full or badly fragmented hard drives or new, memory-hungry applications installed in old, memory-starved PCs. Not all gunk comes from malware. If after you run your antivirus and anti-spyware utilities and find no malware, your PC is still slow and erratic, you should obtain my book *Degunking Windows* (with Joli Ballew; Paraglyph Press, 2004) and run through its cleaning regimen. It's amazing what a little Registry cleaning, disk drive defragmenting, and perhaps a little more memory can do for a sluggish PC!

How to Handle DefCon 1

DefCon 1 happens when your virus or spyware defenses report malware but nothing bad seems to be happening. A lot of people panic when they see a pop-up from their antivirus utility telling them that a virus has been detected. First of all, don't panic! Your antivirus utility is doing what it was designed to do. If it popped up a warning while you were working, it probably detected the virus when the virus was attempting to run, and in all likelihood the antivirus utility prevented the virus from doing any damage at all.

The big question to ask yourself when your antivirus utility reports a virus is this: *What did I do to allow a virus to trigger my defenses?* Were you trying to open an email attachment? Were you trying to install a piece of software? Had you just navigated to a Web site? Viruses generally need some sort of cooperation from you to execute. If possible, learn something from those antivirus warnings. Go back and read Chapters 11 through 13, and adjust your habits accordingly.

If you're running a regular scan of your PC with your antivirus utility and it reports that it has found infected files, again, don't panic. Infected files can land on your PC without the virus executing and taking hold. Most of the time, infected files will be found in your email client's attachments directory and they are infected attachments that came in that you *didn't* open. Your PC isn't infected in the purest sense of the word. Your antivirus utility will probably offer to quarantine or disinfect those files, and if it does, let it do its job. Once the infected files are quarantined or deleted, the danger is over. (Read the documentation for your specific antivirus utility to see if you have anything you need to do to allow the utility to complete its removal of infected files.)

The important thing to remember about DefCon 1 is that it's just daily life in our heavily networked world. Virus files will come to you in spam. Spyware will slip past you. Some personal firewall products (Black Ice Defender is a good example) have tray icons that turn red and flash when they block a probe from a worm or a script. Some people freak out when that happens: *Egad! The bad guys are at the door!* Relax. The bad guys are *always* at the door. That's why you have a firewall. (And that's why ZoneAlarm doesn't give you any indication when it turns back a malware probe. There's nothing you can do that ZoneAlarm hasn't already done, and it doesn't want you to worry.)

Keep your defenses up, don't do stupid things, and with any luck you'll never progress beyond DefCon 1.

How to Handle DefCon 2

When weird (or at the very least, unexpected) things begin to happen on your PC, malware may be at the bottom of it, and that's when you advance to DefCon 2. In DefCon 2, your PC itself seems to be working normally (in terms of speed and reliability) apart from those odd things. Here are some items to watch for:

√ Your network activity tray icon is active all or most of the time. (This is the little icon that looks like two PCs, one slightly behind and to one side of the other.) Be especially wary if it's active when you have no Internet software running, like file sharing utilities, a Web browser, or a VoIP product like Skype.

√ Your antivirus utility or firewall icons suddenly fail to appear in the taskbar tray or appear in their inactive or disabled form. Many modern malware items uninstall or disable antivirus or firewall products so that they can do their work undetected.

√ Unfamiliar dialogs or pop-ups appear that don't seem to be connected with any of your accustomed software products.

√ The "Sent Items" folder in your email client suddenly has dozens or hundreds of new, short messages in it that you don't recall sending. That's a pretty good sign that an address book virus has gotten loose and had its way with your email client.

√ One or more of your friends call you or message you, telling you that they received a virus from you.

Once you start seeing things like this, it's time to take action. Again, don't panic, but don't delay, either. Follow this plan, in order:

1. If your antivirus utility is running (look for its icon in your taskbar tray), bring up its configuration window and request an update from its remote server over the Internet. It's possible that you "lucked in" to a brand-new virus or worm, and if the signature data for that virus or worm was added to the utility's database in the last couple of days, your copy may not yet include it. The idea here is to get your antivirus utility completely up-to-date before running a scan.

2. After your antivirus update has come down, disconnect your PC's network port from the Internet. Literally unplug the cable from the PC or from the cable/DSL modem. If you're connected to the Internet via dialup, close the connection and unplug the PC from the modem and the modem from the wall. If you don't already have a software firewall or a router with a built-in NAT firewall, put one in place (see Chapter 14) before reconnecting to the Internet.

3. Shut down the PC and restart it. (Note well: If you don't already have an antivirus utility installed, run down to the local computer dealer *now*, buy one in a box, and install it, as explained in Chapter 12!)

4. Immediately start a full virus scan of your entire PC. If you're just installing an antivirus utility, you'll be asked for permission to do a full scan during the install. This is important: The utility *must* knock out any running viruses or worms before it can safely install its own files on your PC. It may well find a virus or a worm and then may either automatically or with your permission (through a dialog) begin removing the worm or virus. Let it work. If it displays a dialog indicating the name of a particular worm or virus, write down the information it displays on paper and keep it for future reference.

5. Whether or not your antivirus utility finds a worm or virus, run your anti-spyware utility against your entire hard drive.

6. Back up all of your data from the PC hard drive to a CD-R or some other kind of removable medium, like a Zip cartridge or USB flash drive. (More on this shortly.) This data may be infected with viruses, and you will have to scan the removable medium for viruses after the PC has been set right.

7. Reboot your PC again, and *without reconnecting to the Internet,* get back to your usual work and observe what the PC is doing. Did any of the "odd things" happen again?

8. If you can possibly manage it, wait a day or (ideally) two before reconnecting to the Internet. When you do, update your antivirus utility yet again from its home server and do another scan for viruses, taking notes on anything the utility discovers.

9. Scan your backup (made in Step 6) for viruses. If the backup is on read/write media (like a Zip or flash drive), allow the antivirus utility to disinfect what it finds.

10. Work cautiously, keeping your eyes open for more unusual things happening on your PC. If your antivirus utility is not set to automatically bring down updates on a daily basis, configure it to do so, or at least go up and get an update manually every night and do a scan nightly for the next week to make sure your antivirus utility will catch any brand-new viruses or worms that may have infected your PC.

Most people who find themselves in a DefCon 2 situation do so because they haven't yet installed an antivirus utility or firewall or haven't kept their antivirus utility up-to-date. DefCon 2 is often caused by "stealth" viruses or worms, which have a payload (like a spam relay) that needs to operate in a relatively healthy PC. This forces them to let the PC operate as well as possible, which means they tend not to damage Windows or your data files.

For the most part, what degunking needs to be done is best left to your antivirus and/or anti-spyware utilities. The industry leader products are quite good at stripping out all traces of malware and whatever reconfiguration it has done to your PC. With any luck at all, that's all the degunking that you'll have to do. And if you got to DefCon 2 by neglecting virus or firewall protection, get your shields up and learn from your mistake!

On the other hand, once malware has damaged your data or Windows itself, you've advanced to DefCon 3.

GunkBuster's Notebook: *What Files Should Be Backed Up?*

It may be a little late to be talking about backups here, but better late than never, and a good reminder never hurts. Recovering from malware attacks beyond DefCon 2 often requires restoring from your data backups—and if you never made those backups, your data may be irretrievably lost.

I powerfully recommend keeping as much of your data on removable media as possible rather than leaving it on your hard drive. I have for years kept all my data on Zip cartridges or (more recently) 256 MB Cruzer Mini flash drives, which I plug right into the USB 2.0 ports on the front panel of my main PC. Data that isn't mounted on the PC won't be damaged in a malware attack.

Certain things will remain on your hard drive that should be backed up:

√ Your entire **C:\Documents and Settings** folder and all its subfolders and files should be backed up. Degunk this folder regularly, to reduce clutter and thus the size of the backup and the time it takes to do it.

√ Few people think of this, but your **C:\WINNT\Fonts** folder should be backed up as well. The applications you install may place fonts into this folder, and if a virus destroys the folder, your applications that expect to find their fonts in the folder will not work correctly.

√ If you have digital photos, music files, or other media files, make sure they're backed up. I keep all such files in folders under a folder I created called C:\Media so that they're not scattered all over my hard drive.

√ Back up your mailbase, however it has to be done from the email client that you're using. I spoke of this in detail in Chapter 4.

√ Back up any "install files" that you bought or downloaded, for applications, utilities, or games that did not come on their own installer CDs. I keep all these in a folder I created called **C:\Install Suites** and back it up regularly.

√ Anything else that isn't installed as part of an application (for which you have an install CD or install file) and that you would mind losing if your whole PC went up in flames should be backed up as well.

Let this principle guide you: You want to have a backup of anything that you would need to completely rebuild your PC if necessary or to make a brand new PC the functional equivalent of your old PC.

How to Handle DefCon 3

Now it gets ugly. A DefCon 3 situation means that your PC is malfunctioning in terms of frequent crashes or extremely slow or otherwise erratic operation. Windows still boots, but the machine is slow enough, or crashes enough, so that you're having a hard time getting anything useful done with it.

It's still possible (as I explained earlier in this chapter) that malware is not involved. A PC that has been used for years and years will sometimes gunk up due to "Windows arthritis" (a kind of unavoidable digital entropy) and slow down or begin crashing. This is the topic of my earlier book *Degunking Windows,* and if your antivirus and anti-spyware utilities find no malware, you need to degunk the PC generally, which is outside the topic of this book.

However, once you get to DefCon 3, you may find that your data, or Windows itself, has been damaged. Backups are extremely important here.

Your plan is different from that of DefCon 2 because things are a little more serious:

1. Disconnect your PC from the Internet, just as explained for DefCon 2. If you don't already have a software firewall or router containing a NAT firewall, put one in place before you reconnect to the Internet.

2. If your antivirus utility is installed and still functioning, run a full-system virus scan. Don't try to go online to get an update, and don't reboot. Do a scan right now and let the utility clean up anything it finds.

3. If your antivirus utility doesn't appear to be working, or if you haven't installed one yet, try to get it working or install one. If your antivirus utility isn't present in the taskbar tray or if you can't bring it up from the Start | Programs menu, attempt to reinstall it from the original CD or installer file. During the reinstall (or initial install), allow the utility to do a full-system scan. Write down the names of any malware it identifies in any pop-up alerts.

4. Do a scan for adware and spyware and let the utility clean up anything it finds.

5. Reboot the PC. Back up as much of your data to removable media as the PC will allow. Take note of any file system errors that occur, and on what files. If a data file can't be copied, it may be damaged, and you may need to restore it from your backups, if you have them.

6. Do another full-system scan for viruses and worms. Some malware is diabolical enough to reinstall itself after an attempted removal by an antivirus utility. See if any malware that your antivirus utility claims to have removed in Steps 2 or 3 is back again. If this happens, you may need help from someone technical.

7. If you don't already have a software firewall or a router with a built-in NAT firewall, put one in place (see Chapter 14) before reconnecting to the Internet.

8. Once you have a firewall in place, connect to the Internet and bring down any available updates to your antivirus utility and your anti-spyware utility. Run full-system scans with both utilities and write down the names any viruses or worms that turn up.

9. If you're lucky, your PC will now appear to be working correctly again. Some malware interferes enough with PCs while running to cause them to slow down or crash (especially older machines with little memory), and once the malware has been removed, your PC will recover and no damage may have been done.

10. If you're not lucky, your PC will still be slow and unstable. Give it a week and download an update to your antivirus utility every day just before you do a full-system scan. It may be that a brand-new virus or worm has taken over your PC and your antivirus utility vendor needs some time to catch up and distribute signatures to allow its utilities to catch the new virus or worm.

11. If after a week or so of daily updates and scans your antivirus and anti-spyware utilities still claim that your PC is clean but it continues to run slow and crash, Windows may have been damaged. It's decision time. Read on.

When Do You Yell for Help?

I always advise people to leave as much malware degunking as possible to their antivirus and anti-spyware utilities. Unless you have a technical background, trying to pull malware gunk out of a PC by hand is a dicey business that involves editing the Windows Registry, looking at Windows services that run at startup, and so on. This starts to edge into geek territory, and if you're not a geek, you may be hesitant to go further.

If you have the time and the inclination, giving yourself a little geek training is never a bad thing. There are many books out there about using and configuring Windows, most of which touch on the issue of repairing Windows when parts of it are damaged, whether by malware, disk failure, or some sort of human error. This, however, is a long-term, proactive effort. You don't learn Windows down to the Registry level overnight, and if your PC is croaking every 10 minutes and you have work to do, it's not a practical path to follow. Definitely get help, but *learn whatever you can from the help that you get*—and budget some time to learn even more against the next time your PC goes south.

Most Windows help for nontechnical users comes from that informal helpers network that we all have: family, friends, people at work, people at church, people at school, people at the local user group. Ask around. Recovering from malware is a very common problem, and I'd wager that nearly all of your technical friends and relatives have done it more than once.

If you don't have any technical friends to ask for help, consider paid help. Most computer stores offer repair service that includes virus/worm removal and Windows repair, for fees ranging from $50 to $100. There are even services that will make house calls to fix your PC, though you'll pay more for the convenience. One of the largest is Geeks On Call, which has local affiliates in most larger cities. See their Web site:

www.geeksoncall.com/resserv.htm

How to Handle DefCon 4

The definition of DefCon 4 is that Windows will not boot to the desktop. It may begin its usual process but bog down somewhere along the way, or it may get to what looks like the desktop and then freeze. There are only two possibilities here (along with a ghost of a third) and none of them is good:

√   Windows has been damaged by malware. This means you can't use your antivirus and anti-spyware tools to be rid of the malware.

√ Windows is intact but the malware that has infected your PC has configured Windows to launch it at startup and for some reason the malware crashes Windows as it tries to load and run. Older PCs often don't have the processor power or memory to run modern malware (which is just a species of software), which then goes down and takes Windows with it.

√ In a vanishingly small number of cases, a hardware failure (usually in the hard disk system but sometimes in other places) is keeping Windows from starting normally.

If you haven't already backed up your data to removable media, you could be in a bad situation and may not be able to recover your data. Still, you need a strategy for dealing with DefCon 4, and the following is what I recommend, in this order:

1. Try to get your data off the unbootable PC. Windows may be unbootable, but your data is probably still in there on the hard drive. Some of it may have been damaged by the malware, but most of it is probably still there and usable—if you could only get at it. I'll explain some ways to get at it in the next section.

2. Try to repair Windows by performing a nondestructive reinstallation of the operating system. This is easier than it sounds, and in a great many cases it will make Windows work again and won't damage any data still on your hard drive.

3. If nondestructive reinstallation of Windows doesn't work for some reason (typically a disturbance in the underlying format of your hard drive), you may have no alternative but to "burn down the house," that is, reformat your hard drive completely and reinstall Windows from scratch. This wipes your hard drive clean, and if you have any data there that isn't backed up, well, kiss it goodbye.

I'll spend the rest of this chapter showing you how to do these three things.

Get Your Data Out of a Damaged PC

Needless to say, you should have backed up your data long ago, but what if you didn't and Windows won't boot? There are two things to try, only one of which I can explain in detail here:

√ Try to boot Windows into Safe Mode, and then copy data onto removable media. This will at the very least be your diskette drive, but if you're running Windows 2000 or XP, you may also have access to a USB flash drive, which can contain *much* more data than a single floppy diskette!

√ Obtain a bootable Linux LiveCD, boot your PC into Linux, and then copy files from your hard drive to the diskette drive.

The good news is that if your PC's hardware is still completely functional and your hard drive's logical formatting hasn't been disturbed by the malware, there's a good chance that your data is still intact. The problem lies with Windows, and if you can get Windows running, even minimally, you can rescue your data. Even if you can't make Windows turn over at all, there's still a good chance that you can temporarily boot your PC with another operating system that "understands" a Windows hard drive and then copy your data out to diskette under the control of that operating system.

Booting into Windows Safe Mode

Windows includes a little-known mode designed specifically for system repair and diagnostics—and, not coincidentally, for rescuing data from a damaged system. This mode is Windows Safe Mode, and it exists in all releases of Windows from Windows 95 on. In Safe Mode, Windows loads only a minimal copy of itself. It does not load networking support, so you can't go out on the Internet under Safe Mode. It loads only the least-common-denominator graphics mode that all PC graphics cards understand, in 640x480 resolution. It probably does *not* load drivers for third-party add-on hardware like Zip drives, CD or DVD drives, or other removable media. In Safe Mode under Windows 2000 and XP, you will have drivers for USB flash drives. In older versions of Windows, USB will probably not function at all.

Because Windows running in Safe Mode is simpler than Windows running as its usual self, and because Windows doesn't attempt to do as much in Safe Mode, it's possible that a PC with a damaged version of Windows will boot into Safe Mode when it will not boot completely into normal mode. It's not difficult, and you certainly lose nothing by trying.

Here's how you boot Windows into Safe Mode:

1. Power the PC down completely, and leave it off for at least one minute.
2. Power it up again.
3. After the PC has gone through its power-on self-test (POST) sequence (which, alas, looks different on every brand of PC), typically the floppy drive will "grunt" and the speaker will beep. At that point, POST is over and Windows begins to load.
4. As soon as the PC beeps, begin pressing the F8 key repeatedly. (Don't wait for more than a few seconds or Windows will attempt its normal, failed boot

sequence.) The F8 function key brings up Safe Mode, but on some PCs it's hard to tell when to press it. Your best bet is to press the F8 key about twice per second until the screen clears and you get a text screen (white text on a black background) of Safe Mode options.

5. The options you'll see will vary by Windows version. Some versions allow Safe Mode with networking support, but *don't select that* because your software firewall may not load in Safe Mode and enabling networking support could put you at naked risk for yet more malware! Instead, choose Safe Mode, which is generally the first option in the list.

6. Windows will then attempt to boot into Safe Mode. Let it try for several minutes. On some PCs, Safe Mode takes longer to come up than normal mode. You'll know you're in Safe Mode because the words *Safe Mode* will be visible in text in all four corners of the display. The background will be black and your icons will be all crowded together. It'll be ugly, but that doesn't mean it isn't working.

7. If it looks like Safe Mode came up successfully, launch Windows Explorer and see if you can copy a file to a diskette or (on Windows 2000 and XP) to a USB flash drive. If this works, get busy copying your data out of the wounded PC. When you're done, shut down the PC normally and skip ahead to the section on nondestructive reinstallation of Windows.

If Windows won't boot into Safe Mode, it's been pretty severely damaged. You have one more chance, but fortunately, it's a pretty good one!

Booting Your PC into Linux with a LiveCD

Depending on how technical you are (or how much you're willing to teach yourself), this option may require that you get help from a more technical friend. If your hard drive hasn't been scrambled past readability, you can still copy your data from it onto diskettes and Windows doesn't have to be involved at all. The trick is to boot your PC into a version of the Linux operating system from a Linux *LiveCD,* which is a CD-based copy of Linux that runs in memory only. It boots from the CD and does not write anything onto your hard drive. However, it can *read* files from your hard drive and write files to your diskette drive. It can therefore "rescue" files from an unbootable Windows system. Such LiveCD versions of Linux are thus called *rescue CDs* in some circles and geek types use them a lot.

TIP: *Note well that this technique requires that your PC be able to boot from its CD-ROM drive. Some older PCs cannot, and if yours is one of them, read no further. A geek friend may be able to create a rescue floppy disk and use it to get data off your PC, but this is much more difficult and I can't explain it in this book.*

Using a good LiveCD version of Linux isn't difficult. Your worst problem may simply be obtaining one. LiveCD rescue CDs can be downloaded free from the Internet as ISO CD images. You download the ISO image, burn it to CD, and there's your rescue CD. However, if your PC isn't working, you'll have to ask someone else to download it—and it's important to know that the download could be as much as 700 *megabytes* of data. Even on a broadband connection, that could take 10 or 15 minutes to download. Don't try it on a dialup!

The LiveCD version of Linux that I use is called Knoppix. You can download the ISO image at no charge from the Knoppix Web site:

www.knoppix.net/get.php

The file you're looking to download is this, or something like it (the precise file name changes as the Knoppix version number and release date changes):

KNOPPIX_V3.4–2004–05–17–EN.iso

This version is 690 MB in size. Once you download it, burn the ISO image to a CD. The CD you create will be bootable. To bring up Knoppix, place the bootable LiveCD in your CD drive and power the PC up.

At some point in the Knoppix boot sequence it may seem to pause and wait for input from you (at a prompt labeled "Boot:"). At that point, press Enter and the boot sequence will resume—though in most cases, simply waiting a few seconds will allow Knoppix to continue the boot on its own. Booting into a LiveCD takes a few minutes, especially on a slower PC. It has to run tests to detect and identify all your various hardware devices. Give it all the time it needs before you start to worry—at least 20 minutes. When it's done booting, you'll have what looks like a slightly flashier Windows desktop.

In the upper-left corner of the Knoppix desktop are several icons representing your floppy drive and any hard drives installed in your PC. Your C: drive will be labeled "Hard disk partition [hda1]," and if you click once (don't double-click!) on the hda1 icon, Knoppix will bring up a file explorer utility called Konqueror. This works a lot like Windows Explorer.

TIP: The Knoppix LiveCD uses a desktop system called the K Desktop Environment (KDE), and while it's similar to Windows, it may take a little while to learn by trial and error. If you have a rescue mission to pursue using Knoppix, I recommend getting a book on KDE. Several are available. KDE for Linux for Dummies by Michael Meadhra is good, but nearly any book on using KDE will give you enough information to copy files out of a wounded Windows system.

You navigate in Konqueror by clicking *once* on an icon to open it. You can drag a file from the Konqueror window to the floppy drive icon on the desktop. When you drop it, a context menu will appear. Select Copy and Knoppix will copy the file from your hard drive to the floppy diskette.

KDE will automatically recognize a USB flash drive on most PCs. However, before you can use the USB flash drive you must do two things, in order:

1. First, you must "mount" the USB flash drive, which makes the drive available for access. Right-click on the flash drive's icon on the desktop (look for an icon labeled "Hard disk partition [sdb1]") and select Mount.

2. Second, you must change the read/write permissions on the flash drive to write. By default, USB flash drives are mounted as read-only. Right-click on the flash drive's icon, and select "Change read/write mode." In the dialog that appears, click Yes.

Once you mount and make the USB flash drive writable, you can drag and drop files on it up to its full capacity. I keep several in the drawer with capacities of 128 and 256 MB, just for occasions like this.

Here's a nice Web article on rescuing data from a Windows system with a Knoppix LiveCD:

www.shockfamily.net/cedric/knoppix/

Again, working with Linux is different from working with Windows and takes a little study. Get some experienced help if you must, but if your hard drive is still functional, there's no better way to rescue your data than by using a Linux LiveCD.

Now, once you've gotten your data off your wounded Windows PC, there remains the question of how to make Windows functional again. Let's turn our attention now to fixing Windows.

Repair Windows with a Nondestructive Reinstall

If you can't make Windows boot any way no matter what you try, it's very likely that Windows really is seriously damaged. This is especially true if Windows won't even boot in Safe Mode. Your options are getting a little thin at this point. The next thing to try is what some of us call "nondestructive reinstallation of Windows." What this means is that you'll use your Windows install or recovery CD (or "product recovery system," more on which in a moment) to recopy all of Windows's critical files from the install CD to your hard drive. This can repair the sorts of damage that malware can do to your Windows installation. However, nondestructive reinstallation means that your hard drive is not reformatted and your desktop and data are left alone. (Of course, they may be damaged too. The point here is that Windows is attempting to repair only its own files.) If nondestructive reinstallation allows Windows to run again, your desktop and data may all be there. However, the malware that caused the damage may still be there too and you will have to run your antivirus utility to remove the malware as soon as Windows is able to run again.

TIP: *If you haven't yet been able to get your data off the PC because of the damage to Windows, copy it to removable media as soon as Windows is able to boot!*

Most Windows PCs come with a Windows installation CD. This CD (also called a "recovery CD" for some brands of PC) is how you recover from a malware attack that damages Windows. A few Windows systems (including many of IBM's laptop and notebook PCs) don't have a Windows install or recovery CD. Instead, they have a "product recovery program" that stores all of the Windows recovery files on a hidden partition on the PC hard drive. You initiate the product recovery system by pressing one of the function keys during the early portions of the PC's boot sequence, before Windows attempts to load. Check your PC's documentation to see what Windows recovery technique to use with your individual PC.

Of course, if you bought or inherited your PC as a used unit, you may not have gotten the Windows repair/recovery CD or any documentation at all. If that's the case, you'll need to buy a whole new copy of Windows and use that CD instead.

If you're going to attempt nondestructive repair of Windows, *be careful*. It's done in much the same way as "destructive install," which means that you could accidentally reformat your hard drive and lose all chance of recovering your data. For this reason, I powerfully suggest getting some technical help, ideally from someone who has installed and/or repaired Windows in the past. A computer store with a repair desk will be able to reinstall Windows for you for a fee; typically $50 to $100. (Make sure you tell them that you want a *nondestructive* reinstall so that they don't reformat your hard drive first!)

Unfortunately, I can't give you a step-by-step for every Windows version in this book because they're all different and that would take most of a book in itself. There is a nice site on the Web that does have (rather terse) step-by-step instructions for all Windows versions:

www.windowsreinstall.com/

Of course, if your PC isn't working, you'll need to visit the site from another PC or at a friend's house and print a paper copy of the instructions that you'll need for your particular version of Windows.

Read the site and the instructions carefully; the site's authors do not use the term *nondestructive reinstall* and their use of the word *install* versus the use of *reinstall* is idiosyncratic. There are a lot of instructions on the site that you don't need, especially for destructive reinstallations. To zero in on the correct instructions, I've provided the precise links within the site.

For Windows 95, follow this link:

www.windowsreinstall.com/win95/install/index.htm

For Windows 98, follow this link:

www.win98.windowsreinstall.com/

For Windows ME, follow this link:

www.windowsreinstall.com/install/winme/installme/index.htm

For Windows 2000, follow this link:

www.windowsreinstall.com/install/win2k/repairw2k/page1.htm

For Windows XP Home, follow this link:

www.windowsreinstall.com/winxphome/installxpcdrepair/index.htm

Even with the instructions given on this site, I recommend finding some technical help if you consider yourself a nontechnical Windows user.

Do remember that repairing Windows nondestructively will *not* repair your installed applications or your data, nor will it remove any malware that has infected your PC. As soon as you can get Windows back to a bootable state, run your antivirus utility to remove any malware that may still be present. Once your PC is clean of malware, test your various installed software packages to see if they still run correctly. If they don't, you will probably have to reinstall them as well.

There remains the possibility that your hard drive is messed up so thoroughly that nondestructive reinstallation of Windows is impossible. At that point, you have only one more option—and although it sounds extreme and apocalyptic, in many ways it's the very best way to be rid of malware. Read on.

The Final Solution: "Burning Down the House"

More than once in my long career with Windows, I've run into problems that just won't fix, and after a few days of screwing around, I've decided that to fiddle further is a bad use of my time. At this point, I generally decide to "burn down the house," which is just geek talk for completely reformatting the hard drive and reinstalling Windows (and all my applications and utilities) from scratch.

Ironically, this can be easier (and sometimes faster) than attempting to repair Windows with all of your applications and data still in place. It may also be better, for these reasons:

√   After you reformat your hard drive and reinstall Windows completely, you *know* that all malware is gone. If you reinstall your applications and utilities from known virus-free CDs or installer files, you'll have a malware-free system.

√   Windows may not have been the only thing damaged by malware. Complex modern applications like Microsoft Office, PageMaker, AutoCAD, and their peers consist of many hundreds or even thousands of individual files. If any of those files are damaged by malware, the application may become unstable or fail. Reinstalling everything ensures that all the *effects* of malware—not simply the malware itself—will be gone.

√   Reformatting and reinstalling Windows eliminates several non-malware species of Windows gunk, like Registry clutter, hard disk fragmentation, and gigabytes of unnecessary and abandoned files, including the incompletely uninstalled remnants of software you thought you got rid of ages ago. Your PC will run like it did when it was fresh out of the box.

√   Reformatting and reinstalling everything will make you think about what you need and what you don't. Over time, people tend to install a lot of software that they end up not needing, not liking, and thus not using. This is a species of gunk that may not hurt PC performance, but it takes up space on disk and clutters your desktop with abandoned icons and your Registry with unnecessary keys. As you go to reinstall each piece of software after reformatting and reinstalling Windows, you have that golden opportunity to ask yourself, Is this whatchamacallit really necessary? You'll be surprised at how often you answer with a resounding *No!*

GunkBuster's Notebook: Should You Upgrade to Windows XP?

Many people, when they get to a point where their current copy of Windows will not boot and cannot be repaired, ask themselves whether they should just upgrade to Windows XP. My advice here is pretty simple: *If your PC didn't come with Windows XP, don't install Windows XP on it.*

The reason is this: Windows XP was a pretty aggressive upgrade of Windows. It requires a fast PC with a lot of memory to work well. If you install it on an older PC with a slower processor and less memory, you're not going to be happy with the way it performs. My personal experience has been that Windows XP should *not* be installed on any PC with a processor slower than 1.5 GHz and less than 512 MB of installed memory.

If you have a clobbered copy of Windows 98 on a 400 MHz or faster Pentium and you want to upgrade to something better, find a copy of Windows 2000, which gives you most of the benefits of Windows XP without bogging the hardware down to a crawl. On a PC slower than 400 MHz, the best you'll do is Windows 98. On PCs running at 133 MHz or slower that were running Windows 95, stick with Windows 95.

Oh—one more piece of advice: Never install Windows ME on *anything!*

Of course, if your data isn't somewhere on backups outside the PC, you will lose it, period.

Installing a "fresh" copy of Windows (as Microsoft calls it) is easier than reinstalling Windows nondestructively, but it's still a task for which some technical help will be welcome if you're a nontechnical Windows user. The key difference is that a fresh install requires that you format your hard drive so that it's utterly clean and empty. For Windows 2000 and XP, the Windows installer will do this for you. For Windows 98, you'll need to do the format manually.

There are good instructions on doing a fresh install on **windowsreinstall.com** (see the previous section), and you can download a printable copy of the pertinent instructions at a friend's house and follow those.

Unlike a repair of Windows 2000 or XP, a fresh install of any version will require that you enter the validation code for your copy of Windows. This will be found with the booklet that came with the Windows repair/reinstall CD that came with your PC. There's a "Validation Certificate" somewhere on which the code is printed. Have this handy as you perform the fresh install. At some point Windows will ask for the code and will not proceed without it.

TIP: Some major PC vendors (like Dell and HP) may provide a vendor-labeled recovery CD containing Windows and may provide detailed instructions for Windows recovery in one of the printed manuals shipped with the PC. If you have these instructions, they will help you a lot. Read through the documentation you have before doing anything!

After performing a fresh install of Windows from the CD that you have, *install your firewall* (but not your antivirus utility, which sometimes interferes with Windows Update) and then go up to the Microsoft Web site and initiate Windows Update, which will apply any service packs (SPs) that were not included in the install.

After Windows has been installed and updated, you can begin installing all of your software from the CDs or executable installer files. Install your antivirus utility first. Only when all software has been installed should you copy your data from your backups onto the PC.

Doing a fresh install of Windows is certainly the last word on eliminating stubborn malware from your PC, but be smart: Make sure your personal firewall and antivirus utility are installed, updated, and working before you head back out on the Internet. You don't want to have to do the whole thing again tomorrow!

Summing Up

The work involved in recovering from a malware attack depends completely on what sort of malware it was and how much damage it did to Windows. If Windows remains functional, your antivirus and anti-spyware utilities should be relied upon to get rid of the infection. If Windows has been damaged, you may have to reinstall Windows nondestructively—leaving your applications, settings, and data intact—or, as a last resort, reformat your hard drive entirely and reinstall a "fresh" copy of Windows from scratch.

However you recover, learn from the experience: Make sure you have your antivirus utility and firewall in place before you return to the Internet, and don't allow yourself to do things that open the door to virus and worm infections on your PC.

Index

123 Outlook Express Backup software. *See* AllNetSoft's 123 Outlook Express Backup software.

A

Action, defining, 134
ActiveX components, Internet Explorer and, 246
Ad-Aware software. *See* Lavasoft's Ad-Aware
Address book
    email addresses and, 131–132
    using, 129–132
    whitelist, using as, 131
Adware
    defining, 232
    inoculation against, 242
    phony removers of, 242–243
    preventing installation of, 12
    spyware versus, 232–233
    strategy against, implementing, 243
    understanding, 7, 196–197
    Web sites on, researching, 235–236
    when to keep, 238–239
Alexa software, determining legitimacy of, 243–244
AllNetSoft's 123 Outlook Express Backup software, using, 65
Antispyware software, using, 236–243
Antivirus software
    author recommendations for, 223–224
    cautions to look out for, 221–222
    choosing, 219–225
    free versus commercial, using, 225
    installing, 204, 226–228, 264
    malware and, 311
    Microsoft Internet Explorer (IE) and, relationship between, 221
    multiple utilities, running, 222–223
    one-offs, using, 228–229
    product reviews for, using, 220–221
    testing, 221
    trial utilities, using, 224–225
    updates from, 214–215
Applications, backing up, 309
Art Boese's Museum of Hoaxes Web site, 289
Attachments
    abandoning, avoiding, 52–53
    email clients and, relationship between, 97–98
Attachments folder
    cleaning, 97–101
    virus check on, running, 98
Auto Backup Software. *See* Han-Soft's Auto Backup Software.
Automatic content filtering, problems with, 132–133
.avi extension, nonsupport for viruses, 211

B

Back Doors, understanding, 196
Backups
    applications, 309
    email addresses, role of, 21–22
    media and software, types of, 64
    performing, 308–309
    strategy for, 14
BadTrans virus
    Microsoft Internet Explorer (IE) and, 192
.bas extension, support for viruses, 211
.bat extension, support for viruses, 211
Bayesian spam filtering
    additional information on, 152
    defining, 127
    downside to, 152
    maintaining, 151
    process of, 150–152
Binary attachments, email clients and, 38
Black hats
    antivirus software targeting, 223–224
    identity theft and, 286, 296, 298